Essentials of Statistics for the Social and Behavioral Sciences

Essentials of Behavioral Science Series

Founding Editors, Alan S. Kaufman and Nadeen L. Kaufman

Essentials of Statistics for the Social and Behavioral Sciences
by Barry H. Cohen and R. Brooke Lea

Essentials of Psychological Testing
by Susana Urbina

Essentials of Research Design and Methodology
by Geoffrey R. Marczyk and David DeMatteo

Essentials

of Statistics for the Social and Behavioral Sciences

Barry H. Cohen

R. Brooke Lea

 John Wiley & Sons, Inc.

Published by John Wiley & Sons, Inc., Hoboken, New Jersey.
Published simultaneously in Canada.

This publication is designed to provide accurate and authoritative information in regard to the subject
matter covered. It is sold with the understanding that the publisher is not engaged in rendering
professional services. If legal, accounting, medical, psychological or any other expert assistance is
required, the services of a competent professional person should be sought.

Designations used by companies to distinguish their products are often claimed as trademarks. In all
instances where John Wiley & Sons, Inc. is aware of a claim, the product names appear in initial capital
or all capital letters. Readers, however, should contact the appropriate companies for more complete
information regarding trademarks and registration.

For general information on our other products and services please contact our Customer Care
Department within the U.S. at (800) 762-2974, outside the United States at (317) 572-3993 or fax
(317) 572-4002.

Wiley also publishes its books in a variety of electronic formats. Some content that appears in print
may not be available in electronic books. For more information about Wiley products, visit our
website at www.wiley.com.

Library of Congress Cataloging-in-Publication Data:

Cohen, Barry H., 1949–
    Essentials of statistics for the social and behavioral science / Barry H. Cohen, R. Brooke Lea.
        p. cm. — (Essentials of behavioral sciences series)
    Includes bibliographical references and index.
    ISBN 0-471-22031-0 (pbk. : alk. paper)
        1. Social sciences—Statistical methods.   I. Lea, R. Brooke.   II. Title.   III. Series.

HA29.C65 2003
519.5—dc21   2003049669

Printed in the United States of America.

10   9   8   7   6   5   4   3   2   1

To my dear Aunts: Harriet Anthony and Diana Franzblau

BHC

To Emily and Jackson, the two parameters that keep me normal

RBL

We would like to sincerely thank Irving B. Weiner, Ph.D., ABPP for his assistance as a consulting editor on this project.

Dr. Weiner completed his doctoral studies at the University of Michigan in 1959 and went on to write and edit over 20 books, as well as countless chapters and journal articles. A Diplomate of the American Board of Professional Psychology in both Clinical and Forensic Psychology, he currently serves as Clinical Professor of Psychiatry and Behavioral Medicine at the University of South Florida. Dr. Weiner serves as Chairman of the Wiley Behavioral Sciences Advisory Board and is Editor-in-Chief of the 12-volume Handbook of Psychology, which published in December 2002.

CONTENTS

SERIES PREFACE

I n the *Essentials of Behavioral Science* series, our goal is to provide readers with books that will deliver key practical information in an efficient, accessible style. The series features books on a variety of topics, such as statistics, psychological testing, and research design and methodology, to name just a few. For the experienced professional, books in the series offer a concise yet thorough review of a specific area of expertise, including numerous tips for best practices. Students can turn to series books for a clear and concise overview of the important topics in which they must become proficient to practice skillfully, efficiently, and ethically in their chosen fields.

Wherever feasible, visual cues highlighting key points are utilized alongside systematic, step-by-step guidelines. Chapters are focused and succinct. Topics are organized for an easy understanding of the essential material related to a particular topic. Theory and research are continually woven into the fabric of each book, but always to enhance the practical application of the material, rather than to sidetrack or overwhelm readers. With this series, we aim to challenge and assist readers in the behavioral sciences to aspire to the highest level of competency by arming them with the tools they need for knowledgeable, informed practice.

Essentials of Statistics for the Social and Behavioral Sciences concentrates on drawing connections among seemingly disparate statistical procedures and providing intuitive explanations for how the basic formulas work. The authors weave statistical concepts together and thus make the different procedures seem less arbitrary and isolated. The statistical procedures covered here are those considered *essential* to researchers in the field. Only univariate statistics are presented; topics in multivariate statistics (including multiple regression) deserve a separate volume of their own. Further, this book assumes that the reader has a working knowledge of basic statistics or has ready access to an introductory text. Therefore, this book will not bog down the reader down with computational details. Thus, this book should be ideal as a supplementary text for students struggling to understand the material in an advanced (or sophisticated) undergraduate statistics course, or an intermediate course at the master's level. *Essentials of Statistics* is also ideal for researchers in the social and behavioral sciences who have forgotten some of their statistical training and need to brush up on statistics in order to evaluate data, converse knowledgeably with a statistical consultant, or prepare for licensing exams.

Chapter 1 covers the most often used methods of descriptive statistics, and the next four chapters cover the basics of null hypothesis testing and interval estimation for the one-, two-, and multigroup cases, as well as the case of two continuous variables. Chapter 6 is devoted to the increasingly essential topics of power analysis and effect size estimation for the cases covered in Chapters 2 through 5. Chapters 7 and 8 deal with the complex forms of analysis of variance common in experimental social science research. As appropriate, these chapters include material relevant to the larger topic of research design. Finally, Chapter 9 includes some of the most popular methods in nonparametric statistics. Regrettably, many useful topics had to be omitted for lack of space, but the references and annotated bibliography point the reader toward more comprehensive and more advanced texts to fill any gaps. Indeed, we hope that this book will help the reader understand those more advanced sources. Additional material to help readers of this book understand the statistical topics covered in this book, as well as some related and more advanced topics, are posted on the web and can be accessed by following links from *www.psych.nyu.edu/people/faculty/cohen/statstext.html*.

Alan S. Kaufman, PhD, and Nadeen L. Kaufman, EdD, Founding Editors
Yale University School of Medicine

Essentials of Statistics for the Social and Behavioral Sciences

One

DESCRIPTIVE STATISTICS

Social and behavioral scientists need statistics more than most other scientists, especially the kind of statistics included in this book. For the sake of contrast, consider the subject matter of physics. The nice thing about protons and electrons, for instance, is that all protons have the same mass; electrons are a lot lighter, but they also are all identical to each other in mass. This is not to imply that physics is easier than any of the social or behavioral sciences, but the fact that animals and especially humans vary so much from each other along every conceivable dimension creates a particular need to summarize all this variability in order to make sense of it.

The purpose of descriptive statistics is to use just a few numbers to capture the meaning of a much larger collection of observations on many different cases. These cases could be people, animals, or even cities or colleges; or the same cases on many different occasions; or some combination of the two. Often, computing descriptive statistics is just your first step in a process that uses more advanced statistical methods to make estimates about cases that you will never have the opportunity to measure directly. This chapter will cover only descriptive statistics. The remaining chapters will be devoted to more advanced methods called *inferential* statistics.

SAMPLES AND POPULATIONS

Sometimes you have all of the observations in which you are interested, but this is rare. For instance, a school psychologist may have scores on some standardized test for every sixth grader in Springfield County and her only concern is studying and comparing students within the County. These test scores would be thought of as her *population*. More often, you have just a subset of the observations in which you are interested. For instance, a market researcher randomly selects and calls 100 people in Springfield County and asks all of them about their use of the Internet. The 100 observations obtained (Springfield residents are very cooperative) do not include all of the individuals in which the researcher is interested. The

100 observations would be thought of as a *sample* of a larger population.

If as a researcher you are interested in the Internet habits of people in Springfield County, your population consists of all the people in that county. If you are really interested in the Internet habits of people in the United States, then that is your population. In the latter case your sample may not be a good representation of the population. But for the purposes of descriptive statistics, populations and samples are dealt with in similar ways. The distinction between *sample* and *population* will become important in the next chapter, when we introduce the topic of *inferential statistics*. For now, we will treat any collection of numbers that you have as a population.

The most obvious descriptive statistic is one that summarizes all of the observations with a single number—one that is the most typical or that best locates the middle of all the numbers. Such a statistic is called a measure of *central tendency*. The best-known measure of central tendency is the arithmetic mean: the statistic you get if you add up all the scores in your sample (or population) and divide by the number of different scores you added. When people use the term *mean* you can be quite sure that they are referring to the arithmetic mean. There are other statistics that are called means; these include the geometric and the harmonic mean (the latter will be discussed in Chapter 5). However, whenever we use the term *mean* by itself we will be referring to the arithmetic mean. Although the mean is calculated the same way for a sample as a population, it is symbolized as $\overline{X}$ (pronounced "X bar") or M when it describes a sample, and μ (the lowercase Greek letter mu; pronounced "myoo") when it describes a population. In general, numbers that summarize the scores in a sample are called statistics (e.g., $\overline{X}$ is a statistic), whereas numbers that summarize an entire population are called parameters (e.g., μ is a parameter).

SCALES OF MEASUREMENT

When we calculate the mean for a set of numbers we are assuming that these numbers represent a precise scale of measurement. For instance, the average of 61 inches and 63 inches is 62 inches, and we know that 62 is exactly in the middle of 61 and 63 because an inch is always the same size (the inch that's between 61 and 62 is precisely the same size as the inch between 62 and 63). In this case we can say that our measurement scale has the *interval* property. This property is necessary to justify and give meaning to calculating means and many other statistics on the measurements that we have. However, in the social sciences we often use numbers to measure a variable in a way that is not as precise as measuring in inches. For instance, a researcher may ask a student to express his or her agreement with some political statement (e.g., I think U.S. senators should be limited to two 6-year terms) on a scale that consists of the following choices: 1 = strongly disagree; 2 = somewhat disagree; 3 = neutral; 4 = somewhat agree; 5 = strongly agree. [This kind of scale is called a *Likert scale,* after its inventor, Rensis Likert (1932).]

Ordinal Scales

You might say that a person who strongly agrees and one who is neutral, when averaged together, are equivalent to someone who somewhat agrees, because the mean of 1 and 3 is 2. But this assumes that "somewhat agree" is just as close to "strongly agree" as it is to neutral—that is, that the intervals on the scale are all equal. All we can really be sure of in this case is the order of the responses—that as the responses progress from 1 to 5 there is more agreement with the statement. A scale like the one described is therefore classified as an *ordinal scale.* The more points such a scale has (e.g., a 1 to 10 rating scale for attractiveness), the more likely social scientists are to treat the scale as though it were not just an ordinal scale, but an interval scale, and therefore calculate statistics such as the mean on the numbers that are reported by participants in the study. In fact, it is even common to treat the numbers from a 5-point Likert scale in that way, even though statisticians argue against it. This is one of many areas in which you will see that common practice among social scientists does not agree with the recommendations of many statisticians (and measurement experts) as reported in textbooks and journal articles.

Another way that an ordinal scale arises is through ranking. A researcher observing 12 children in a playground might order them in terms of aggressiveness, so that the most aggressive child receives a rank of 1 and the least aggressive gets a 12. One cannot say that the children ranked 1 and 2 differ by the same amount as the children ranked 11 and 12; all you know is that the child ranked 5, for instance, has been judged more aggressive than the one ranked 6. Sometimes measurements that come from an interval scale (e.g., time in seconds to solve a puzzle) are converted to ranks, because of extreme scores and other problems (e.g., most participants solve the puzzle in about 10 seconds, but a few take several minutes). There is a whole set of procedures for dealing with ranked data, some of which are described in Chapter 9. Some statisticians would argue that these rank-order statistics should be applied to Likert-scale data, but this is rarely done for reasons that will be clearer after reading that chapter.

Nominal Scales

Some of the distinctions that social scientists need to make are just qualitative—they do not have a quantitative aspect, so the categories that are used to distinguish people have no order, let alone equal intervals. For instance, psychiatrists diagnose people with symptoms of mental illness and assign them to a category. The collection of all these categories can be thought of as a *categorical* or *nominal scale* (the latter name indicates that the categories have names rather than numbers) for mental illness. Even when the categories are given numbers (e.g., the *Diagnostic and Statistical Manual of Mental Disorders* used by psychologists and psychiatrists has a number for each diagnosis), these numbers are not meant to be used mathematically (e.g., it doesn't make sense to add the numbers together) and do not even imply any ordering of the categories (e.g., according to the *Diagnostic and Statistical Manual of Mental Disorders,* fourth edition [*DSM-IV*], Obsessive-Compulsive Disorder is 300.3, and Depressive Disorder is 311; but the diagnostic category for someone suffering from Obsessive-Compulsive Disorder *and* Depressive Disorder is not 611.3, nor is it 305.65, the sum and mean of the categories, respectively).

Although you cannot calculate statistics such as the mean when dealing with categorical data, you can compare frequencies and percentages in a useful way. For instance, the percentages of patients that fall into each *DSM-IV* diagnosis can be compared from one country to another to see if symptoms are interpreted differently in different cultures, or perhaps to see if people in some countries are more susceptible to some forms of mental illness than the people of other countries. Statistical methods for dealing with data from both categorical and ordinal scales will be described in Chapter 9.

Ratio Scales

The three scales of measurement described so far are the nominal (categories that have no quantitative order), the ordinal (the values of the scale have an order, but the intervals may not be equal), and the interval scale (a change of one unit on the scale represents the same amount of change anywhere along the scale). One scale we have not yet mentioned is the *ratio scale*. This is an interval scale that has a true zero point (i.e., zero on the scale represents a total absence of the variable being

≡Rapid Reference 1.1

Measurement Scales

Nominal: Observations are assigned to categories that differ qualitatively but have no quantitative order (e.g., depressed, phobic, obsessive, etc.).

Ordinal: The values have an order that can be represented by numbers, but the numbers cannot be used mathematically, because the intervals may not be equal (e.g., assigning ranks according to the ability of gymnasts on a team).

Interval: One unit on this scale is the same size anywhere along the scale, so values can be treated mathematically (e.g., averaged), but zero on the scale does not indicate a total absence of the variable being measured (e.g., IQ scores).

Ratio: This scale has the interval property plus the zero point is not arbitrary; it represents a true absence of the variable being measured. For instance, weight in pounds has this property, so that if object A is measured as twice as many pounds as object B, then object A has twice as much weight. (You cannot say that someone with an IQ of 120 is twice as smart as someone with an IQ of 60.)

measured). For instance, neither the Celsius nor Fahrenheit scales for measuring temperature qualify as ratio scales, because both have arbitrary zero points. The Kelvin temperature scale is a ratio scale because on that scale zero is absolute zero, the point at which all molecular motion, and therefore all heat, ceases. The statistical methods described in this book do not distinguish between the interval and ratio scales, so it is common to drop the distinction and refer to interval/ratio data. A summary of the different measurement scales is given in Rapid Reference 1.1.

DISPLAYING YOUR DATA

When describing data there are many options for interval/ratio data, such as the mean, but relatively few options for nominal or ordinal data. However, regardless of the scale you are dealing with, the most basic way to look at your data is in terms of frequencies.

Bar Charts

If you have nominal data, a simple *bar chart* is a good place to start. Along a horizontal axis you write out the different categories in any order that is convenient. The height of the bar above each category should be proportional to the number of your cases that fall into that category. If 20 of the patients you studied were phobic and 10 were depressed, the vertical bar rising above "phobic" would be twice as high as the bar above "depressed." Of course, the chart can be rotated to make the bars horizontal, or a pie chart or some other display can be used instead, but the bar chart is probably the most common form of display for nominal data in the social sciences.

Because the ordering of the categories in a bar chart of nominal data is arbitrary, it doesn't quite make sense to talk of the central tendency of the data. However, if you want to talk about the most typical value, it makes some sense to identify the category that is the most popular (i.e., the one with the highest bar). The category with the highest frequency of occurrence is called the *mode*. For instance, among patients at a psychiatric hospital the modal diagnosis is usually schizophrenia (unless this category is broken into subtypes).

The bar chart is also a good way to display data from an ordinal scale, but because the values now have an order, we can talk meaningfully about central tendency. You can still determine the mode—the value with the highest bar (i.e., frequency)—but the mode need not be near the middle of your bar chart (although it usually will be). However, with an ordinal scale you can add up frequencies and percentages in a way that doesn't make sense with a nominal scale. First, let us look at the convenience of dealing with percentages.

Percentile Ranks and the Median

Suppose 44 people in your sample "strongly agree" with a particular statement; this is more impressive in a sample of 142 participants than in a sample of 245 participants (note: in keeping with recent custom in the field of psychology, we will usually use the term *participant* to avoid the connotations of the older term *subject*). The easiest way to see that is to note that in the first case the 44 participants are 31% of the total sample; in the second case, they are only 18%. The percentages make sense without knowing the sample size. Percentages are useful with a nominal scale (e.g., 45% of the patients were schizophrenic), but with an ordinal scale there is the added advantage that the percentages can be summed. For example, suppose that 100 people respond to a single question on a Likert scale with the following percentages: 5% strongly disagree; 9% somewhat disagree; 36% are neutral; 40% agree; and 10% strongly agree. We can then say that 14% (5 + 9) of the people are on the disagree side, or that 14% are below neutral (it's arbitrary, but we are assigning higher values in the agree direction).

We can assign a *percentile rank* (PR) to a value on the scale such that the PR equals the percentage of the sample (or population) that is at or below that value. The PR is 5 for strongly disagree, 14 for somewhat disagree, 50 for neutral, 90 for agree, and 100 for strongly agree (it is always 100, of course, for the highest value represented in your set of scores). A particularly useful value in any set of scores is called the *median*. The median is defined as the middle score, such that half the scores are higher, and half are lower. In other words, the median is the value whose PR is 50. In this example the median is "neutral." The median is a useful measure of central tendency that can be determined with an ordinal, but not a nominal, scale. According to this definition, the median in the preceding example would be somewhere between "neutral" and "somewhat agree." If "neutral" is 3 and "somewhat" agree is 4 on the scale, then some researchers would say that the median is 3.5. But unless you are dealing with an interval scale you cannot use the numbers of your scale so precisely. If all your scores are different, it is easy to see which score is the middle score. If there are only a few different scores (e.g., 1 to 5) but many responses, there will be many scores that are tied, making it less clear which score is in the middle.

Histograms

A slight modification of the bar chart is traditionally used when dealing with interval/ratio data. On a bar chart for nominal or ordinal data there should be some space between any two adjacent bars, but for interval/ratio data it is usually appropriate for each bar to touch the bars on either side of it. When the bars touch, the chart is called a *histogram*. To understand when it makes sense for the bars to touch, you need to know a little about *continuous* and *discrete* scales, and therefore something about discrete and continuous variables. A variable is discrete when it can only take certain values, with none between. Appropriately, it is measured on a discrete scale (whole numbers—no fractions allowed). For example, family size is a discrete variable because a family can consist of three or four or five members, but it cannot consist of 3.76 members.

Height is a continuous variable because for any two people (no matter how close in height) it is theoretically possible to find someone between them in height. So height should be measured on a continuous scale (e.g., number of inches to as many decimal places as necessary). Of course, no scale is perfectly continuous (infinitely precise), but measuring height in tiny fractions of inches can be considered continuous for our purposes. Note that some continuous variables cannot at present be measured on a continuous scale. A variable like charisma may vary continuously, but it can only be measured with a rather crude, discrete scale (e.g., virtually no charisma, a little charisma, moderate charisma, etc.). Data from a continuous scale are particularly appropriate for a histogram.

Consider what a histogram might look like for the heights of 100 randomly selected men (for simplicity, we will look at one gender at a time). If the men range from 62 to 76 inches, the simplest scheme would be to have a total of 15 bars, the first ranging from 61.5 to 62.5 inches, the second from 62.5 to 63.5 inches, and so on until the 15th bar, which goes from 75.5 to 76.5 inches. Looking at Figure 1.1, notice how the bars are higher near the middle, as is the case for many variables (the mode in this case is 69 inches). Now suppose that these men range in weight from 131 to 218 pounds. One bar per pound would require 88 bars (218 − 131 + 1), and many of the bars (especially near either end) would be empty. The solution is to group together values into class intervals. For the weight example, 10-pound intervals starting with 130–139 and ending with 210–219 for a total of nine intervals would be reasonable. A total of eighteen 5-pound intervals (130–134 to 215–219) would give more detail and would also be reasonable. The common guidelines are to use between 10 and 20 intervals, and when possible to start or end the intervals with zeroes or fives (e.g., 160–164 or 161–165).

Note that if you look at what are called the *apparent limits* of two adjacent class intervals, they don't appear to touch—for example, 130–134 and 135–139. However, measurements are being rounded off to the nearest unit, so the *real limits* of the intervals just mentioned are 129.5–134.5 and 134.5–139.5, which obviously do touch. We don't worry about anyone who is exactly 134.5 pounds; we just

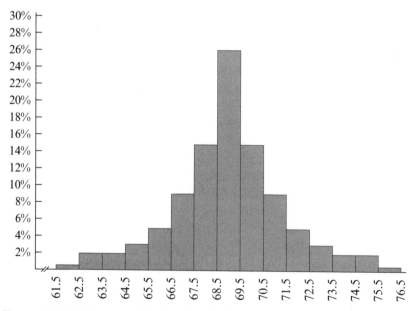

Figure 1.1 A histogram of the heights (in inches) of 100 randomly selected men

assume that if we measure precisely
enough, that person will fall into one
interval or the other.

Percentiles

Percentages can be added, just as
with the ordinal scale, to create percentile ranks. For instance, looking at
Figure 1.1, we can add the percentages of the first five bars (1 + 2 + 2
+ 3 + 5) to find that the PR for 66

inches is 13% (actually 13% is the PR for 66.5 inches, because you have to go to
the upper real limit of the interval to ensure that you have surpassed everyone in
that interval). Conversely, one can define a *percentile* as a score that has a particular PR. For example, the 22nd percentile is 67 (actually 67.5), because the PR of
67 is 22. The percentiles of greatest interest are the deciles (10%, 20%, etc.), and
the quartiles (25%, 50%, 75%).

Unfortunately, these particular percentiles are not likely to fall right in the
middle of a bar or right between two bars. For instance, for the data in Figure 1.1,
the 1st quartile (25%) is somewhere between 67.5 (PR = 22) and 68.5 (PR = 37).
It is common to interpolate linearly between these two points. Because 25 is one
fifth of the way from 22 to 37, we say that the 25th percentile is about one fifth
of the way from 67.5 to 68.5 or about 67.7. The formula for linear interpolation
is given in most introductory statistics texts. Probably the most important percentile of all is the 50th; as we mentioned before, this percentile is called the median. For Figure 1.1, the median is 69.0—that is, half the men have heights below
69.0 inches, and half are taller than 69.0 inches. The mode is the interval represented by 69 inches—that is, 68.5 to 69.5 inches.

Distributions

Figure 1.1 shows you that height is a variable; if it were a constant, all people
would have the same height (the number of chambers in the human heart is a
constant—everybody has four). Figure 1.1 shows how the values for height are
distributed in the sample of 100 men that were measured. A set of values from a
variable together with the relative frequency associated with each value is called
a *distribution*. Except for the last chapter of the book, all of the statistical methods
we will present involve distributions. If all of the heights from 62 to 76 inches
were equally represented, all of the bars would be at the same height, and it would

be said that we have a *uniform distribution*. That form of distribution is not likely when dealing with the variables usually measured for people. Often, the distribution of a variable is shaped something like a bell, as in Figure 1.1, and has one mode somewhere in the middle. Values further from the middle are progressively less popular.

Shapes of Distributions

Imagine the distribution of 60 students who took a statistics exam. If the class consisted mostly of math majors and English majors the distribution might have two equally high bars, and therefore two modes—one more to the right for the math majors and one more to the left for the English majors, with a dip in between. This distribution would be called *bimodal* (even if the two modes were not exactly equal in frequency), whereas the distribution in Figure 1.1 is called *unimodal*. It is possible for a distribution to have even more than two modes, but we will be dealing only with unimodal distributions. Now imagine that the statistics exam was very easy (if you can). The scores would be bunched up (producing high bars) in the 90s with relatively few low scores trailing off in the negative direction. The mode would be decidedly to one side (the right, or positive, side in this case), and the distribution would appear to have a tail (a series of relatively low bars) on the left. Such a distribution is said to be *negatively skewed,* because the tail is in the negative direction. This kind of distribution often arises when a large portion of the scores are approaching the highest possible score (i.e., there is a ceiling effect).

Positively skewed distributions are probably more common in the social sciences than those with a negative skew. Annual income is a good example. The majority of people in the United States, for instance, are much closer to the lowest possible income (we'll say it is zero and ignore the possibility of negative income) than to the highest known income. Clearly, there is a floor for income, but no clearly defined ceiling, so the income distribution has a tail that points in the positive direction. The annual incomes for a randomly selected group of people would therefore be very likely to form a positively skewed distribution, as illustrated in Figure 1.2.

CHOOSING A MEASURE OF CENTRAL TENDENCY

One of the most important reasons to draw (or have a computer draw) a histogram is to look at the shape of the distribution with which you are dealing. With a very large sample—and especially with a population—the distribution will be fairly smooth and very likely unimodal with an approximate bell shape. However, the shape may be symmetrical or skewed (either positively or negatively). The shape can be important: For example, strong skewing can affect your choice of

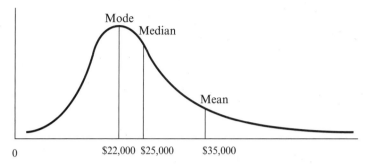

Figure 1.2 Distribution of annual income (in dollars) for a large sample of U.S. citizens

descriptive statistics. In a symmetrical, unimodal distribution the three measures of central tendency we have described—the mean, the median, and the mode—will all be in the same spot, so it doesn't matter which you choose. However, in a skewed distribution extreme scores have a larger effect on the mean than on the median, so while both of these measures are pulled away from the mode, the mean is pulled further. This is illustrated in Figure 1.2.

It is easy to understand why the skewing does not move the median much. Although the long positive tail includes some very high values, the tail represents only a small percentage of the sample. Moving the median just a little in the hump of the distribution (where the bars are high) can have a large effect on the percentage on each side of the median. Moving the median a little toward the tail can compensate for the small extra percentage that is contained in the tail. Once a score is to the right of the median, moving it much further to the right has no effect on the median, because that wouldn't change the fact that 50% of the scores are still on each side of the median. The mean, however, is sensitive to the actual values of all the scores, and a few very large scores on one side of the distribution can noticeably pull the mean to that side. That's why for some purposes the mean can be considered a misleading measure of central tendency, as we will explain next.

Suppose that Figure 1.2 displays the incomes of employees for one particular company. To make the argument that the employees are well paid, the company president would be happy to report that the mean annual income is $35,000. However, you can see that the vast majority of employees earn less than this amount; the mean is being unduly influenced by the incomes of a relatively few executives at the company. The regular workers of the company would prefer to use the median as a description of the average salary. Whereas the majority of the scores in a distribution can be above or below the mean, the median is always near the middle because 50% of the scores are above and 50% below it.

When a news report refers to an average or mean number, it is usually refer-ring to the arithmetic mean, but read closely: The author could be referring to a median or even a mode or other measure in an imprecise way (the measures of central tendency just described are summarized in Rapid Reference 1.2). How-ever, regardless of which measure of central tendency is being used, you should notice that the wider the distribution, the harder it can be to describe it with just one number: The endpoints of the distribution can be very far from the middle, no matter how the middle is defined. Measuring the width of the distribution can be an important complement to locating the middle. This is our next topic.

MEASURES OF VARIABILITY

As a sixth-grade English teacher, which class of 20 students would you rather teach, one whose average reading score is 6.3 (a bit above grade level) or 5.8 (a bit below)? Perhaps you like a challenge, but you would probably guess that the 6.3 class would be easier to teach. But what if we tell you that the students in the "5.8" class range from 5.6 to 6.0, whereas the "6.3" class ranges from 5.7 to 6.9? Given these ranges, the more homogeneous ("5.8") class would likely be the easier to teach.

The Range and Semi-Interquartile Range

The simplest way to measure the width of a distribution is to calculate its *range*. The range is just the highest minus the lowest score, plus one unit if you are deal-ing with a continuous scale (e.g., the range of the 5.8 class is $6.0 - 5.6 + .1 = .4 + .1 = .5$, because the upper limit of 6.0 is really 6.05 and the lower real limit of 5.6 is 5.55). The problem with the range is that it can be dramatically influenced by one extreme score. Add a 7.0 reader to the 5.8 class and the 5.8 class will now have a larger range than the 6.3 class. However, the range of the 5.8 class would then be misleading; it is still a very homogeneous class, with just one very ad-vanced student who needs to be dealt with separately.

One way to modify the range so that it is not affected by extreme scores is to measure the range of the middle 50% of the scores. This modified range is found by subtracting the 25th percentile of the distribution from the 75th percentile. Hence, it is called the *interquartile range*. If you divide this range by 2, you get a mea-sure called the *semi-interquartile range* (SIQ), which is roughly the average of the dis-tances from the median to the 25th and 75th percentiles. The SIQ gives you a typ-ical amount by which scores tend to differ from the median (about half are closer and half are further away than the SIQ), and this is one very useful way to describe the variability of a distribution. The SIQ range can be very useful for descriptive purposes, especially when dealing with ordinal data or with a distribution that has extreme scores on one or both sides of its median. Measures that make use of all of the scores at hand are usually more useful for describing the spread of the scores when you want to extrapolate from your sample to a larger population. We will describe such a measure shortly.

The Summation Sign

An obvious way to measure the amount of variability in a distribution is to find the distance of each score from some measure of central tendency, and then average these differences together to find a typical amount of deviation from the middle. If your variability measure will use all of your scores it makes sense to anchor it to a measure of central tendency that does the same—that is, the mean. Expressed in words, we can propose a measure of variability that is equal to the average of all of the scores' deviations from the mean. At this point, mathematical notation, which so many students find annoying, can be really helpful in defining complex statistics in a compact and unambiguous way. The uppercase Greek letter sigma (Σ) is often used as a way of telling you to add your scores together; it is therefore called, in this context, the *summation sign*. If you follow the summation sign with a letter representing the variable you are measuring (e.g., ΣX), this is a shorthand way of telling you to add all of your scores together. This notation allows us to write a very simple formula for the mean of a set of scores:

$$\mu = \frac{\Sigma X_i}{N} \tag{1.1}$$

The subscript i associated with X is there to remind you that there is more than just one X; there are a whole series of values to be added up. Statistical purists would like us to put "$i = 1$" under the summation sign and N above it (to remind you to start adding with the first score and not to stop until you have added the Nth score), but we will always use Σ to mean "add them all up," so that extra notation won't be necessary. Note that Formula 1.1 is a very convenient way of saying that if you add up all of your scores, and then divide by the number (N) of scores that you added, the result will equal the mean.

The Mean Deviation

Next, we can apply Formula 1.1 to the deviations of scores from the mean rather than to the scores themselves. This can be expressed symbolically as follows:

$$\frac{\Sigma(X_i - \mu)}{N}$$

The problem with the above expression is that it is always equal to zero. This is actually an important property of the mean—that it is a balance point in any distribution, such that the sum of deviations above it equals the sum of deviations below it. However, if we want to know the average distance of scores from the mean we are not concerned with the sign of a deviation, just its magnitude. That idea can be expressed mathematically in the following formula:

$$\text{MD} = \frac{\sum |X_i - \mu|}{N} \tag{1.2}$$

MD stands for the *mean deviation,* and the vertical bars around $X_i - \mu$ tell us to take the absolute value of the deviation. Since the deviations are now all positive, they don't cancel each other out, and we are left with a number that is literally the average of the absolute deviations from the mean. The mean deviation gives us a good description of the variability in a set of scores, and one that makes a good deal of sense. Unfortunately, it is rarely used, mainly because MD is not useful when extrapolating from samples to populations. The reason we are describing MD to you is that the most common measure of variability is just like the MD, only a little different.

Variance and Standard Deviation

If you were to square the deviations instead of taking their absolute values, and then average these squared deviations, not only would you get rid of the negative deviations, but the result would be an important measure of variability called the *variance;* it is symbolized by a lowercase sigma being squared, as in the following formula:

$$\sigma^2 = \frac{\sum (X_i - \mu)^2}{N} \tag{1.3}$$

The numerator of this expression, the sum of the squared deviations from the mean, has its own abbreviation; it is known as the sum of squares, or even more briefly as SS. The variance is useful in advanced statistics, but it is not helpful as a descriptive measure of your set of scores, because it is in terms of squared scores. Taking the square root of the variance produces a good descriptive measure of variability that can also be useful for advanced statistics. The resulting measure is called the *standard deviation,* and it is symbolized by a lowercase sigma (without being squared), as in Formula 1.4.

$$\sigma = \sqrt{\frac{\sum (X_i - \mu)^2}{N}} \tag{1.4}$$

It is important to realize that taking the square root *after* averaging the squared deviations does not entirely remove the effect of squaring. Otherwise, the standard deviation would always be the same as the mean deviation. Although MD and σ can be the same for a set of scores (e.g., when there are only two scores), σ is usually larger and can be quite a bit larger if there are a few extreme scores. In fact, the sensitivity of σ to extreme scores can be seen as a drawback. Just as the median can be a better descriptive measure than the mean when there are extreme scores, so too MD (or the SIQ) can be better than σ for descriptive purposes. But as we shall see shortly, σ plays a role in a very common distribution that makes it more useful than MD in advanced statistics. And even though σ is usually larger than MD for the same set of scores, σ is usually in the same ballpark, and therefore a good descriptive measure. The variability measures just described are summarized in Rapid Reference 1.2.

≡Rapid Reference 1.2

Measures of Central Tendency

The *mode* can be found with any scale of measurement; it is the only measure of typicality that can be used with a nominal scale.

The *median* can be used with ordinal, as well as interval/ratio, scales. It can even be used with scales that have open-ended categories at either end (e.g., 10 or more). It is not greatly affected by outliers, and it can be a good descriptive statistic for a strongly skewed distribution.

The *mean* can only be used with interval or ratio scales. It is affected by every score in the distribution, and it can be strongly affected by outliers. It may not be a good descriptive statistic for a skewed distribution, but it plays an important role in advanced statistics.

Measures of Variability

The *range* tells you the largest difference that you have among your scores. It is strongly affected by outliers, and being based on only two scores, it can be very unreliable.

The *SIQ range* has the same properties as described for the median, and is often used as a companion measure to the median.

The *mean deviation,* and the two measures that follow, can only be used with interval/ratio scales. It is a good descriptive measure, which is less affected by outliers than the standard deviation, but it is not used in advanced statistics.

The *variance* is not appropriate for descriptive purposes, but it plays an important role in advanced statistics.

The *standard deviation* is a good descriptive measure of variability, although it can be affected strongly by outliers. It plays an important role in advanced statistics.

THE NORMAL DISTRIBUTION

The best-known mathematical distribution and the one that is the most often ap-
plicable to variables in the social sciences is the one called the *normal distribution*.
The normal distribution (ND), or *normal curve* as it is often called, has many convenient mathematical properties, but the one that is most relevant to us at this
point is that the ND is completely determined by two of its characteristics (called
parameters): its mean and its standard deviation. In other words, if two NDs have
exactly the same μ and σ, they will overlap each other perfectly. You can see how
the ND depends on μ and σ by looking at the mathematical equation for the ND:

$$f(x) = \frac{1}{\sqrt{2\pi\sigma^2}}\, e^{-(x-\mu)^2/2\sigma^2} \qquad (1.5)$$

$f(x)$ is short for "function of" and it translates into y, the vertical height of the
curve at that value for x; e, like π, is a constant ($e = 2.718\ldots$). The exponent next
to e has a minus sign, so the smaller the exponent, the higher the curve. The exponent is smallest when it is zero ($e^0 = 1.0$), which occurs when $X = \mu$, so the
curve has its mode when X is at the mean.

　　One of the reasons the ND is so important to science (both physical and social) is that many variables in nature have distributions that look a lot like the ND.
A common way that the ND arises is when many different independent factors
contribute to the value of a variable, and each factor can just as easily contribute
positively or negatively in any given case. If 20 factors contribute to a variable, a
common result is 10 factors contributing positively and 10 negatively, leading to
a middle value. Cases in which all 20 factors pull in the same direction will be rare
and, therefore, so will extreme values on the variable. Something like this is probably acting to determine the heights of adult humans.

　　Let's look at a likely distribution of the heights for an entire population of adult
women (once again, it is simpler to look at one gender at a time; see Figure 1.3).
The height distribution looks a lot like the ND, except for one simple fact: The
height distribution ends on either side—there is no chance of finding an adult
woman less than 2 feet or more than 9 feet tall. The true ND never ends; looking
again at Formula 1.5, we see that the height of the curve does not fall to zero until the negative exponent of e, and therefore the value of X, reaches infinity. Moreover, the actual height distribution may not be perfectly symmetrical, and the
curve may bend in a way that is slightly different from the ND. Still, it is so much
easier to deal with the ND than real population distributions that it is common
just to assume that the ND applies (with the same μ and σ as the real distribution) and ignore the relatively small discrepancies that inevitably exist between
the real distribution and the ND.

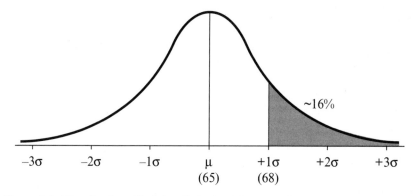

Figure 1.3 Distribution of heights (in inches) for an entire population of women

Areas under the Normal Curve

Let us look at how the ND can help us deal with the distribution of heights for the female population. Suppose we have measured the heights of enough women that we have excellent estimates of μ and σ, and that they are 65 inches and 3 inches, respectively. Now imagine that we want to know the percentile rank of a woman who is 68 inches. Without using the ND, we would need a histogram of the entire population so we could add the percentages of all the bars up to 68 inches (and you would want lots of skinny bars—perhaps tenths of inches—for greater accuracy). If we use the ND instead you don't need a whole population of height measurements. You have a smooth curve that follows a mathematical equation; you can use the calculus to integrate the area of the curve from negative infinity up to 68 inches. Fortunately, you don't need to know what calculus is to use the ND, because the work has already been done for you.

Take a look at Figure 1.3. A woman who is 68 inches tall is one σ (3 inches) above μ (65 inches). Note that all NDs have the same shape, so a score that is one σ above μ always has about 84% of the distribution below (to the left of) it and about 16% above, regardless of the variable being measured. Before computers could easily figure out the proportion of the ND below any particular score, tables were calculated to give proportions of the ND in terms of different fractions of σ. To understand these tables you need to be introduced to z scores, our next topic.

STANDARDIZED SCORES

A normal distribution can have any values for its mean and standard deviation, but once you mark off the x-axis in terms of μ and σ (as in Figure 1.3), all NDs look alike (e.g., as you move to the right of the mean the curve falls more and more sharply until you get to one σ, then the rate of the curve's descent stops increasing and starts decreasing). When a raw score (e.g., 68 inches) is expressed in terms of σ (e.g., one σ above the mean), we say it has been transformed to a *standardized score*. The common symbol for a standardized score is a lower case z. If a score is one σ above the mean, we say that $z = +1$. If the score is one σ below the mean, $z = -1$. Any raw score can be transformed to a z score by using the following simple formula:

$$z = \frac{X - \mu}{\sigma} \qquad (1.6)$$

For instance, for the height distribution described above, a woman who is 63 inches tall would have a z score of $(63-65)/3 = -2/3 = -.67$ (approximately).

The Table for the Standard Normal Distribution

Your variable of interest does not have to follow the ND for z scores to be useful. If a friend tells you that she got a 72 on her last physics exam, this is not as informative as her telling you that her z score for the exam was $-.2$ (below the mean, but only one fifth of σ below). But if your variable *does* follow the ND the z score can be looked up in a table that will tell you what proportion of the ND is above or below that score. A common form of the ND table gives proportions between the mean and every z score from 0 to about 4.00 to two decimal places (see Table A.1 in Appendix A). You don't need to have negative z scores in the table, because the ND is perfectly symmetrical (e.g., the proportion between the mean and $z = +.5$ is exactly the same as the proportion between the mean and $z = -.5$). The table usually stops at around 4.0 because the proportion of the ND above $z = 4.0$ is only .00003. The ND table we included in the appendix gives not only the proportion between the mean and z, but also the proportion beyond z: that is, the proportion from z to infinity (in the direction of the right tail of the ND).

Note that Table A.1 corresponds to an ND with a mean of zero and an SD of 1.0; this ND is called the *standard normal distribution*. However, any ND can be transformed into the standard ND by converting all of the scores into z scores. Fortunately, to answer common questions about your data, you don't need to convert all of your scores to z scores—only the ones you have questions about.

Also note that the equation for the ND can be written in terms of z scores (compare Formula 1.5' to Formula 1.5).

$$f(x) = \frac{1}{\sqrt{2\pi\sigma^2}} e^{-z^2/2} \tag{1.5'}$$

You can see that the function is largest when z is zero (the exponent of e is at its least negative), and that it is symmetric. Because z is squared, the function has the same height whether a particular z is positive or negative.

Properties of z Scores

Because z scores work so well with the ND, some students get the erroneous impression that converting a set of scores to z scores makes them follow the ND. In reality, converting to z scores does not change the shape of your distribution at all. However, it does change the μ and σ of your distribution. The mean for a set of z scores will always be zero, because subtracting a constant from your scores subtracts the same constant from your mean. If the constant you're subtracting *is* the mean (as in Formula 1.6), then your new mean will be $\mu - \mu$, which equals zero. The standard deviation for a set of z scores will always be 1.0 because dividing your scores by a constant results in σ being divided by that constant; if the constant you're dividing by *is* σ (as in Formula 1.6), then your new σ will be σ/σ, which equals 1.0.

However, if your distribution is negatively skewed your z scores will be negatively skewed as well, and you will have a few large negative z scores, but no really large positive z scores (of course, the reverse is true for a positively skewed distribution). If you know that someone's z score on a test is large and positive you won't know quite what to make of it unless you know something about the skewness of the distribution. If you know the distribution is normal, you know exactly where in the distribution that z score falls. It is also important to note that adding, subtracting, multiplying, or dividing all of your scores by a constant (or any combination of the above) will not change the z scores associated with any of your scores. Adding or subtracting a constant changes a score, but it changes the mean by the same amount, so the difference between the score and the mean (which is the numerator of the z score) is not changed. Nor is the denominator of the z score changed, because the standard deviation is not affected by the addition or subtraction of constants. Multiplying or dividing by a constant will change the numerator of the z score (e.g., $60 - 40$ is greater than $6 - 4$), but the denominator will change proportionally, so again the z score stays the same. Your weight can be measured in pounds or kilograms, but your z score in a particular group of people will be the same either way. The mathematical properties of z scores are summarized along with the properties of the mean and standard deviation in Rapid Reference 1.3.

Rapid Reference 1.3

Properties of the Mean, Standard Deviation, and Standardized Scores

Mean. Adding or subtracting a constant from the scores changes the mean in the same way. Multiplying or dividing by a constant also changes the mean in the same way. The sum of squared deviations is smaller around the mean than any other point in the distribution.

Standard deviation. Adding or subtracting a constant from the scores does not change the standard deviation. However, multiplying or dividing by a constant means that the standard deviation will be multiplied or divided by the same constant. The standard deviation is smaller when calculated around the mean than any other point in the distribution.

Standardized scores. Adding, subtracting, multiplying or dividing the scores by a constant does not change the standardized scores. The mean of a set of z scores is zero, and the standard deviation is 1.0.

DEALING WITH DEPARTURES FROM THE NORMAL DISTRIBUTION

For some variables, like height, blood pressure, and IQ scores, we have enough data that we can be confident that the true population distribution looks so much like the mathematical normal distribution that the latter can be used as a good approximation of the former. However, social scientists often study variables about which there may be very few data, such as the number of close friends people have, or variables that are measured in a new way (e.g., the recall of a list of words created for a new study). Unfortunately, the fewer the data you have for a particular variable, the less confidence you can have about guessing the shape of the population distribution from which you are sampling. In the next chapter we will discuss why the shape of your population distribution is not as important as you might think for advanced statistics. But it certainly can be useful to use whatever data you have to judge whether the ND is a fairly close approximation of your population distribution.

The first step is to take a really careful look at your data. One way is to draw a histogram or frequency polygon. In recent years a whole branch of statistics, *exploratory data analysis* (EDA), has been devised to create better ways to display data and highlight important trends (Behrens, 1997). We will talk about EDA shortly, but first we want to mention some traditional ways to compare your data to the ND.

Measuring Skewness

Probably the most frequent departure from the ND that is seen in the distributions with which social scientists work is skewness, often due to floor or ceiling effects. A common measure of skewness involves finding the average of the cubed rather than squared (i.e., raising to the 3rd rather than 2nd power) deviations from the mean, and comparing this average to the variance. Cubing a deviation, unlike squaring, preserves its sign (e.g., $-2^3 = -8$), so large scores on the left (negative) side of the distribution, not balanced by similar scores on the right side, will lead to negative skewness, whereas the reverse situation will produce positive skewness. A symmetrical distribution like the ND will have zero skewness. A skewness measure for a set of data can be tested to see if it is unreasonable to use a symmetrical distribution as an approximation. But these tests are not very helpful when they are most needed—when the sample is fairly small—so they are not often used.

Measuring Kurtosis

Another departure from normality that may be seen in a real distribution is the percentage of scores that would be considered extreme. A distribution could be relatively flat, or there could be a concentration of scores in the middle, with a sharp drop-off at moderate distances from the mean, and a relatively high proportion of extreme scores. This kind of pattern can be assessed by a measure called *kurtosis,* which is based on averaging deviations from the mean raised to the 4th power and comparing that average to the variance. It is said that kurtosis is based on the fourth *moment* of the distribution, skewness on the third, the variance on the second (and the mean on the first). There are no popular measures based on any moment higher than the fourth. Raising to the 4th power gives more weight to extreme scores than squaring. So distributions with thicker tails (i.e., a higher percentage of extreme scores) than the ND, such as the *t* distribution (introduced in Chapter 3), have positive kurtosis (if kurtosis is adjusted to zero for the ND), and they are called *leptokurtic.* Relatively flat distributions have negative kurtosis and are called *platykurtic* (the ND is defined as being in the middle, or *mesokurtic*).

As with skewness, the kurtosis of a data set can be tested to see if the ND is a reasonable approximation, but for the same reason as the skewness test, it is rarely done. There are more direct tests of the resemblance to a theoretical distribution; probably the most common is the *Kolmogorov-Smirnov test.* Although this is an appropriate test, researchers are more likely to just eyeball their data and become concerned about their distribution only if it seems as though their data could not possibly be coming from a distribution that looks like the ND.

Trimming Your Data

What can researchers do if they are concerned that their data do not look normal (i.e., like the ND)? If the data look fairly consistent with the ND except for a few extreme scores, it makes sense to try to find a good reason to drop the outliers (e.g., the respondent didn't understand the instructions, got drowsy, etc.). If no independent reason can be found for dropping outliers, sometimes researchers trim their data, eliminating the highest (or most extreme) 5 or 10% of the scores. This method is especially acceptable if one can anticipate outliers based on previous experiments (this is particularly common when measuring reaction times) and plan the trimming in advance. Trimming your data leads to some complications in applying more advanced statistical analysis to your results, but in recent years there has been a good deal of progress in developing methods for dealing with *robust statistics* (Wilcox, 1998). When the mean, for instance, is calculated for trimmed data, it is called a *trimmed mean;* this is a robust statistic in that outliers do not affect it.

Data Transformations

If instead of having a few distinct outliers your data have a strong skew to one side or the other, you can make your distribution more normal by applying a mathematical transformation to all of the scores in your data set. Suppose that children from different economic backgrounds are sketching the same coin from memory and you are measuring the areas of the circle they are drawing. The data for five children could be 4, 9, 9, 16, and 100 squared centimeters. The strong positive skew of the data can be reduced by taking the square root of each number; the data would be transformed to 2, 3, 3, 4, and 10. In this case you have switched from measuring the area of the coins to a measure that is propor-

> ### CAUTION
>
> For more advanced statistics it is often helpful to be dealing with a normal distribution. If your distribution contains outliers, or has a skewness or kurtosis very different from the ND, you may want to either *trim* your data or *transform* your data. However, trimmed data require special robust methods of data analysis, and statistical results on transformed data can be difficult to interpret.

tional to the diameter of the coins. Unfortunately, data transformations usually do not have such a simple interpretation, but they are fairly common and considered quite legitimate nonetheless. In cases of extreme skewing, a data transformation can allow you to use advanced statistics based on the ND and can prevent you from resorting to the less powerful techniques described in the final chapter of this text. The value of data transformations will become clearer as we discuss more advanced statistical methods in later chapters.

EXPLORATORY DATA ANALYSIS

Whether or not you are looking at your data in order to decide if your values could have come easily from an ND, it is a good idea to look carefully at your data before rushing to summarize them with a few statistics, such as the mean and standard deviation. To encourage researchers to explore their data thoroughly before calculating summary statistics, John Tukey (1969, 1977) devised several techniques, mostly involving visual displays of data, that form the basis of EDA, as mentioned previously.

Stem-and-Leaf Plots

One of the simplest of the EDA techniques is an alternative to the histogram called the *stem-and-leaf plot*, or stemplot, for short. If the IQ scores for 30 students in a sixth-grade class ranged from 94 to 136, the stems would be the numbers 9 through 13, arranged vertically, and the leaves would be the final digits of each IQ score (e.g., 4 for the lowest, and 6 for the highest IQ). The entire stemplot is shown in Figure 1.4. Notice how the stemplot exhibits the shape of the distribution (unimodal, skewed) while at the same time containing all of the actual values.

```
13 | 0  6
12 | 0  1  6
11 | 1  3  3  7  7  9
10 | 0  1  2  2  3  4  4  4  6  7  7  9
 9 | 4  5  6  6  7  9  9
```

Figure 1.4 Stem-and-leaf plot for 30 IQ scores

The height of a histogram bar may tell you how many students scored in the 120s, but not what the actual scores were, whereas in Figure 1.4, you can see that the three scores in the 120s were 120, 121, and 126. It would be easy to compare last year's class to this year's by using the same stems for both classes and putting the leaves for last year's class to the left and those for this year's class to the right. There are numerous variations for getting a convenient number of stems depending on how your data range, but this technique is not feasible for really large data sets. Another popular form of display that is suitable for any size data set is described next.

Box-and-Whisker Plots

A very convenient and descriptive way to summarize a set of data is with a *box-and-whisker plot,* or boxplot, for short. If the values of the dependent variable are placed along the horizontal axis, the vertical sides of the box (called the hinges), are placed at the 25th and 75th percentiles. (The exact definition of the hinges, according to Tukey [1977] is a bit different, but the 1st and 3rd quartiles are a good approximation.) The distance between the hinges (called the *h-spread*) is therefore the same as the interquartile (IQ) range. The median is also drawn as a vertical line within the box. In a positively skewed distribution, the median will be closer to the left than the right side of the box; the reverse pattern holds for a negatively skewed distribution. The whisker on the right side of the box extends horizontally until it hits the highest value in the distribution that isn't further than 1.5 times the *h*-spread, and similarly on the left side of the box (the locations that are 1.5 *h*-spreads from either side of the box are called the *inner fences,* and the most extreme values on either side that are not past the inner fences are called the *adjacent values*). Points that lie beyond the inner fences in either direction are considered outliers and are drawn individually as points in the boxplot. The features of a typical boxplot are shown in Figure 1.5.

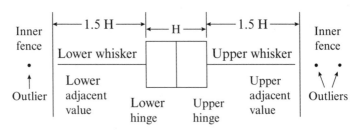

Figure 1.5 Complete boxplot

The boxplot shows at a glance the skewing of the distribution (the position of the median inside the box, the relative lengths of the whiskers on either side) and the presence of outliers. At the same time it provides the locations of all the quartiles and the full range of the scores in the data set. There are many possible variations involving the details of the boxplot. For instance, drawing the boxplots vertically (the DV is on the y-axis of the graph) can be particularly convenient when comparing several boxplots from different data sets.

Boxplots and stemplots are only two of many graphic methods that are part of exploratory data analysis, but they are among the most popular. These methods are helpful when you have many measurements and need to see how they are distributed. However, these methods become even more important if you need to make inferences about the population from which your data have come. The reasons for this will become clear in the next chapter.

Putting It Into Practice

1. Imagine that you are an anthropologist who has discovered a group of never-before-seen people who are native to the continent of Antarctica. You suspect that because they live in such a cold climate, their normal body temperatures differ from other human beings. To test that hypothesis, you manage to measure the body temperatures (in degrees Fahrenheit) of 25 Antarcticans. The measurements are listed below: 97.6, 98.7, 96.9, 99.0, 93.2, 97.1, 98.5, 97.8, 94.5, 90.8, 99.7, 96.6, 97.8, 94.3, 91.7, 98.2, 95.3, 97.9, 99.6, 89.5, 93.0, 96.4, 94.8, 95.7, 97.4.

    (a) What are the mode, median, and mean for the data above? Which way does the distribution seem to be skewed?

    (b) What are the range, mean deviation, and standard deviation?

2. (a) Create a histogram, stemplot, and boxplot for the data.

    (b) What is the percentile rank for a temperature of 95.0°? Of 98.6°?

    (c) What temperature is at the 30th percentile? The 65th percentile?

3. (a) What is the z score for a body temperature of 95.0°? For 98.6°?

    (b) What body temperature has a z score of $+1.5$? Of -0.8?

4. For the following questions, assume a normal distribution for Antarcticans, with a mean and SD equal to the values you found for the sample above.

    (a) What percentage of Antarcticans would have body temperatures above 95.0°? Above 98.6°?

    (b) What percentage of Antarcticans would have body temperatures *below* 95.0°? How does this compare to the PR you found for 95.0° in 2b? Explain the relationship between the two answers.

🦎 TEST YOURSELF 🦎

1. **Even if your data consist of numbers, it is not valid to perform arithmetic operations on those numbers if your data were derived from**

    (a) a nominal scale.

    (b) a discrete scale.

    (c) a ratio scale.

    (d) an interval scale.

2. **If a participant's attitude toward the death penalty is assessed on a scale that consists of strongly opposed, somewhat opposed, slightly opposed, neutral, slightly for, somewhat for, and strongly for, which of the following types of scales is being used?**

    (a) A nominal scale

    (b) An ordinal scale

    (c) An interval scale

    (d) A ratio scale

3. **If your data have been measured on an ordinal scale, an appropriate way to display the distribution is by means of**

    (a) a frequency polygon.

    (b) a histogram.

    (c) a bar graph.

    (d) an ogive.

4. **A major advantage of the stem-and-leaf plot as compared to other methods for displaying data is that**

    (a) all of the original data are preserved.

    (b) any skewing of the distribution will be evident.

    (c) it takes up less space.

    (d) it displays data horizontally rather than vertically.

5. **Which of the following will definitely be affected by taking an extreme point and making it even more extreme?**

    (a) The mean

    (b) The median

    (c) The mode

    (d) None of the above will be affected

6. **It is not possible for more than half of the scores in a distribution to be above**

    (a) the mode.

    (b) the median.

    (c) the mean.

    (d) the mode, median, or mean.

7. **Which of the following is unaffected by extreme scores?**
   (a) The range
   (b) The interquartile range
   (c) The mean deviation
   (d) The standard deviation

8. **If a constant is subtracted from all of the scores in a distribution,**
   (a) the standard deviation will be negative.
   (b) that constant will be subtracted from the standard deviation.
   (c) that constant will be added to the standard deviation.
   (d) the standard deviation will be unchanged.

9. **By inspecting a boxplot of your data, you can see**
   (a) all of the individual scores.
   (b) the skewness of your distribution.
   (c) the mean and SD of your distribution.
   (d) the mode and mean deviation of your distribution.

10. **If a distribution of raw scores is positively skewed, the distribution after converting to z scores will be**
   (a) positively skewed.
   (b) the standard normal distribution.
   (c) negatively skewed.
   (d) less skewed than the original distribution.

Answers: 1. a; 2. b; 3. c; 4. a; 5. a; 6. b; 7. b; 8. d; 9. b; 10. a.

Two

INTRODUCTION TO NULL HYPOTHESIS TESTING

I n the previous chapter we mentioned several times that some statistics play a more important role in the area of advanced statistics than others (e.g., the standard deviation). When we used the term *advanced statistics* we were referring to a branch of statistics called *inferential statistics,* which we introduce in this chapter. Although sometimes you may want to do nothing more than describe the scores that you have, more often it is not practical to measure everyone in the population of interest, so you'll want to use a sample to make a guess (an inference) about the population. The methods of inferential statistics can help you to do that as accurately as possible. The type of inferential statistics we will be dealing with in this chapter is called *parametric statistics,* because it involves estimating (or drawing inferences about) the parameters of a distribution—in this case, the normal distribution (whose parameters are the mean and standard deviation). Parametric statistics requires that your dependent variable be measured on an interval or ratio scale, and that will be one of the assumptions underlying the statistical methods in all of the following chapters except for the last. The last chapter will cover the topic of nonparametric statistics.

SAMPLES AND POPULATIONS

Probably the simplest example of statistical inference is trying to guess the mean of a population on a variable that has not been studied very extensively. For instance, as a market researcher you may want to know the average number of hours per week that Americans spend browsing the web. Obviously you're not going to be able to measure *everybody!* So if you want to estimate that quantity using the standard methods of inferential statistics as described in this book, the first step is to decide on a sample size and then to obtain a *random sample* of the population in which you are interested (in this case, Americans). Let us say that you have decided to sample 100 residents of the United States. This is not a trivial matter. To obtain a truly random sample you must strictly obey two rules:

(1) Everyone in the population must have an equal chance of getting sampled; and (2) selecting one particular person must not affect the chances of any other person's being selected. The second rule prevents you from selecting whole families at a time, for instance, or setting quotas (e.g., saying you have too many men at one point so you must sample more women). The resulting sample would be called a simple or *independent random sample*.

Random Sampling

Let us look at the difficulties involved in obtaining a "simple" random

> ### DON'T FORGET
> ....
>
> **When Will I Use the Statistics in This Chapter?**
>
> You have measured a quantitative variable on a random sample of cases, and you want to use the information you have to estimate the mean or variance of the population from which the sample was drawn. Alternatively, the sample may have been given an experimental treatment, or sampled from a subgroup of the population, and you want to determine if your sample truly represents the larger population, or whether it can best be considered as coming from a population with a different mean.

sample. You would have to have the name of every U.S. resident (not just those with web access) in your database. A computer could do a pretty good job of picking 100 names at random, but you would have to contact every person selected and get web-browsing information from each one. If anyone refuses to give the required information, or cannot be contacted, the sample will not be truly random (even if you replace those people with other randomly selected people). To be truly random the sample must include the kinds of people who refuse to participate in such surveys (those people might be higher or lower than the average in their web browsing habits). Compliance is a greater problem in studies that require even more active participation than answering a few survey questions. Although the accuracy of inferential statistics formulas rely, in part, on the assumption that the samples have been randomly selected, such sampling is rare in the social sciences—and yet these formulas are often used anyway. We'll point out as we go along how the lack of random sampling may impact your statistical inferences in different types of research, and how researchers try to avoid the problem.

If you are trying to estimate the mean web-browsing time for the population from the data from a random sample the next step is to calculate the mean of the sample. The sample mean (symbolized as $\overline{X}$ or M) provides a good *point estimate* of the population mean (you will learn how to suplement your point estimate with an interval estimate later in this chapter). Let us say that the average for your sample is 3.2 hours per week. Our best guess (i.e., point estimate) for the population mean, therefore, is 3.2. Suppose, however, that instead of sampling 100 people, you decided to ask only 10 people. Should an estimate based on 10 people be taken as seriously as an estimate based on one hundred people, or a thousand? The answer is clearly no. To understand how seriously to take any estimate of a population mean that is based on a random sample we need to understand how different random samples from the same population can differ in the estimates they produce. That is our next topic.

Sampling Distributions

Even though the population mean is a fixed number, different samples from that population will almost always have different means. To see how much sample means vary, first imagine that our random samples are the same size and that we draw very many of them (always replacing the people drawn from one sample before drawing the next sample) from the same population. When we have enough sample means they will form a fairly smooth histogram that represents the distribution of the sample means. This distribution is called the *sampling distribution of the mean*. If we instead found the median of each sample, these sample medians would pile up into something called the *sampling distribution of the median*. However, the sampling distribution of the mean (SDM) follows some simple statistical laws that make it particularly easy to deal with.

One of these laws states that if the population follows an ND, then the SDM will follow the ND as well. Although none of the variables of social science research follow the ND exactly, some, like height, are pretty close, so we can be sure that if we found the mean heights for equal-sized samples then these sample means would follow a distribution very similar to the ND. In fact, even variables whose distributions are far from the ND can have SDMs similar to the ND, thanks to a very helpful statistical law known as the *Central Limit Theorem* (CLT).

The Central Limit Theorem

The CLT states that, regardless of the shape of the population distribution, the SDM will approach the ND as the size of the samples (not the number of samples, which is assumed to be infinite, but the *size* of each of the equal-sized samples) approaches infinity. For some very strangely shaped population distributions the sample size may have to be quite large before the SDM begins to resemble the ND. But it is fortunate that for roughly bell-shaped, unimodal distributions, even if quite skewed, the SDM begins to look surprisingly similar to the ND even for modest sample sizes that are no more than 30 or 40.

As an example, let us look at annual income for households in the United States. The population distribution is very (positively) skewed, as you can see in panel A of Figure 2.1. However, if you take random samples of 40 households each, the means of these samples will form a distribution that is much less skewed, as shown in panel B of Figure 2.1. It may not be unusual to find one household whose annual income is over $100,000, but if you select 40 households at random and average their incomes together it is very unlikely that the mean of this sample will exceed $100,000. Even if one of the 40 households has a very large income it is likely that the other 39 households will be relatively close to the population mean, thus limiting the influence of that one wealthy family on the sample mean. You may notice that the SDM is not only more symmetric than the population distribution of individuals, it is also less spread out. That is the next point to be discussed.

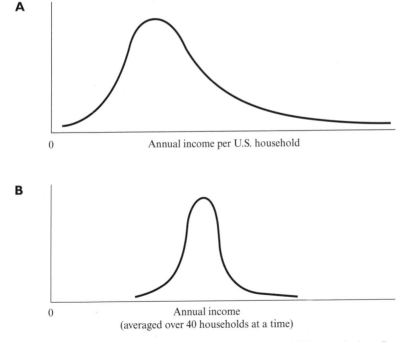

Figure 2.1 A, Distribution of annual income for the U.S. population; B, sampling distribution of the mean for N = 40

Standard Error of the Mean

The laws of statistics tell us not only that the SDM will be more like the ND than is the population distribution and that this resemblance increases with sample size; they also tell us what the mean and standard deviation of the SDM will be. The mean is easy. Is there any reason that the mean of all the sample means should be any different from the population mean? (For example, if the mean annual household income in the United States were $35,000, why would samples of 40 households each consistently average to some lower or higher amount?) So it should be easy to remember that the mean of the SDM is μ, the mean of the population. However, sample means won't *vary* as much as individual scores will. Suppose that you draw random samples of 1,000 men at a time and calculate the mean height for the men in each sample. Can you imagine these sample means varying much from each other? The larger the samples, the less their means will vary. There is a simple law that connects the variability of the sample means to the sample size, and it is expressed in the following formula:

$$\sigma_{\bar{x}} = \frac{\sigma}{\sqrt{N}} \tag{2.1}$$

The symbol $\sigma_{\bar{x}}$ stands for the standard deviation of the sample means, and it has its own name; for purely historical reasons, $\sigma_{\bar{x}}$ is called the *standard error of the mean* (but it is literally the standard deviation of all the sample means). If, for instance, σ for the height of men is 2.5 inches, $\sigma_{\bar{x}}$ for samples of 100 men each would be a quarter of an inch ($2.5/\sqrt{100} = 2.5/10 = .25$). Therefore, it would be very unusual for a random sample of 100 men to have a mean that is more than, say, one inch from the population mean. In fact, we can estimate just how unusual that sample would be using methods we will describe next.

DON'T FORGET

Compared to the distribution of individuals in the population, the sampling distribution of the mean (i.e., the distribution of the means of random groups from the population) is (1) less skewed (unless, of course, the population distribution is not skewed at all); and (2) less spread out (i.e., its standard deviation, called the standard error of the mean, is less).

The z Score for Groups

To determine how unusual a particular sample is in terms of its mean on some variable, we can calculate its z score just as we would for individuals. The z score, modified for groups, is as follows:

$$z = \frac{\overline{X} - \mu}{\sigma_{\overline{x}}} \qquad (2.2)$$

Substituting Formula 2.1 into 2.2 yields Formula 2.2′:

$$z = \frac{\overline{X} - \mu}{\dfrac{\sigma}{\sqrt{N}}} \qquad (2.2′)$$

For instance, if the mean height of all men (μ) is 69 inches with a standard deviation (σ) of 2.5 inches, and a random sample of 100 men has a mean height of 70 inches, the z score for the random sample, according to Formula 2.2′ is

$$z = \frac{70 - 69}{\dfrac{2.5}{\sqrt{100}}} = \frac{1}{\dfrac{2.5}{10}} = \frac{1}{.25} = 4.0$$

Translating that z score into a statement about probability is easy because the distribution of sample means for groups of 100 men (randomly sampled) measured on height will be so close to the ND that we can use the table of the standard ND without worry. Looking up $z = 4.0$ in Table A.1 shows us that only .00003 (three out of one hundred thousand) or .003% of all such random samples will be taller than the one we are testing. Therefore, the probability of selecting a random sample that is taller than the one we are testing is .00003—a very unlikely occurrence. It is safe to say that the sample we are looking at is unusual.

The z score for groups is not used very often in the social sciences, but more complex variations of it are used very often as part of a system known as *null hypothesis testing* (NHT). In this chapter we will introduce the concepts of NHT in the context of the z score for groups. In subsequent chapters the z score formula will grow in complexity (and change its name), but the concepts of NHT will remain essentially the same. To explain the need for NHT we first have to describe a simple social science experiment.

NULL HYPOTHESIS TESTING

Suppose that you have invented a new method for teaching children how to read. How would you go about testing its effectiveness? You would probably teach a few students individually to perfect the technique, but ultimately you would want to test the method on a randomly selected class of students. In fact, most experiments in the social sciences are performed on groups of people rather than on a few individuals. Researchers prefer groups in part because often they are looking for small or variable changes that are easier to see in a group than in a few individuals. For example, if you're testing a drug that turns out to have an effect on most but not all people, you might miss the effect if you looked at just a few individuals who happened to be part of the minority that does not respond to the drug.

So now imagine that you have used your method to teach a class of 25 randomly selected students and, at the end of the year, you gave them a standard reading test. Of course, your first step would be to calculate the mean of the 25 scores. Let's say the mean is 3.2. If the national average is 3.0 (these are students in the third grade), you might find these results encouraging. However, many criticisms of your experiment could be raised, and some of these would involve the randomness of your sample. It is hard to obtain a truly random sample of the population of interest, but even if you had, there's a surprisingly simple objection that can be raised if you try to conclude that your class scored above the national average because of your new method. The fact is that, as we have mentioned before, the means of random samples will not all be exactly the same as the population mean. Even among random classes taught by the standard method, some will score below and some above the 3.0 average. Some may even score above the 3.2 attained by the class taught by the new method. How can you know that the class scoring 3.2 would not have scored just as highly if taught by the traditional method? (The hypothesis that there is *no* difference between the new and the traditional method is called the *null hypothesis*.)

Unfortunately, you can never know the answer to that question with certainty. However, it is rather easy to use the methods we have already discussed to determine the probability of a random sample taught by the traditional method scoring a mean of 3.2 or higher. The lower that probability, the more confident you can feel that your result is not an accident due to sampling. To find that probability you must first find the z score for your class. If the national average on the test is 3.0 and σ equals .6, and a class of 25 (N) has a mean ($\overline{X}$) of 3.2, the z for that class is:

$$z = \frac{3.2 - 3.0}{\dfrac{.6}{\sqrt{25}}} = \frac{.2}{\dfrac{.6}{5}} = \frac{.2}{.12} = 1.67$$

If we assume that the sample means will follow a normal distribution (a fairly safe assumption for $N = 25$), we can use the standard normal table to look for the proportion of the ND beyond $z = 1.67$. That proportion, as can be seen in Table A.1, is .0475. Therefore, if we select at random one sample of 25 students and teach them by the traditional method, the probability is .0475 (a little less than 1 in 20) that that sample will score 3.2 or higher and thus tie or beat our experimental group.

Alpha Levels and Type I Errors

We call this probability the *p value* for our experiment, and we hope that *p* will be so low that we can ignore the possibility that our experimental results could be produced by an unusually good class taught by the traditional method. How low is low enough? This is a fairly arbitrary decision, but the widely held convention in the social sciences is to use a probability of .05 as the cutoff. This probability is called an *alpha level*. If the *p* for your experiment is lower than the alpha level you are using, you can declare your results *statistically significant,* which basically means that you are willing to ignore the objection that your results are really just a lucky accident. To state that your results are statistically significant is to *reject the null hypothesis* (in this case, the hypothesis that the new method would make no difference if you could test everyone in the population); it is always possible that the null is true for your experiment, and that your significant results are really just a lucky accident, but we have to draw a line and decide to take that risk at some point.

   If it turns out that you were wrong in dismissing the lucky-accident (i.e., null) hypothesis, you have made what is commonly called a *Type I error.* In most cases you never get to know for sure whether or not you have committed a Type I error, but to understand why social scientists are so concerned about deciding whether their results can be called statistically significant or not it helps to understand statistical significance within the context of the scientific research community.

The Logic of Null Hypothesis Testing

Imagine that out of the thousands of social science experiments performed each year some unknown percentage consists of null experiments. By a null experiment we mean that the method or treatment being used is *completely* ineffective— that is, it is no better than a placebo or whatever control condition it is being compared to. The problem is that in many of these experiments it will look like the experiment worked a bit just from luck (e.g., in the new reading method experiment it could be that half the population actually performs better with the standard method, but the selected sample accidentally has an unusually high number of students who prefer the new method). If the experiment produced positive results purely by accident, it would be misleading if the results were published, which would suggest that the treatment does work. It would be a good idea to screen out as large a percentage of these null experiments as possible in order to prevent them from being published in a way that suggests the treatment is effective. This is where NHT comes in.

It is generally easier to find the distribution of null experiments than a distribution of experiments in which the treatments work. For a one-group experiment involving a variable whose population mean and standard deviation are known, the distribution of null experiments, known as the *null hypothesis distribution* (NHD) is simply the distribution of (random) sample means from the population (i.e., the sampling distribution of the mean). If we allow only the top 5% of the NHD to be called statistically significant, we are screening out 95% of the null experiments. The 5% of null experiments that pass the test and get called statistically significant are Type I errors because they are really null experiments. Setting alpha at .05 means that we are setting the Type I error rate at 5%—that we have decided to let the best 5% of null experiments be called statistically significant, implying that their treatments do work at least a bit, even though they really don't.

Type II Errors

At this point you might well be thinking, "Why allow any null experiments to be called statistically significant? Why not screen them all out?" The problem is that we almost never know for sure when we are dealing with a null experiment. No matter how good a result looks, there is always some chance (even if it is very tiny) that it comes from a null experiment. So we cannot screen out all null experiments without screening out *all* experiments. Perhaps you are thinking instead: "Okay, but why allow a 5% rate of Type I errors? Why not reduce the rate to 1% or even less?" To understand the consequences of making alpha smaller you must keep in mind that it isn't only null experiments that are being subjected to NHT; experiments performed on treatments that really do work are subjected to the same test. If a treatment works only slightly, it can easily produce results that do not pass the test (i.e., the null hypothesis is not rejected), because the results look like those often obtained by accident from null experiments. When a non-null experiment does *not* get called statistically significant, another type of error has been made: the *Type II error*.

Reducing alpha would require results to be stronger to pass the test, so a larger percentage of weak but non-null experiments would fail the test, increasing the rate of Type II errors (that rate is symbolized by the Greek letter beta, β). The .05 alpha level is widely considered a reasonable compromise that keeps the Type I error rate fairly low without letting the Type II error rate get too high. The Type II error rate depends, in part, on just how "non-null" an experiment is (i.e., how effective the treatment is). Because that is something we can only guess about in a given case, we can only estimate Type II error rates roughly. Such estimations

≡ Rapid Reference 2.1

The Probabilities Involved in Null Hypothesis Testing

	Null Hypothesis Is Really True	Null Hypothesis Is Really False
Results declared not significant	Correct decision (1 − alpha)	Type II error (beta)
Results declared significant	Type I error (alpha)	Correct decision (1 = beta 5 power of test)

Note: Alpha is set by the experimenter (usually the widely accepted .05 level). Beta is determined by several factors, including the degree to which the null hypothesis is false (which is generally not known), and can only be estimated roughly (this estimation will be covered in Chapter 6). The probabilities can be meaningfully added down each column, but not across the rows. Each probability can be thought of as the proportion of events in that column that will fall under that decision. For instance, 1 − alpha is the proportion of null experiments that will be declared not significant.

will be postponed until Chapter 6, when the topic of *power* will be discussed. The probabilities involved in null hypothesis testing are summarized in Rapid Reference 2.1.

Critical Values

In our example, in which the effectiveness of a new reading method was tested, the z score we calculated was looked up in Table A.1 to find the p value. This step can be skipped if we find the z score that falls exactly on the borderline for our alpha level. If we look for .0500 in the "beyond z" column of Table A.1 we find that it falls between $z = 1.64$ (.0505) and $z = 1.65$ (.0495), so we can say that a z score of 1.645 falls on the borderline. Any z score larger than 1.645 (e.g., 1.65) will be associated with a p less than .05 and will therefore be significant at the .05 level. Any z score less than 1.645 (e.g., 1.64) will have a p greater than .05, and will fail to reach significance at the .05 level. This borderline z score is called a *critical z score;* for example, $z = 1.645$ is the critical z for a .05 test (symbolized $z_{.05}$) that is one-tailed (one- and two-tailed tests will be explained in the next paragraph).

Knowing the critical z for your alpha level saves you the trouble of looking up the p value that corresponds to the z score for your experimental group. If your calculated z is greater than the critical z, you know that your p value will be less than alpha, and you can therefore reject the null hypothesis. Looking up critical values is not necessary when you perform a statistical test by computer because your statistical program will give you the exact p value that corresponds to your z score. However, occasionally you may need to calculate a statistical test by hand, and if you need to compare your result to a distribution other than the normal, a table of critical values can be very convenient, as you will see in subsequent chapters.

One- versus Two-Tailed Tests

There is one complication of the z test that we haven't yet addressed. What if the class taught by your new method obtained a mean of only 2.5? Would you want to test it to see if this mean is significantly *less* than what is expected from the traditional method? Probably not. You would probably just work on figuring out what went wrong. But if you were testing some controversial method that could be counterproductive, you might be interested in testing both good (i.e., above 3.0) and bad results (it would be important to know that the new method is making learning significantly worse than the traditional method). In this case, 5% of the null hypothesis distribution reaches significance on the positive side, and another 5% reaches significance on the negative side (see panel A of Figure 2.2).

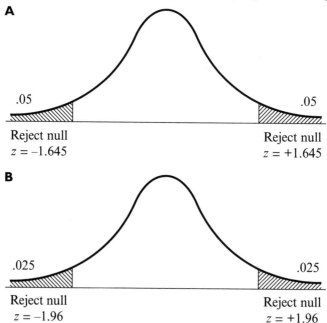

Figure 2.2 A, A one-tailed .05 test in both directions leads to a total alpha of .10; **B,** in a two-tailed .05 test, .025 (half of alpha) is placed in each tail

The Type I error rate and, therefore, your alpha, would be .10 instead of .05 because you are performing a *two-tailed* test.

To keep alpha down to .05 when performing a two-tailed test you have to divide alpha in half and put .025 area in each tail (as in panel B of Figure 2.2). The critical zs for the two-tailed .05 test are $+1.96$ and -1.96 (you can see in Table A.1 that the area beyond $z = 1.96$ is .0250). The price you pay for being able to test a result in both directions is that you need a stronger result to reach significance.

The one- and two-tailed distinction affects p values as well as the critical values. When we looked up the area beyond $z = 1.67$ and found that our p value was .0475 we were finding a one-tailed p value. The two-tailed p value would be twice as much (we are allowing for results as extreme as ours on *both* sides of the distribution): the two-tailed p equals $2 \cdot .0475 = .095$. Notice that a z of 1.67 is significant if a one-tailed test is performed ($p = .0475 < .05$), but not for a two-tailed test ($p = .095 > .05$). Thus, it is understandable that statistics texts often tell students that a two-tailed test should only be performed when you have no hypothesis about which way the results will go, and that a one-tailed test should be used when you have a clear prediction about the direction of the results. However, this is another one of those cases where common practice tends not to match the textbooks.

It is rare that a researcher compares two experimental conditions without hypothesizing about which condition will have the higher mean on some dependent variable. However, it is also true that paradoxical results are common in the social sciences. The publication of one-tailed tests implies a trust that the researcher would not have tested results in the unpredicted direction no matter how interesting. If, for instance, researchers routinely performed one-tailed .05 tests for results in the predicted direction, and then turned around and performed two-tailed tests whenever the results turned out opposite to prediction, the overall Type I error rate would really be $.05 + .025 = .075$, more than the generally agreed-upon alpha of .05.

To be *conservative* (in statistics, this means being especially cautious about Type I errors), the more prestigious journals usually require the two-tailed test to be used as the default and allow one-tailed tests only in special circumstances (e.g., results in the opposite direction would not only be unpredicted, but they would be ridiculous or entirely uninteresting). If you did plan to use a one-tailed test but the results came out significant in

CAUTION

To find a critical value for a two-tailed test, first *divide* alpha by two, and then find the z score with *half* of alpha in the "beyond z" column of Table A.1.

To find a two-tailed p value, first find the area "beyond" your z score, and then *multiply* that area by two.

the other direction, you must repeat the experiment and replicate the results if you want to publish them.

Problems with One-Sample Tests

Tests involving the comparison of the mean of a single sample to the population mean offer a simple way to introduce NHT because the null hypothesis distribution is simply the sampling distribution of the mean. However, such experiments are rarely performed. The biggest problem is finding a truly random sample. If the group getting the new reading method is not a random sample of the population it is not fair to compare its mean with the mean of the population. The group with the new method may be from a geographical area that is more affluent or that differs in other ways from the population as a whole. This argument also applies to nonexperimental cases. If you want to prove that left-handed students read better than the national average you have to be sure that your sample of lefties is truly representative of all lefties in the population and is not more affluent, better educated, and the like.

Another problem that involves one-group experiments in particular is the lack of a control group. Is it the specifics of the new teaching method that has increased reading scores, or would any experimental treatment make the students feel special and increase their motivation to learn? With a carefully designed control condition this question would not arise. Finally, it was easy to find the NHD because our example was dealing with a variable (reading scores) so well studied in the population that we can assume we know its mean and standard deviation. More often, researchers are dealing with a variable for which μ and σ are not

DON'T FORGET

The procedure of finding a z score for groups for your experimental sample, and then determining whether it is statistically significant, requires the following assumptions to be true:

1. The sample must have been obtained by independent, random sampling of the population to which you are comparing it.
2. The variable you are measuring should have a normal distribution in the population, but (thanks to the Central Limit Theorem) little accuracy is lost if the distribution is not extremely different from the ND and the sample size is at least about 30.
3. The standard deviation of the new population, represented by the sample, is not different from the standard deviation of the population to which you are comparing it. Of course, the mean of the new population may be different—that is what you are testing.

known. However, If the goal is to estimate the population mean, the z score for groups can be used in a backward way to provide an answer. This will be described next.

INTERVAL ESTIMATION

Earlier we mentioned that the mean of a random sample can be used as a point estimate of the population mean but that the drawback of this is that no distinction is made between estimates from small samples and estimates from large samples. The solution is to supplement your point estimate with an *interval estimate* that does account for sample size. The larger the interval that we use for estimation, the surer we can be that the population mean is in that interval, but, of course, smaller intervals are more useful, so some compromise must be made. If, for instance, the probability is .95 that the population mean is in the stated interval (over many intervals), then we say that our confidence level is 95%. The interval is therefore called a 95% *confidence interval* (CI). This implies that 5% of our CIs will be wrong: They will not contain the population mean. You will recall that 5% is the rate commonly tolerated for Type I errors, so it should not be surprising that the 95% CI is the most common one. Once a CI percentage is chosen, the width of the CI depends in part on the sample size, as we will see next.

Creating Confidence Intervals

The first step in constructing a CI is to put the sample mean in the middle. We can then imagine that the possible values for the population mean form a normal distribution around that point, as in Figure 2.3. To create a 95% CI we want to capture the middle 95% of this distribution, which means that .025 area will be in each tail. The z scores that fall on these boundaries are −1.96 and +1.96. You should recognize these as the critical zs for a .05, two-tailed significance test. The final step is to convert these z scores back into raw scores. Because we are deal-

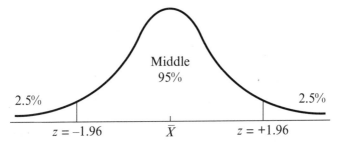

Middle
95%

2.5%   2.5%

$z = -1.96$ $\overline{X}$ $z = +1.96$

Figure 2.3 The 95% confidence interval

ing with sample means instead of individual scores it is the z score for groups that must be used. If we solve Formula 2.2 for μ, which is what we are trying to find, we get:

$$\mu = \overline{X} \pm z_{crit}\, \sigma_{\overline{x}} \qquad (2.3)$$

The plus-and-minus sign reminds you to solve the formula twice: With the minus sign you get the lower boundary of the CI (μ_{lower}), and with the plus sign the upper boundary (μ_{upper}).

Let's calculate an example. Suppose that 100 people are sampled at random and their average web browsing time per week is 3.2 hours ($\overline{X}$) with a standard deviation of 2.5 hours (σ). Because we don't know σ for the population, we have to use σ from our sample as an estimate. Thus, the estimated standard error is $\sigma_{\overline{x}} = 2.5/\sqrt{100} = 2.5/10 = .25$. According to Formula 2.3, the limits of the 95% CI are

$$\mu_{lower} = 3.2 - 1.96(.25) = 3.2 - .49 = 2.71$$

$$\mu_{upper} = 3.2 + 1.96(.25) = 3.2 + .49 = 3.69$$

The Size of Confidence Intervals

We can now say with 95% confidence that the mean of the population we sampled is somewhere between 2.71 and 3.69. Put another way, if we constructed 95% CIs for a living, 95% of them would contain the population mean and 5% would not. If we want to make fewer mistakes, say, only 1%, we would have to construct 99% CIs, which would entail using $z_{.01}$, two-tailed (± 2.575), instead of $z_{.05}$, two-tailed. For the example above, the 99% CI would be 2.56 to 3.84.

One way to make your CI narrower is to decrease the confidence level (e.g., 90%), but this can produce an unacceptably high rate of errors. A better way to narrow your CI, if it is economically feasible, is to increase your sample size. In the above example if your sample size were 400 with the same $\overline{X}$ and σ, the estimated

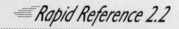

Rapid Reference 2.2

Factors Affecting the Size of a Confidence Interval

• You can make your CI smaller by decreasing your confidence (e.g., from 95% to 90%), but this will increase errors (CIs that don't contain the population mean).

• You can make your CI smaller by increasing your sample size (which decreases the standard error), but this can be too expensive.

• Your CI will be smaller when you are dealing with a variable that has a smaller standard deviation, but that is not a factor that you can control.

standard error would be reduced to .125, so the 95% CI would then range from 2.955 to 3.445 (multiplying your sample size by a constant C divides the width of your CI by the square root of C, so in this case, multiplying N by 4 resulted in a CI half as wide). The factors affecting the size of a CI are summarized in Rapid Reference 2.2.

ESTIMATING THE POPULATION VARIANCE

In the preceding example we used σ from a sample to estimate the population σ. If your sample is very large, the amount of error involved in this estimation may be small enough to ignore. This would be the case in most marketing research aimed at estimating a population mean (sample sizes typically are in the hundreds if not the thousands). However, social scientists are sometimes stuck with small samples (e.g., patients with a rare disease; fossilized jawbones from a particular prehistoric animal) and yet they would still like to estimate a population parameter. In such cases the error involved in estimating a population σ from a sample can be too great to ignore. In the next chapter, you will learn how to compensate for estimates made from small samples. In the meantime, we need to point out that σ from a sample tends, on average, to *underestimate* the σ of the corresponding population (the problem gets worse as the sample gets smaller). This problem is easily corrected for, as we show next.

The Unbiased Sample Variance

Mathematically, it is often easier to work with variances than SDs, so we begin by pointing out that σ^2 from a sample tends to *underestimate* the σ^2 of the corresponding population. This makes σ^2 from a sample a *biased estimator* of the population σ^2. This is not a desirable property of an estimator, but fortunately the bias in this case is easily corrected. It turns out that the mean of all the possible sample σ^2s is $(N-1)/N$ times the population σ^2. Therefore, if we multiply each σ^2 by $N/(N-1)$, we can compensate for this bias, and the average of our sample variances will be exactly equal to the population variance. Let's see what that does to our formula for the sample variance. Multiplying Formula 1.3 by the compensating factor we get

$$\text{Unbiased sample variance} = \left(\frac{N}{N-1}\right)\frac{\sum(X_i - \mu)^2}{N} = \frac{\sum(X_i - \mu)^2}{N}$$

Because this new formula gives us a different (slightly larger) value for the variance of a sample, it should have a different symbol. In keeping with a general trend to use Greek letters for population parameters and corresponding Roman letters for the sample statistics that estimate them, the unbiased estimator of sample variance will be symbolized by s^2. This gives us the following new formula:

$$s^2 = \frac{\sum(X_i - \overline{X})^2}{N - 1} \tag{2.4}$$

Note that $\overline{X}$ is substituted for μ because when we don't know the variance of the population we usually don't know μ either, but when we have a sample we can always calculate the $\overline{X}$ for that sample and then calculate s^2 around $\overline{X}$. Some texts use two versions of s^2 (e.g., one with a "hat" and one without; one capitalized, and one not; etc.) to represent the two ways of calculating the variance of a sample— that is, biased (Formula 1.3 with $\overline{X}$ instead of μ) or unbiased (Formula 2.4). However, we see so little use for the biased sample variance that we will not bother introducing a separate symbol for it. When you see σ^2 in this text you'll know that the set of numbers it is based on is being viewed as a population, and just N is in the denominator. When you see s^2 you'll know that it represents the SD of a sample, and that $N - 1$ is being used in the denominator, as in Formula 2.4.

The Unbiased Standard Deviation

The correction factor for sample variance can be applied just as easily to the standard deviation of a sample. In particular, the result of the following formula is commonly referred to as the *unbiased estimate of the standard deviation* or the *unbiased standard deviation*.

$$s = \sqrt{\frac{\sum(X_i - \overline{X})^2}{N - 1}} \tag{2.5}$$

Although s is not a perfectly unbiased estimate of the population σ, it is close enough for practical purposes and is much better than using Formula 1.4 with $\overline{X}$ for μ. (The reason that s is not perfectly unbiased when s^2 is involves the fact that the square root of an average is not the same as averaging the square roots. For example, if you start with 16, 25, and 36, the average of the square roots is exactly 5, but the square root of the average of these three numbers is 5.0666.) Bear in mind that σ is fine for descriptive purposes, but when drawing inferences about the population, especially from small samples, using s is more accurate.

The Concept of Degrees of Freedom

The use of $N - 1$ as a substitute for N to correct the bias problem is usually explained in terms of an important concept known as *degrees of freedom*, or df for short.

You can see from the formulas that s and s^2 are based on deviations from the mean of a sample. However, if you have 10 scores in a sample and you have calculated $\overline{X}$, only nine deviations from the mean (df $= N - 1$) are free to vary. Once you know the mean and nine of the deviations, the 10th deviation will be whatever must be added to the other nine to make zero. This also works in terms of the scores themselves. If I tell you that the mean of five scores is 6 and that four of the scores are 4, 4, 5, and 9, you should be able to tell me that the fifth score is an 8 (the sum is $N\overline{X} = 5 \cdot 6 = 30$, so $4 + 4 + 5 + 9 + X = 30$, so X must equal 8).

If we define the sum of squares (SS) for a sample as $\Sigma(X - \overline{X})^2$, the unbiased variance can be expressed as $s^2 = \text{SS}/\text{df}$, and the unbiased SD as $s = \sqrt{\text{SS}/df}$. Another way to understand the concept of df is that it is the number of pieces of information you get about the population σ from a sample when you don't know the population mean. Recall the exercise at the end of the previous chapter and imagine that you discover just one Antarctican, and you measure his or her body temperature. If you know the population mean for Antarcticans (perhaps it is 98.6°F), then you have one piece of information about variability. However, if you have no idea what the population mean might be, one Antarctican gives you no information about variability at all (but you do have one piece of information about what the population mean might be). It is when you have two Antarcticans that you have one piece of information about population variance, namely the difference in temperature between the two of them (df $= N - 1 = 2 - 1 = 1$). Only if you knew the population mean would two Antarcticans provide two pieces of information about σ.

Putting It Into Practice

1. In the previous chapter you were given body temperatures for 25 Antarcticans and asked to calculate descriptive statistics. Now you can test whether the Antarcticans differ from the known human population.
   (a) Using the mean and the *unbiased* standard deviation of the 25 scores, calculate a z score comparing the sample to a population that has a mean of 98.6 degrees, and then test that z score for statistical significance at the .05 level with a two-tailed test (in the next chapter, you will learn a more accurate way to test for significance when you don't know the population standard deviation and your sample size is fairly small, as in this exercise).
   (b) If the sample were 100 instead of 25, but with the same sample mean and unbiased SD, what would be its z score? Would the results be significant at the .01 level with a two-tailed test? With a .01 one-tailed test in the correct direction? (Optional: What shortcut could you have used to find the new z score without using the whole z score formula?)

(continued)

   (c) Based on the 25 scores, find the 95% CI for the mean body temperature of all Antarcticans. How can you tell from this CI whether the results in part a would be significant at the .05 level?

   (d) For the example in 1b—$N = 100$—find the 99% CI.

2. Suppose that the movie industry wants to know how often college students go to the movies. Sixteen college students are selected at random from the United States and asked how many movies they have seen in a theater in the previous year. The data are as follows: 7, 13, 0, 10, 2, 8, 4, 11, 0, 5, 16, 6, 2, 12, 9, 0.

   (a) What is your point estimate for the mean number of movie theater visits by all college students in a year?

   (b) Find the 95% confidence interval for the mean of all college students.

   (c) Suppose that the U.S. national average for movie visits in a year is 9.0. If alpha is set to .05, can you reject the null hypothesis that the population mean for college students is the same as the mean for the general population, using a two-tailed test? Show how you can use the CI you found in 2b to answer this part.

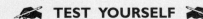 TEST YOURSELF

1. **A sampling distribution is**

   (a) the distribution within any one sample from a population.

   (b) one distribution randomly selected from many possible distributions.

   (c) a distribution in which each of the individuals has been sampled from the same population.

   (d) a distribution of sample statistics, each from a different random sample of the same population.

2. **The standard error of the mean will be approximately equal to**

   (a) the standard deviation of many sample means.

   (b) the mean of many sample standard deviations.

   (c) the mean of many sample means.

   (d) the standard deviation of many sample standard deviations.

3. **The Central Limit Theorem applies only when**

   (a) the size of the samples is infinite.

   (b) the variance of the population distribution is infinite.

   (c) the shape of the population distribution is normal.

   (d) each selection in a sample is independent of all other selections.

4. **Which of the following conditions requires that rather large sample sizes must be used before the sampling distribution resembles the normal distribution?**

   (a) A strongly skewed population distribution

   (b) A very large population variance

   (c) A small, finite population

   (d) All of the above

5. **If the population distribution is positively skewed, which of the following will be true about the shape of the sampling distribution of the mean for a sample size of 10?**
   (a) It will be the same as the population distribution.
   (b) It will be less positively skewed than the population distribution.
   (c) It will be negatively skewed.
   (d) It will be the same as the normal distribution.

6. **Heart rates for a group of 25 joggers were measured, and the mean of the group was found to be 65 beats per minute (bpm). If the mean of the population is 72 bpm with a standard deviation of 10, what is the z score for this group compared to other groups of the same size?**
   (a) $-.7$
   (b) -3.5
   (c) -7.0
   (d) -17.5

7. **The main advantage of a one-tailed test over a two-tailed test is that**
   (a) only half the calculation is required.
   (b) only half of the calculated t value is required.
   (c) there is only half the risk of a Type I error.
   (d) a smaller critical value must be exceeded.

8. **As the calculated z score for a one-sample test gets larger,**
   (a) p gets larger.
   (b) p gets smaller.
   (c) p remains the same, but alpha gets larger.
   (d) p remains the same, but alpha gets smaller.

9. **Compared to Type II errors, Type I errors**
   (a) are more directly controlled by null hypothesis testing.
   (b) are more difficult to detect.
   (c) are more likely to lead to the abandonment of a line of research.
   (d) are far more common in psychological research.

10. **Of all the 95% confidence intervals for the population mean that you construct, about what percent will contain the sample mean?**
   (a) About 5%
   (b) About 95%
   (c) 100%
   (d) It depends on the sample sizes that were used.

Answers: 1. d; 2. a; 3. d; 4. a; 5. b; 6. b; 7. d; 8. b; 9. a; 10. c.

Three

THE TWO-GROUP *t* TEST

THE INDEPENDENT-GROUPS *t* TEST

In the previous chapter, we described one-group hypothesis tests and explained why they are rarely performed. Indeed, the value of knowing about one-group tests has less to do with applying them to data sets than it has to do with the basis they provide for understanding more advanced hypothesis tests. Fortunately, the NHT concepts explained in the previous chapter will apply, with very little modification, to the two-group case, which *is* frequently used. In fact, when participants are *matched* in a two-group test, the procedure reduces to a one-group test, as will be described later in this chapter. We will begin this chapter by describing a possible one-group experiment, and then we will show you how to create and analyze a two-group experiment, as a better alternative.

Many drugs are now available for lowering blood pressure, but suppose that you have been asked to develop a drug for those suffering from low blood pressure. That is, you want a drug that *raises* blood pressure. As an initial test of your new drug, you could give it to a random sample of people, measure their blood pressure after the drug has taken effect, and perform a one-sample significance test against the average blood pressure for the population to see if the null hypothesis (that the drug doesn't work at all) can be rejected. We can perform a one-group test because blood pressure has been measured so extensively that we have a very good estimate of the mean and standard deviation in the population. But a significant result for our test would hardly be conclusive. Did the blood pressure in your sample rise because the drug worked or because the participants were reacting fearfully to being given a dose of some new drug? You can't say for sure. Is your sample truly a random one from the population? Practical considerations make that very unlikely. It is possible that you accidentally drew your sample from a segment of the population that is particularly responsive with respect to blood pressure.

DON'T FORGET

When Will I Use the Statistics in This Chapter?

You are measuring one outcome (i.e., dependent) variable on a quantitative scale, and

- You are comparing the means of two groups that represent existing populations (e.g., cholesterol levels of vegetarians and people who eat meat).
- You have randomly assigned participants to one or the other of two experimental treatments or conditions (e.g., drug group and placebo group). The participants may be matched in pairs before being randomly assigned to the two groups, or the two groups may be completely independent.
- You are measuring the same participants under two different conditions (e.g., each participant performs a task while listening to music and also performs the same task in silence), or before and after some treatment (e.g., the intensity of a phobia is measured before a new type of therapy, and then again after the patient has been in that therapy for six months).

The Two-Group Experiment

A much better way to do the blood pressure experiment is with two groups. One random sample gets the drug, while the other random sample is given a pill that looks and tastes the same but has no active ingredients (i.e., a placebo). Now if the drug group ends up with higher blood pressure on average it can't be due to the situation of taking a new drug. (The ideal way of doing this experiment is called *double-blind*—neither the participants nor the experimenters know who is getting the drug and who is getting the placebo [code numbers are used to keep track] until the experiment is completely finished.) The problem of truly random samples is solved by selecting one large *sample of convenience* (in this case, perhaps people seeking treatment for low blood pressure) and then randomly assigning participants to the two conditions (e.g., drug or placebo). This method isn't perfect (as we will point out later, in our discussion of assumptions), but it does ensure that the groups will almost always be very similar and that, over many experiments, there will not be a systematic bias favoring either the drug or the placebo group. A two-group experiment could be comparing two experimental treatments (e.g., a new form of therapy and a traditional form of therapy) or one experimental treatment with a control group, as in our blood pressure example.

The Two-Group z Score

Suppose that your drug group ends up, on the average, with higher blood pressure than the placebo group. You still have to answer the criticism that your results could be due entirely to chance (e.g., it may be that the blood pressure increases you observed in the participants of both groups are due to fear reactions, and that by accident the drug control group wound up with more fearful participants than the placebo group). In order to dismiss the possibility that you got your good-looking results by accident (i.e., the null hypothesis), you first have to figure out the distribution of null experiments (i.e., experiments just like yours except neither group gets any treatment).

In the two-group case, you could find this distribution (i.e., the NHD) by taking two samples from the same distribution, subtracting their means, and doing this over and over. Fortunately, you don't have to. We know that these differences of means usually will pile up into an approximate normal distribution, and if the two samples are coming from the same population (or two populations with the same mean—we will point out the distinction later), this distribution will be centered at zero. So all we need to know for our hypothesis test is the standard deviation of this NHD, which is called the standard error of the difference ($\sigma_{\overline{X}_1-\overline{X}_2}$). Then we can create a z score for our experimental results as follows:

$$z = \frac{(\overline{X}_1 - \overline{X}_2) - (\mu_1 - \mu_2)}{\sigma_{\overline{X}_1-\overline{X}_2}} \quad (3.1)$$

Compared to the one-group test (Formula 2.2, Chapter 2), it's like seeing double.

In the one-group case, the numerator of the z score is the difference between your specially treated (or selected) group and the mean you would expect to get if the null hypothesis were true. The denominator (i.e., the standard error of the mean) is a typical difference you would get for the numerator when the null hypothesis is true (according to the normal distribution, about two thirds of the numerator differences will be smaller than the typical difference in the denominator, and one third will be larger). In the two-group case, the numerator is the difference between the difference of groups you observed ($\overline{X}_1 - \overline{X}_2$) and the difference you expected ($\mu_1 - \mu_2$). Because the expected difference (i.e., the null hypothesis) is almost always zero for the two-group case (H_0: $\mu_1 = \mu_2$, so $\mu_1 - \mu_2 = 0$), we will leave that term out of the numerator in the future. The denominator is a typical difference of two sample means when H_0 is true.

The Standard Error of the Difference

To find $\sigma_{\overline{X}}$ (the standard error of the mean) in Chapter 2 we used a simple law, $\sigma_{\overline{X}} = \sigma/\sqrt{N}$. There is a similar law that applies to the two-group case. But to make sure you see the similarity, let us change the formula for the standard error of the mean to this equivalent form:

$$\sigma_{\bar{X}} = \sqrt{\frac{\sigma^2}{N}}$$

(the square root of a ratio equals the ratio of the two square roots).

The formula for the standard error of the difference is

$$\sigma_{\bar{X}_1 - \bar{X}_2} = \sqrt{\frac{\sigma_1^2}{n_1} + \frac{\sigma_2^2}{n_2}} \tag{3.2}$$

The notation n_1 and n_2 represents the sample sizes for the two groups and allows for the fact that your drug and placebo groups could have different numbers of participants. The subscripts on σ^2 allow for the case in which you are sampling from two different populations with the same mean but different variances. This is a situation that will be explained later under the topic of homogeneity of variance.

Calculating a Test Comparing Two Groups

In the case of blood pressure, we can use the variance in the general population for both σ_1^2 and σ_2^2. Let's say we are measuring systolic blood pressure (the peak pressure in each heart beat cycle) in mm Hg (millimeters of mercury), and we know the standard deviation in the population to be 20, so $\sigma^2 = 400$. If after taking the drug, 15 participants average 143 mm Hg, and after taking placebos, a separate set of 10 participants averages 125, the z score would be

$$z = \frac{143 - 125}{\sqrt{\dfrac{400}{15} + \dfrac{400}{10}}} = \frac{18}{\sqrt{26.7 + 40}} = \frac{18}{8.17} = 2.2.$$

With an 18-point difference between the two means we can reject the null hypothesis ($2.20 > 1.96$) and conclude that the drug led to significantly higher blood pressure.

The problem with Formula 3.2 is that it requires that you know the population variance. There are very few variables that meet this criterion, other than well-studied aspects of human physiology. If two groups of participants memorize a list of words created for your study—one group while listening to happy music, and the other while listening to sad music—you cannot use Formula 3.2 to find the standard error for comparing their means for recall of those words: No one knows what σ^2 is in this case! However, if your groups are very large (e.g., if both are in the hundreds), the variances of the recall scores within the groups are good estimates of their respective population variances, so you can use a slight modification of Formula 3.2. Inserting the modified version of Formula 3.2 into Formula 3.1 yields

$$z = \frac{\overline{X}_1 - \overline{X}_2}{\sqrt{\dfrac{s_1^2}{n_1} + \dfrac{s_2^2}{n_2}}} \tag{3.3}$$

where s_1^2 and s_2^2 are the unbiased variances of the scores within each group.

On the other hand, if your groups are small (as in the blood pressure example), the sample variances cannot be trusted very well as estimates of the population variance, and this introduces some additional error into your z scores. Occasionally, your z score will be accidentally very large (or very small) because the sample variances are accidentally very large (or very small), and not because of a very large (or very small) difference in the means. Because z scores calculated by Formula 3.3 do not follow the normal distribution very well when the samples are small, you cannot use the critical values for the normal distribution to make your statistical decisions. Fortunately, there is a well-understood distribution, similar to the normal distribution, which can be used in this case. To explain this new distribution, it will help to go back to the one-group case.

The t Distribution

If you are drawing random samples from the population, one sample at a time, and you calculate your group z scores using s from the sample instead of σ from the population—$z = (\overline{X} - \mu)/s/\sqrt{N}$—these z scores will follow a distribution that has more values that are extreme than the normal distribution (thicker tails of the distribution, because some z's are large due to accidentally small s's), and more tiny values (sharper peak in the middle caused by accidentally large s's), and fewer moderate values. This distribution is called the *t distribution;* it is sometimes called *Student's* t *distribution,* because William Gossett, who first described the application of this distribution to null hypothesis testing, published his paper under the pseudonym "Student" (the beer company he worked for in the early 1900s wouldn't allow him to publish under his own name). Actually, there is a whole family of *t* distributions; as the samples get smaller, the s's become more unreliable as estimates of σ and the tails of the *t* distribution get thicker.

Mathematically, the *t* distributions are described in terms of a single parameter—not the size of the samples exactly, but the degrees of freedom that divides the SS to create s^2. Fortunately, the degrees of freedom are just $N-1$ in the one-sample case. Before it became routine to calculate *t* tests by computer, researchers relied on a table of critical values for the *t* distribution to make their decisions. Such a table is included in Appendix A. Looking at Table A.2, you can see that as df gets larger (because *N* is getting larger), the critical values get smaller (because the tails of the distribution are getting thinner) until they are very similar to the critical values of the normal distribution. In fact, when df becomes infinitely large (indicated by the infinity symbol, ∞), the *t* distribution becomes identical to the normal distribution; the bottom row of the *t* table contains the critical values for the normal distribution. Notice that as alpha gets smaller, the critical values get larger—you have to go further out on the tail to reduce the area beyond the critical value. Also notice that the critical value for a .025 one-tailed test is the same as for a .05 two-tailed test (except that for the two-tailed test you actually have two critical values: the value in the table preceded by either a negative or a positive sign).

The Separate-Variances t Test Formula

Strictly speaking, Formula 3.3 follows a normal distribution only for infinitely large samples, but it always follows a *t* distribution. So a more general formula would change the z to *t*:

$$ t = \frac{\overline{X}_1 - \overline{X}_2}{\sqrt{\dfrac{s_1^2}{n_1} + \dfrac{s_2^2}{n_2}}} \tag{3.4} $$

The only question is which *t* distribution is appropriate for this formula—that is, what are the df in this case? You might think that for two groups, df $= n_1 + n_2 - 2$, and sometimes that is true, but that value for df is usually not appropriate when using Formula 3.4. This formula produces what is called the *separate-variances* (s-v) *t* test, and unfortunately, finding the df for this test can be tricky. Generally, the df must be reduced below $n_1 + n_2 - 2$ for the s-v test (the df can get as low as $n_1 - 1$ or $n_2 - 1$, whichever is smaller). The logic of exactly why this correction is necessary and the details of its calculation are beyond the scope of this book, but these areas are covered well in other texts (e.g., Howell, 2002). Although computers can now easily find an approximate value for df to test the *t* from Formula 3.4, the more traditional solution is to calculate the *t* test a different way, so that the df come out to a simple $n_1 + n_2 - 2$. This solution requires that we assume that the two populations from which we are sampling have the same variance. This assumption is called *homogeneity of variance,* and we will have a good deal to say about it shortly.

The Pooled-Variances t Test Formula

If you assume that both populations have the same variance (σ^2), you can assume that s_1^2 and s_2^2 are estimating the same thing (i.e., σ^2). It follows then that an average of the two sample variances is a better estimate of σ^2 than either alone. However, if one sample is larger than the other, it makes sense that the larger sample be weighted more heavily in the average. The weighted average of the two sample variances is called the pooled variance and is calculated according to Formula 3.5:

$$s_p^2 = \frac{(n_1 - 1)\, s_1^2 + (n_2 - 1)\, s_2^2}{n_1 + n_2 - 2} \tag{3.5}$$

Because $s^2/(n-1) = SS$, you are really adding the SSs of the two groups and then dividing by their total df. If you substitute the pooled variance (s_p^2) for each of the variances in Formula 3.4, you get the formula for the pooled-variances (p-v) t test:

$$t = \frac{\overline{X}_1 - \overline{X}_2}{\sqrt{\dfrac{s_p^2}{n_1} + \dfrac{s_p^2}{n_2}}}$$

Because mathematical people love to factor out common terms, the formula is more frequently written in this form:

$$t = \frac{(\overline{X}_1 - \overline{X}_2)}{\sqrt{s_p^2\left(\dfrac{1}{n_1} + \dfrac{1}{n_2}\right)}} \tag{3.6}$$

The nice thing about this formula is that it follows the t distribution with df $= n_1 + n_2 - 2$ when the two populations have the same variance. The procedures for both the p-v and s-v t tests are summarized in Rapid Reference 3.1.

Rapid Reference 3.1

To calculate a pooled-variance t test: Use Formulas 3.5 and 3.6, and df $= n_1 + n_2 - 2$. You can look up a critical value in Table A.2.

To calculate a separate-variances t test: You can use Formula 3.4, but it is best to let a computer calculate the adjusted df and corresponding p value.

Testing for Homogeneity of Variance

If both of your samples are the same size, you will get the same t value whether you use the p-v or s-v formula, and it is well agreed that you can use $2n - 2$ as your df (where n is the size of *each* of your groups). However, if your sample sizes are not the same, the two procedures will give different *t* values, so you have to decide which to use. If it is reasonable to assume that the two populations have the same variance, the p-v test is more powerful (i.e., more likely to yield significance when appropriate); if that assumption is not reasonable, the p-v test may be too liberal (i.e., loose about Type I errors), making the s-v test the safer bet. (Although your two groups of participants may literally come from the same population, it is possible that one treatment affects variance more than the other, even if there is no difference in population means.) When the *n*'s are not equal, it is important to compare the two sample variances to see if they could both reasonably represent the same population variance.

If one variance is less than two times the other, you should probably use the p-v test, but fortunately statistical software can perform a significance test for you to determine whether homogeneity of variance is a reasonable assumption given your sample variances and sample sizes. For example, the Statistical Package for the Social Sciences (SPSS) automatically tests your variances for equality whenever you do a *t* test: You don't even have to ask for it! The test that SPSS uses is called *Levene's test,* and it tests the null hypothesis that your variances are equal. If Levene's test produces a significant result ($p < .05$), you should proceed as though the population variances are not equal, and perform the s-v *t* test. It is also fortunate that most statistical packages can find the df and *p* value for an s-v test, in case Levene's test is significant. (SPSS automatically computes both the p-v *t* test [labeled *equal variances assumed*] and the s-v *t* test [labeled *equal variances not assumed*] whenever a *t* test is requested.) However, the results of only one of these tests should be reported in a research article; a simple rule for when to report the results of a p-v or s-v *t* test is given in Rapid Reference 3.2.

Interpreting the Results of a Homogeneity of Variance Test

It makes sense to compare your variances with a homogeneity test not just to help you decide which type of *t* test to use, but, more interestingly, to see if your treatment may be pushing your participant's scores further apart, or even homogenizing the scores (moving participants at either extreme closer to the middle). For instance, it has been found that just taking a depression test can make

Rapid Reference 3.2

When to Use the Pooled- or Separate-Variances *t* Test

Report the pooled-variance t test if your sample sizes are equal *or* your sample sizes are not equal, but your sample variances do not differ significantly.

Report the separate-variance t test if your sample sizes are not equal and your sample variances differ significantly.

slightly depressed participants more depressed and happy participants even happier, thus increasing variance. Giving amphetamines to young boys can reduce activity in the hyperactive ones and raise the activity in the quiet ones, possibly reducing variance. A homogeneity of variance (HOV) test like Levene's test can indicate that something like this is happening, even when there is little difference in the means of the two groups.

On the other hand, a significant difference in the two variances does not always signify an interesting result. Variances are very susceptible to outliers (extreme scores), and having a skewed distribution or just a few outliers in one group but not the other can cause a significant difference in variances. The outliers may or may not reflect some interesting result (e.g., the instructions may be more complicated in one condition than another, leading to some extreme mistakes in that condition). Whereas it is always a good idea to look at the distribution of scores in each of your samples to see if anything strange is going on, a significant HOV test is a strong signal that you *must* take such a look. Sometimes a data transformation that minimizes extreme scores, or a justified elimination of outliers, will render the two variances homogeneous and suitable for a p-v test. Other times it is appropriate to sort the participants in your study according to their responses to your treatment and try to account for these differences with whatever information you have about your participants. This can lead to the design of a follow-up study.

Reporting Your Calculated t Value

Let us say that you have calculated a *t* value of 2.4 for an experiment comparing a group of 20 participants with a group of 30 participants, and you want to report it. The format used by the style manual of the American Psychological Association (2001) is the following: $t(48) = 2.4, p < .05$. The "48" represents the df for the p-v test, $n_1 + n_2 - 2$. If you were reporting an s-v test, you would include instead the df reported by your statistical package, which will be somewhere between 19 (the df for the smaller group alone) and 48 (the df for the pooled test) and is likely to involve a fractional value (e.g., 37.6). Reporting that your *p* is $< .05$ makes it clear that your results are statistically significant at the .05 level; otherwise, you might state "$p > .05$" or "n.s." (short for "not significant"). Note, however, that two trends are becoming increasingly common due to the use of statistical software: (1) reporting *p* exactly as given in your computer output (e.g., $p = .003$), or (2) reporting *p* in terms of the lowest possible alpha at which it would be significant (e.g., $p < .005$ or $p < .0001$). Exact *p*'s are rarely reported for $p > .05$, unless *p* is close to the borderline of significance and the author wants you to notice this (e.g., $p = .055$ or, perhaps, $p < .07$).

The Assumptions of the Two-Group t Test

1. *The DV is measured on an interval or ratio scale.* As mentioned in the previous chapter, this level of measurement is required to validly calculate means and standard deviations, and therefore to perform parametric statistics. If you can place your participants in order on your DV (e.g., rank them for creativity shown in writing a story) but cannot quantify the DV more precisely than that, you can use a nonparametric version of the *t* test (e.g., the Mann-Whitney test), as described in Chapter 9.

2. *The DV has a normal distribution in both populations.* If the DV is normally distributed in both populations (e.g., drug and placebo), the differences of the sample means will also follow a normal distribution, and when divided by the appropriate estimate of the standard error of the difference will follow a *t* distribution. Fortunately, just as in the one-sample case, the CLT implies that with large enough sample sizes we can use the *t* distribution for our critical values even though our DVs are not very normal. This is fortunate because social scientists often deal with DVs that have skewed distributions, like annual income. Even with extremely skewed distributions, samples of at least 30 or 40 participants each lead to *t* statistics that follow the *t* distribution quite well. However, if the distribution of your DV is very far from normal and you are using small sample sizes, you should consider using either a data transformation that normalizes your distribution or a nonparametric version of the *t* test, as mentioned under assumption 1 (once you ignore the actual scores and just place your participants in rank order, the original distribution becomes irrelevant).

3. *Your samples were selected at random from their respective populations.* The importance of this assumption should be obvious when you are sampling from preexisting populations. If you want to determine whether men or women, in general, have greater manual dexterity on a particular type of task, you would need to select truly random samples from each population. In practice, this is extremely difficult, so an attempt is made to ensure that the two samples are similar on various relevant characteristics (such as age, in this example).

In the case of a true experiment, social scientists expect to make valid causal conclusions despite the fact that they usually know that their samples were not selected at random from the entire population. The validity of the experiment is ensured by selecting one sample and then randomly assigning participants to one condition or the other (the validity of your conclusions would be threatened, for example, if you used a sample of participants who signed up for a morning session under one condition, while using a

3

8

0ESSENTIALS OF STATISTICS

sample of afternoon participants under the other condition). If the one sample that you are dividing is not very representative of the entire population (e.g., college sophomores who volunteer for a psychology experiment), you must be cautious about generalizing your results to very different participants (e.g., migrant farm workers), especially if your DV measures social attitudes rather than a more basic human function, like visual perception. Nonetheless, the random division of your sample allows you to make valid conclusions about your variables, at least for participants similar to those in your sample.

There is a technical problem involved, however, in applying the *t* formulas to samples created by random assignment. Strictly speaking, the *t* formulas apply to the case of two truly random samples each assigned to a different condition. However, it turns out that random assignment from one larger sample does not generally produce more Type I errors than using two separate random samples, so you needn't be concerned about this distinction (Reichardt & Gollob, 1999).

4. *The p-v* t *test requires the assumption of homogeneity of variance.* We have already discussed this assumption in some detail.

Interpreting a Significant t Test

Let us say you are satisfied that the assumptions of the *t* test apply to your situation, and your *t* statistic is statistically significant. What can you conclude? You are entitled to say (at the risk of a Type I error) that the means of the two populations, represented by your two samples, are different. The practical meaning of that statement depends on the situation. First, we need to consider whether you were sampling from two already existing populations or randomly assigning your participants to different conditions.

For instance, if you take a random sample of people who regularly exercise and compare their cholesterol levels (CL) to a random sample of people who don't exercise, a significant *t* allows you to conclude that the average CL of all exercisers in the population (from which you are sampling) is different from the average for the population of nonexercisers. However, you cannot conclude that exercise directly affects CL. It is quite possible, for example, that exercisers tend to eat different foods and that the different diet accounts for any difference in CL. Observational or correlational studies (or quasi-experiments) like the one just described are relatively easy to perform, and they can indicate useful avenues for future research, but they are not conclusive with respect to causality.

To prove that exercise affects CL, you would take one sample (as representative of the population as possible, but more commonly a sample that is convenient), divide it randomly into two groups, enforce an exercise regimen on one group, while disallowing exercise in the other, and then measure CL after an appropriate amount of time. A significant t for a real experiment, such as the one just described, allows you to conclude that the difference in treatments *caused* the difference in the dependent variable (to be sure it is the actual exercise producing the difference, your nonexercise group should receive some control treatment, with similar expectations being raised; this is easier to say than to do). Now, let us say that your t is significant for the experiment just described, and that exercise lowers CL. Can you recommend that people who don't exercise should adopt your regimen to reduce their cholesterol levels?

The Confidence Interval for the Two-Group Case

It seems harmless enough to recommend exercise, but what if, instead of exercise, your experiment showed decreased CL for a group assigned to a moderate level of alcohol ingestion as compared to a nondrinking group? What is missing from a statement that your t statistic is significant is any mention of how large the difference is between the two groups. Asking people who don't drink to begin to drink moderately may make sense if the reduction in cholesterol is large, but it is questionable if the difference is tiny. Can a tiny difference between samples produce significant results? Yes. Even if a difference of the means is a tiny fraction of the standard deviation in either sample, t can be large if the samples are large. It is usually meaningless to report the size of your t statistic without also giving the means of the two samples. The reader can then calculate the difference and decide if this difference is large enough to be practical.

Of course, the difference of your two sample means is only an estimate of the difference in the population means. This estimate becomes more reliable as the samples increase in size. Just as a CI can be used to estimate the mean of a population, as in the previous chapter, it can also be used to estimate the difference between two population means. Let us take another look at Formula 2.3. This formula is appropriate for very large sample sizes, but if one were forced to estimate a population mean from a small sample (e.g., a small collection of skulls found in an archaeological site), the z_{crit} would have to be replaced with t_{crit} based on df $= N-1$, as in Formula 3.7:

$$\mu = \overline{X} \pm t_{crit} s_{\overline{X}} \qquad (3.7)$$

The formula for the difference in the population means is very similar:

$$\mu_1 - \mu_2 = \overline{X}_1 - \overline{X}_2 \pm t_{crit} s_{\overline{X}_1 - \overline{X}_2} \qquad (3.8)$$

(This is just the generic two-group t test formula twisted around.)

CAUTION

An experiment may result in a very large *t* value and a very tiny *p* value, even though there is little difference between the two groups (this can happen when the samples are very large). A CI can give a more accurate picture, but if the units of the DV are not meaningful or familiar, a measure of effect size can be helpful.

The difference of your two sample means is always at the center of the CI. For a 95% CI with a not very tiny sample, you would add and subtract about 2 standard errors of the difference (the denominator of the *t* test) from the difference of the sample means to find the upper and lower boundaries of the interval. For the exercise experiment, your CI might allow you to say that you are 95% certain that the cholesterol reduction due to your exercise regimen is somewhere between 12 and 24 points. This is much more informative than just saying that exercise makes some difference, and even more informative than just saying the difference is probably about 18 points.

Note that if zero is in the 95% CI (one boundary is positive and the other is negative), a *t* test of the usual null hypothesis ($\mu_1 - \mu_2 = 0$) will not reach significance at the .05 level (two tailed); if zero is not in the interval, the test will be significant. In this way, constructing a CI gives you null hypothesis testing for free. Because a CI is so much more informative than just a significance test, many researchers are arguing that CIs should be reported whenever possible and that significance tests are not even necessary.

The Effect Size in a Two-Group Experiment

Confidence intervals are particularly helpful when the units of the dependent variable are well known. For instance, we know how many pounds must be lost for a new weight loss method to be of practical use. Confidence intervals are less helpful when the DV is specific to a particular experiment. It may be of theoretical interest that participants recall more words from a list that had once been played to them while asleep than a similar list that had not, but if the 95% CI ranges from a two- to a six-word difference, are you impressed? Standardizing this difference by dividing it by the average standard deviation of the two lists (more exactly by the square root of the pooled variance) yields a more universally meaningful measure known as the effect size. The effect size seen in the sample is often called *g*, and the simplest formula is as follows:

$$g = \frac{\overline{X}_1 - \overline{X}_2}{s_p} \tag{3.9}$$

This measure, g, can be used as a point estimate of the effect size in the entire population, usually called d (and usually written in bold to indicate that it applies to a population, and not just your own data). The formula for the t test can be written in terms of g; the formula is particularly simple when the sample sizes are equal:

$$t = g\sqrt{\frac{n}{2}} \qquad (3.10)$$

Note that even when g is very tiny, t can be large if n is very large. When $n_1 = n_2$ and t has already been calculated, g can be found from the following formula:

$$g = t\sqrt{\frac{2}{n}} \qquad (3.11)$$

When g equals 1.0, it means that the mean of one sample is a whole standard deviation above or below the other sample, and that tells us that the two samples are rather well separated on the DV, no matter what the DV is or what units are used to measure it. Creating a CI around g to estimate that d is, for example, between .7 and 1.3, is very informative and in this case assures us that we are likely dealing with an impressive difference between the two populations. Creating CIs for g was difficult until quite recently. We will have a good deal to say about the meaning of effect size and its utility in power analysis when we get to Chapter 6.

REPEATED-MEASURES OR MATCHED t TEST

Formula 3.10 shows us that when g is on the small side you need rather large samples to obtain a t value large enough to be significant. However, social science researchers often deal with small effects that are likely to lead to small g's, and yet using large samples can be prohibitively expensive and time-consuming. Fortunately, there are ways to increase your t value without using large samples, so that you have a good chance of showing that an effect is not zero, even when it is fairly small. The most

CAUTION

When comparing a statistically significant t test with one that is not, don't assume that the two tests are telling you very different things. For example, if a test of exercisers versus nonexercisers on cholesterol levels yields $t(48) = 2.1, p < .05$ for male participants, and $t(44) = 1.8, p > .05$ (not significant) for female participants, this does not mean exercise affects cholesterol significantly more for men than for women. In fact, the two p's (about .04 and .06 respectively) are similar, as are the g's. To test whether the results for men differ significantly from those for women you can use a two-way analysis of variance, as described in Chapter 7.

powerful of these ways is the repeated-measures (RM) design. There are many experiments for which this design would not be convenient, or even possible, but when it can be reasonably applied it is often very effective. Let us look at an example of how this design can lead to a larger *t* value than you would expect.

One Type of Repeated-Measures Design: The Before-After Design

Suppose that you are conducting a weight loss experiment with 10 participants whose average weight is about 200 pounds, and who vary such that their standard deviation is about 45 pounds. After 6 months, every participant has lost about 2 pounds (the weight loss method might be to spend an hour a day vividly imagining that you are exercising). Assuming that the variance at the end of 6 months is the same as at the beginning—about 2,000 (we are squaring 45 and then rounding off)—we can use Formula 3.6 to see how large our *t* value would be. The denominator of the formula is the square root of 2,000 times 0.2, which equals the square root of 400, which equals 20. If the numerator is 2 (an average of 2 pounds lost), *t* would be 2 over 20, which is only .1. This is nowhere near statistical significance.

In fact, with a denominator of 20 you would need to find a weight loss of more than 40 pounds to attain a significant *t* statistic. If you are stuck with a *g* of 2/45 = .044, as in this example, you would need a sample of about 4,000 participants to attain a significant *t*. The person-to-person variability is large in this example, but it would be large in any realistic weight loss experiment and in many other experiments in the social sciences. The advantage of the RM design (in this example, every participant would be measured twice: before and after the 6-month weight loss program) is that it allows you to avoid the person-to-person variability, as we will show next.

The null hypothesis for the weight loss experiment is that the weight loss program is totally ineffective. The two group *t* test we just performed suggests that it is easy to get a 2-pound difference by chance with so few participants and so much variability among participants. However, something happened in our hypothetical experiment that is not likely to happen by chance, but was missed by the two-group *t* test. All of the participants lost weight. If the null hypothesis were true you might expect about half of the participants to *gain* rather than lose weight over a 6-month period (actually, for this experiment you would need a control group, but for many other RM designs, the null hypothesis would dictate a fifty-fifty split in the results).

If you expect only half of the participants to lose weight by chance, the odds against all 10 of them losing weight by chance is about 1,000 to 1. Moreover, all of the participants lost about the same amount of weight: 2 pounds. The more similar the participants are to each other in the amount of weight loss, the less likely it is that this can happen by accident. What is needed is a *t* test that can capture these consistencies when they occur in an RM design and determine how likely they are to occur by chance. Such a *t* test exists, and it is actually simpler than you would expect, as you will see next.

The Formula for the Repeated-Measures t Test

The way you look for and capture the consistencies in an RM design is to look at the difference scores—that is, the differences between the two measurements (for this example, the before-after differences, which are the amounts of weight lost for each participant). By doing this, you are changing two groups of scores into just one group. The null hypothesis is still the same: that the differences are as likely to be negative as positive, and that their mean across the entire population would be zero. To test the null hypothesis you will need to determine whether the mean of your difference scores is so far from zero that there is little chance of getting this value by accident. This calls for a one-sample *t* test, where your difference scores are the one sample. Therefore, you can use Formula 2.2. We will repeat that formula below, but we modify the notation to reflect the fact that your scores are actually difference scores.

$$t = \frac{\overline{D} - \mu_D}{s_{\overline{D}}}$$

The mean of the difference scores according to the null hypothesis, μ_D, does not have to be zero—but it so often is that we can leave that term out of the formula. Expressing the standard error in terms of the standard deviation and sample size leads to the following practical formula for calculating the RM *t* test.

$$t = \frac{\overline{D}}{\frac{s_D}{\sqrt{N}}} \tag{3.12}$$

Because this is a one-sample *t* test, we don't have to worry about homogeneity of variance. We can simply look up the critical *t* by noting that the degrees of freedom equal $N - 1$, where N is the number of difference scores. Note that by looking only at the difference scores rather than the before and after scores we are actually reducing our df. For the two-group *t* test we performed on the before and after scores, df $= n_1 + n_2 - 2 = 10 + 10 - 2 = 18$, so $t_{.05} = 2.19$. For the RM *t* test, df $= 10 - 1 = 9$, so $t_{.05}$ is 2.26. The RM *t* test reduces your df by half, so unless you are dealing with hundreds of participants, the critical *t* for the RM test will be noticeably higher than for the corresponding two-group test. A higher critical *t* is not good, but the calculated RM *t* value is usually so much higher than the calculated two-group *t* value that the difference in critical values becomes unimportant. That is certainly the case in our weight loss example, as you will see next.

Calculating the Repeated-Measures t Test

Let us apply Formula 3.12 to the weight loss example. The numerator of the test is the mean of the difference scores, which is 2 (pounds). Note that the RM *t* test always has the same numerator as the corresponding two-group test because the difference of the two means is always the same as the mean of the differences (i.e., if you subtract the mean of the after scores from the mean of the before scores, you get the same result as subtracting the after score from the before score separately for each participant and then averaging these difference scores). The advantage of the RM test is in the denominator. The two-group *t* test is based on the variability from person to person under each condition; for our example, the SD was about 45 pounds. The RM *t* test is based instead on the variability of the difference scores. We have been saying that everyone lost "about" 2 pounds. To be more specific, let's say that the SD for the difference scores is 1.0 pounds (so most participants lost between 1 and 3 pounds). Using Formula 3.12,

$$t = \frac{2}{\dfrac{1}{\sqrt{10}}} = \frac{2}{.316} = 6.33$$

The RM *t* value is more than 60 times greater than the corresponding two-group *t* value because the RM test avoids the large amount of person-to-person variability and benefits from the consistency of the difference scores. Adding one 500-pound person who loses 2 pounds would make the two-group *t* statistic even smaller but would have very little effect on the RM test (in this case the effect would be positive because adding a difference score of −2 would only make the SD smaller; plus you'd gain a degree of freedom). Of course, the difference scores are not usually as consistent as in our example, but when it makes sense to create an RM design, the RM *t* statistic is almost always considerably larger than the corresponding independent-group *t*.

Other Repeated-Measures Designs

The before-after design is not the best example of the RM *t* test because a control group usually is required, which means that *two* groups are being measured at two points in time, and this adds some complication (this will be dealt with in Chapter 8). A more typical use for the RM design is to compare the means for two experimental conditions both of which are given to all of the participants—for instance, comparing the recall for happy and sad words. Happy and sad words can be mixed in a single list that participants memorize (the *simultaneous RM design*). For each participant the number of sad words recalled can be subtracted from the number of happy words recalled, and then an RM *t* test can be calculated on these difference scores.

A somewhat more problematic design is needed if each participant is tested on two lists—one studied while listening to happy music and one during sad music. You can't mix the happy and sad music together, so one condition will have to be presented before the other (the *successive RM design*), which can give that condition (e.g., type of music) an advantage or disadvantage due to an *order effect* (e.g., practice or fatigue). This problem is dealt with by *counterbalancing:* Half of the participants get the happy music condition first, whereas the other half of the participants get the sad condition first.

Dealing with Order Effects
If you have collected data from a counterbalanced design you should look to see if your order effects are symmetrical. Suppose half the participants receive a happy condition first followed by a sad condition, whereas the other half get the reverse order. If you average all the happy scores separately for those getting happy first and for those getting happy second, you can see the order effect for the happy condition. If you do this again for sad, you can compare the order effects for the two conditions. If they are very different, it seems you have *differential carryover effects* (e.g., sadness may dribble into the following happy condition more than the other way around), which can bias your results (we will discuss how to test this for significance in Chapter 8). You may need to look only at the condition each participant had first. This changes your design from RM to one based on independent groups, and it can greatly lower your calculated *t*, but it eliminates the bias in the results that can be produced by asymmetrical carryover effects and that can threaten the validity of your results. Even if the two order effects are the same, if they are large they can increase the denominator of your RM *t* test quite a bit. We will discuss how to remove this effect when we describe the Latin Square design in Chapter 8.

The Matched-Pairs Design
There are many cases when counterbalancing is obviously inappropriate from the outset. Imagine that you want to compare two methods for teaching long division to children to see which works more quickly. If both methods are fairly effective,

DON'T FORGET

There are a variety of situations in which the appropriate result is an RM t value:

1. The before-after design (but it is usually important to include a control group).
2. The RM simultaneous design (two different conditions are mixed together).
3. The RM successive design (it is usually important to counterbalance the conditions).
4. The matched-pairs design (the scores from the two matched participants are treated as though they were both from one participant).

it doesn't make sense to try to teach the children a second time. However, one can still get much of the benefit of the RM t test in this situation. The trick is to match the children in pairs based on similar performance on previous math tests; then, for each pair, one member is assigned to each method, in a random way. After performance is measured, difference scores are created by subtracting the two scores for each pair (as though the two scores were from the very same participant), always in the same direction, of course (e.g., Method 1 minus Method 2). The t test performed on these difference scores is called a *matched-pairs t test* (or just a *matched t test*), but it is calculated exactly the same way as the RM t test, so either name can be used to refer to Formula 3.12.

It doesn't matter if some pairs are much better at math than others, as long as one method is fairly consistent in being better within each pair. The better the matching of the pairs, the more this design resembles the RM design. Sometimes you can't measure the same participant twice and you don't have any basis for matching the participants. Then you are stuck with the independent-groups design, and you will need large samples if the effect size you are exploring is fairly small.

The Assumptions of the Repeated-Measures t Test

You should also inspect the distribution of your difference scores for severe skewing and for outliers. If your sample size is small, such problems can render the matched t test inappropriate for your data (the chief assumption of the matched t test is that the difference scores are normally distributed, and the CLT won't help you with this if your sample is very small). An alternative is to rank-order your difference scores and perform Wilcoxon's matched-pairs signed ranks test, as described in Chapter 9. A cruder alternative is to simply count the number of differences favoring one condition or the other and perform a binomial (or sign) test, also described in Chapter 9. Underlying the RM design is the assumption that the pairs of scores will exhibit a fairly high linear correlation. In fact, an alternative way of calculating the RM t test is in terms of that correlation (see

B. Cohen, 2000). The quantification of linear correlation is the topic of the next chapter.

Confidence Intervals for the Repeated Measures or Matched Design

Repeated measures and matched designs make it possible to obtain large t statistics without using large samples and without obtaining a large difference between the means of the two conditions. As we mentioned earlier, a before-after (or well-matched) design can produce a large and statistically significant t value even if very little weight is lost. Therefore, it is often important to find a confidence interval for the difference of the means when significant results are obtained. The CI in this case is centered around $\overline{D}$, and its formula is just the formula for the CI for the population mean (Formula 2.3) with different notation.

$$\mu_{lower} = \overline{D} - t_{crit} s_{\overline{D}}$$
$$\mu_{upper} = \overline{D} + t_{crit} s_{\overline{D}} \qquad (3.13)$$

When the units of the dependent variable are not familiar (e.g., number of words recalled from a list created for the experiment), it makes sense to look at effect size measures. The effect size and power associated with the RM t test will be discussed in Chapter 6.

Putting It Into Practice

1. The following table is being reprinted from Gist, Rosen, and Schwoerer (1988).* Participants in this study were trained on a particular computer skill by one of two methods, and were classified into one of two age groups. Mean performance (along with SD and n) on the computer task is given for each of the four subgroups (cells).

| | Younger | | Older | |
	Modeling	Tutorial	Modeling	Tutorial
Mean	36.74	32.14	29.63	26.04
SD	6.69	7.19	8.51	7.29
Cell n	52	45	20	30

(a) In the article, the above data were appropriately analyzed as a two-way analysis of variance (we will return to these data in Chapter 7). However, as an exercise, calculate the four t tests that make sense (i.e., compare the

(continued)

two age levels for each method, and compare the two methods for each age level). Calculate both the p-v and s-v t test in each case and test the p-v t for significance. Which seems more appropriate for these t tests? If the method comparison is significant at the .05 level for one age level but not the other, can you conclude that age affects the difference between the two methods? Explain.

(b) Calculate g for each of the pooled-variance t tests in 1a. Comment on the size of g in each case.

(c) Find the 95% CI for the difference of the two methods just for the younger participants (using the p-v error term).

2. A cognitive psychologist is investigating the effects of giving imagery instructions on paired-associates recall. Eight participants are given a recall test for a list of 20 word pairs, first with no imagery instructions, and then again (with a different list) after instructions on how to use imagery to link the words together. The numbers of paired-associates recalled for each participant for each condition are given in the table below.

Participant No.	No Imagery	Imagery
1	8	14
2	11	15
3	7	5
4	10	16
5	9	9
6	15	16
7	7	8
8	16	20

(a) Calculate the RM t value for these data. For a two-tailed test, are the results statistically significant at the .05 level? At the .01 level?

(b) Using the standard error from 2a, find the 99% confidence interval for the imagery/no imagery difference in the population. Is your CI consistent with your answers to 2a? Explain.

(c) Assuming the results of the above experiment are significant, can you conclude that imagery instructions *caused* an increase in recall? What alternative explanations are available?

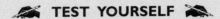

TEST YOURSELF

1. **The usual null hypothesis of the two-group t test is that**
   (a) the two sample means are the same.
   (b) the two population means are the same.
   (c) the two sample standard deviations are the same.
   (d) the two population standard deviations are the same.

2. **You need to use the t distribution as your null hypothesis distribution whenever**
   (a) the population mean and variance are unknown.
   (b) the population mean is unknown and the sample size is small.
   (c) the population variance is small and the sample size is unknown.
   (d) the population variance is unknown and the sample size is small.

3. **Pooling the variances is**
   (a) not necessary when $N_1 = N_2$.
   (b) not appropriate unless homogeneity of variance can be assumed.
   (c) not optimal unless a weighted average is taken.
   (d) all of the above.

4. **The denominator of the pooled-variances t test will equal the denominator of the separate-variances t test when**
   (a) the sample means are equal.
   (b) the population variances are equal.
   (c) the sample sizes are equal.
   (d) any of the above are true.

5. **All else remaining equal, as the sample variances in a two-group t test increase,**
   (a) the critical *t* value increases.
   (b) the calculated *t* value decreases.
   (c) the estimate of the standard error of the difference (i.e., $s_{\bar{X}_1-\bar{X}_2}$) decreases.
   (d) all of the above.

6. **If a homogeneity of variance test is associated with a p value less than alpha, which of the following should be performed?**
   (a) Nothing—it is not valid to proceed with the *t* test
   (b) Nothing—the null hypothesis of the *t* test can be rejected
   (c) The pooled-variances *t* test
   (d) The separate-variances *t* test

(continued)

7. Compared to an independent-samples *t* test on the same data, the matched *t* test will always yield

(a) a smaller critical *t*.

(b) a larger critical *t*.

(c) a smaller calculated *t*.

(d) none of the above.

8. The purpose of counterbalancing is

(a) to average out order effects.

(b) to eliminate the need for a control group.

(c) to increase the chance of getting a significant *t* value.

(d) none of the above.

9. Drawing conclusions from a before-after design can be misleading if

(a) the same participants are measured twice.

(b) there is a large amount of person-to-person variability.

(c) the confidence interval for the difference of means is very small.

(d) there is no control group.

10. Matching participants in pairs is usually preferable to repeated measures on the same participants, whenever

(a) there are simple order effects.

(b) there are differential carryover effects.

(c) there is a large amount of person-to-person variability.

(d) all of the above.

Answers: 1. b; 2. d; 3. d; 4. c; 5. b; 6. d; 7. b; 8. a; 9. d; 10. b.

Four

CORRELATION AND REGRESSION

CORRELATION

Correlation, like the mean, is a concept that you were probably familiar with before taking a statistics course. If we tell you that music ability is correlated with mathematical ability you may be skeptical, but it is very likely that you know what we mean. If we don't say that the two variables are negatively correlated, it is reasonable to assume that we are implying that the variables are positively correlated; that is, when someone has a good deal of musical ability he or she tends to be good at math (and vice versa), while low musical ability tends to go with low math ability. And if we say that depression and college grades are negatively correlated, you probably know that this means low scores on one variable tend to be paired with high scores on the other. The main purpose of this chapter is to show you how to quantify the amount of correlation and then use this amount to make predictions or inferences concerning the population. In this chapter we will be dealing only with *bivariate correlation* (i.e., two variables at a time). Multiple correlation (e.g., one variable being predicted by a combination of two or more variables) is beyond the scope of this book.

Perfect Correlation

To explain how we can measure the degree of correlation between two variables it will be helpful to begin with describing perfect correlation. Suppose that students in a statistics class take both a midterm and a final; both are exams that are graded from 0 to 100. If every student gets the same score on the final that he or she got on the midterm, the midterm scores will be perfectly correlated with the final scores. However, getting the same score is not necessary for perfect correlation. If every student scores five points higher on the final than on the midterm the correlation will still be perfect; given a student's midterm score (MT) you know exactly what that student's final score is (MT + 5). The relationship between the two variables could get very complicated, and yet by using some fancy

DON'T FORGET

When Will I Use the Statistics in This Chapter?

You are measuring one or two variables on a quantitative scale.

One variable: You are measuring the same variable on two different occasions (test-retest reliability), or comparing one part of the measure with another part (internal reliability).

Two variables: You are comparing a new measure with a more established measure (validity), or looking at the relation between two completely different variables (e.g., you want to see if charisma is related to annual income). Or you are looking at the relation between a continuous experimental variable (e.g., participants are assigned to different amounts of weekly exercise) and an outcome variable (e.g., resting heart rate; cholesterol level).

Prediction: You want to use the magnitude of one variable to predict the magnitude of another. Or you want to use those predictions to remove the effect of one variable on another (e.g., age-adjusting memory scores in the elderly by predicting the memory score from age, and then using only the part of the memory score *not* predicted by age).

math you might be able to predict the second score exactly from knowing the first (and vice versa). Fortunately, we will not be dealing with all kinds of (perfect) correlation in this chapter. This chapter is only about *linear correlation* and *linear regression,* so we need only define perfect linear correlation, which we will do next.

Two variables will have a perfect linear correlation together if each variable is a *linear transformation* of the other. Any combination of adding, subtracting, multiplying, and dividing a variable by constants will result in a linear transformation of the variable. Any linear transformation can be summarized by the following equation: $Y = bX + a$. (You may recognize this as the equation for a straight line, which is not a coincidence, as we will explain shortly.) When two variables have a linear relationship, the increase (or decrease) in one variable is always the same amount for a one-unit increase in the other variable, no matter what value of the other variable you are starting out with (this will be clearer when we show graphs of linear relationships later in this chapter).

The z score is a linear transformation of a score (you subtract a constant, μ, and then divide by a constant, σ). Therefore, a score and its z score are always perfectly correlated. This may seem obvious, but it leads to a simple and meaningful definition of perfect linear correlation. If everyone in the population has the same z score for one variable as they do on the other, the two variables will have a perfect positive linear correlation in the population (from now on in this chapter when we use the term *correlation* we will mean *linear correlation*).

It is just as easy to define perfect negative correlation. If everyone has the same z score for both variables, but the z scores are always opposite in sign, the two variables will have a perfect negative correlation. If depression and GPA were perfectly negatively correlated, you would know that someone who is 1 standard deviation above the mean for depression (i.e., $z = +1$) is 1 standard deviation below the mean for GPA (i.e., $z = -1$). Thus, negative correlation can be just as perfect (in terms of predictability) as positive correlation.

Height and weight are not perfectly correlated in the human population, but they could be. Imagine, for instance, that Antarcticans all have the same body type, differing only in height. If height and weight were perfectly correlated for these people you would be able to find an equation of the form $W = bH + a$, so that you could multiply an Antarctican's height in inches by a certain constant and then add a constant (possibly a negative number) to get his or her weight. This equation is called a *linear regression* equation, and it is used to make predictions even when correlation is far from perfect, as you will see later in this chapter. Note that measuring height in centimeters instead of inches and weight in kilograms instead of pounds won't change anyone's z score for height or weight, so it won't change the correlation (but it will change the constants in the equation above). Whatever amount of correlation there is between two variables, linearly transforming one or both of them will not change that amount. Now it is time to describe how the amount of correlation can be quantified when it is less than perfect.

Pearson's Correlation Coefficient

In the late 1800s Sir Francis Galton was studying heredity in England, and attempted to quantify various correlations, such as the correlation between the heights of fathers and their sons. He used a lowercase letter r to symbolize his coefficient of correlation (Cowles, 2001). Karl Pearson improved the mathematical formulation of Galton's correlation coefficient just before the end of the nineteenth century. Because it is Pearson's formula that we now use, the coefficient for linear correlation is usually referred to as *Pearson's r* (it is sometimes called the *product-moment correlation coefficient* for reasons too technical to explain here). In terms of z scores Pearson's formula is remarkably simple, as shown below:

$$r = \frac{\sum z_x z_y}{N} \tag{4.1}$$

where the subscripts x and y represent the two variables.

The formula tells us that for each person in the population we take his or her

z scores on both variables and multiply them together. Then we average these cross products (i.e., add them up and divide by the number of cross products). This coefficient reaches its greatest magnitude when everyone has the same z score on both variables. In that case the formula reduces to $\Sigma z^2/N$, which always equals exactly 1.0 (the variance of a set of z scores is $\Sigma(z-\bar{z}^2)/N$, which always equals 1.0, but $\bar{z}$ is always zero, so $\Sigma z^2/N = 1.0$). If everyone has the same z score on both variables, but with opposite signs, r equals $-\Sigma z^2/N = -1.0$. For less than perfect correlation the magnitude of r will be less than 1.0 and can be as small as zero when the two variables have no correlation at all.

Computational Formulas

Formula 4.1 is easy to understand, but it is not convenient for calculation. Substituting the corresponding z score formulas for the X and Y variables and rearranging algebraically yields the following convenient formula:

$$r = \frac{\dfrac{\Sigma XY}{N} - \mu_x \mu_y}{\sigma_x \sigma_y} \qquad (4.2)$$

Expressed verbally this formula tells us to average the cross products of the scores and subtract the product of the population averages, and then divide by the product of the two population standard deviations. This formula is instructive. The numerator is called the *covariance,* and it determines the sign of the correlation. When a number that is relatively large for one variable tends to be paired with a relatively large number for the other variable (and, of course, small with small), the average of the cross products tends to be higher than the product of the averages, yielding a positive correlation. When relatively large numbers for one variable are consistently paired with relatively small numbers for the other; $\Sigma XY/N$ will be smaller than $\mu_x \mu_y$, producing a negative correlation. When values for the two variables are paired at random, the two terms in the numerator tend to be the same size, resulting in a zero or near-zero value for r. The denominator of Formula 4.2, the product of the two standard deviations, tells you just how large the covariance can get in either the positive or negative direction. When the covariance reaches its maximum negatively or positively, r will equal -1 or $+1$, respectively.

The only aspect of Formula 4.2 that is not convenient is that it assumes that you are treating your set of scores as a population and have therefore calculated the standard deviations with N, rather than $N-1$, in the denominator (as in Formula 1.4). In most research settings, however, you will be treating your scores as a sample, and it is likely that you will want to calculate s rather than σ for each of your variables. If you want to use $s_x s_y$ in the denominator of Formula 4.2, you will have to adjust the numerator accordingly, as in the formula below:

$$r = \frac{\frac{1}{N-1}\left(\sum XY - N\overline{X}\,\overline{Y}\right)}{s_x s_y} \tag{4.3}$$

Note that we changed μ_x and μ_y to $\overline{X}$ and $\overline{Y}$ in Formula 4.3 to reflect the fact that we are viewing our data set as a sample, even though the values for the mean will be the same. Note especially that Formula 4.3 always yields exactly the same value for r as Formula 4.2, so it doesn't matter which you use. Formula 4.3 is just more convenient to use if you have s's instead of σ's handy. The numerator of Formula 4.2 is the *biased* covariance, but dividing it by the product of two biased SDs cancels out the bias and yields the same r as Formula 4.3. There are several other formulas for Pearson's r that may be more convenient for calculation without a computer (and, of course, all produce the same value), but they are not very instructive, so we will not bother to show them.

Uses for Correlation: Reliability and Validity

Correlation coefficients are used for many purposes in social science research. For some of these purposes it is important that r have a large positive value, perhaps between .7 and 1.0. For instance, suppose children are being rated for aggressiveness as they interact in a playground. No matter how experienced your rater might be, you would probably want the same children rated by two independent raters so that you can then look at the correlation between the two sets of ratings. Only a high r would reassure you that you have good *interrater reliability,* which is necessary if you expect your experimental findings to be replicated by other researchers.

A large value for r is also important when measuring the reliability of some self-report measuring instrument. Suppose that you are interested in measuring generosity with a new questionnaire. If you assume that a person's generosity is a trait that remains relatively stable over time, you will likely want to demonstrate that your new questionnaire measures generosity in a stable fashion. If you measure each person in your sample for generosity at time one (G1) and then again, say 6 months later (G2), and then calculate the correlation between G1 and G2, the resulting r will be a measure of *test-retest reliability.* The closer r is to 1.0, the more stable your measure of generosity is. This does not prove you have a good measure of generosity, but it is an important first step.

You can also measure the *internal reliability* of your questionnaire by summing the odd-numbered items to get one score (O), and the even items to get a second score (E). A large *r* between O and E shows that your measure has good *split-half reliability*, implying that your questionnaire is measuring just one trait (statistical software now makes it easy to calculate more sophisticated measures of internal reliability, such as the statistic known as Cronbach's alpha).

The correlation coefficient for the *validity* of your generosity questionnaire is not expected to be as high as it is for the test's reliability, but it is important that it be fairly high. One test of validity would be to measure participants with the generosity questionnaire and then in a seemingly unrelated way tell them that you are running low on funds for your experiment and ask if they would take less payment themselves so you can run more participants. If the correlation is high between their generosity score and the amount of money they are willing to give back to the experimenter, there is good support for the validity of your questionnaire. Another way to validate your new generosity questionnaire is by demonstrating that there is a high correlation between it and an older generosity questionnaire previously shown to be both reliable and behaviorally valid. These and other uses for Pearson's *r* will be summarized in Rapid Reference 4.1.

Testing Pearson's *r* for Statistical Significance

When calculating the correlation between two completely different psychological variables it can be interesting that they have any correlation more than zero, or to see whether the correlation is positive or negative. However, if in a sample of 30 people the correlation between mathematical and musical abilities is $+.3$ that does not prove that the correlation in the population from which that sample was drawn is $+.3$, or even that it is positive (or anything other than zero). In keeping with the use of Greek letters for population parameters, the correlation of a population is symbolized by ρ, the lower-case Greek letter r, pronounced "rho." It is certainly possible to get a sample *r* of .3 by accident even when ρ for the two variables is zero. As you might guess, the usual null hypothesis is that the two variables in question have a zero correlation in the population (symbolically, $H_0: \rho = 0$).

To test the null hypothesis you need to know the null hypothesis distribution (NHD). Fortunately, it is known that if you take many samples of 30 each, for example, and H_0 is true, the *r*'s of the samples will form an approximately normal distribution around a mean of zero. Therefore, all you need is the standard error of this NHD, and you can create a z score and make a statistical decision. A good estimate of this standard error is given by the expression

$$\sqrt{\frac{1 - r^2}{N - 2}}$$

To test your single sample against your null hypothesis for the population you can put this expression in the denominator of a ratio to form a z score for groups (similar to Formula 2.2′). However, the problem with using z scores for such a formula is that r is different for every sample, so not only does the numerator of the formula keep changing, but the denominator does as well (we faced a similar problem when we used the sample SD to estimate σ in the last chapter). Fortunately, the solution in the previous chapter applies: We can use the t distribution. So the formula for testing the significance of a Pearson r is

$$t = \frac{r - \rho_0}{\sqrt{\dfrac{1 - r^2}{N - 2}}} , \tag{4.4}$$

where ρ_0 is the correlation in the population, according to the null hypothesis. The denominator of the denominator in Formula 4.4 can be moved to the numerator to create an alternative (but equivalent) version of the formula:

$$t = \frac{r\sqrt{N - 2}}{\sqrt{1 - r^2}} \tag{4.4′}$$

Any t test formula can be rearranged so that the sample size is in the numerator (ρ_0 was left out of this version, because it is so often zero). This version makes it clearer that, all else being equal, the larger the sample the larger the t, and the greater the chance for statistical significance.

An Example of Calculating a Significance Test

Let's test the r of .3 in our example for significance.

$$t = \frac{.3}{\sqrt{\dfrac{1 - .3^2}{28}}} = \frac{.3}{\sqrt{\dfrac{.91}{28}}} = \frac{.3}{\sqrt{.0325}} = \frac{.3}{.18} = 1.66$$

To compare this result to a critical value of t we need to know the appropriate degrees of freedom. For bivariate correlation df $= N - 2$ (this will be explained in a later section). In this case, df $= 30 - 2 = 28$, so t_{crit} for a .05 test, two-tailed, is 2.048 (from Table A.2). Our calculated t is well below this so we cannot reject the null hypothesis. Our results are not strong enough to make us confident that mathematical and musical abilities definitely have more than a zero correlation in the population. Our results are almost significant by a one-tailed test, but it would be hard to justify a one-tailed test in this situation. Our sample r would have to be about .362 to reach significance with a two-tailed test (you can use Formula 4.4 or 4.4' to verify this for yourself). You can see from looking at Formula 4.4' that any r, other than zero, can reach significance with a large enough sample (e.g., it takes an N of about 400 for $r = .1$ to become significant at the .05 level, two-tailed). On the other hand, with a sample size of only four, even an r of .9 is not significant.

Correlation and Causation

It can be nice to find a significant correlation between two variables that are not obviously related, especially if r is fairly high (according to the guidelines of J. Cohen (1988), .5 is a large r, .3 is moderate, and .1 is small). However, what usually makes the correlation interesting is the possibility of some causal connection between the two variables. Although high correlations give us good leads for finding causal connections, we must be very cautious not to leap to unwarranted conclusions. Suppose that we find a high negative correlation between the number of hours a person exercises per week and his or her serum cholesterol level (SCL). It is tempting to conclude that exercise *causes* a reduction in SCL, but it is also possible that people who exercise more also eat less fat, or experience less stress, and that it is these factors, rather than the exercise itself, that reduces cholesterol. It is important to know the causal mechanism before recommending lifestyle changes. If it is the reduced fat intake of exercisers rather than their exercise that is reducing SCL, you wouldn't then recommend exercise to people who need to reduce their SCL without making it clear that exercise alone won't do the job— they must reduce their fat intake. The only way to rule out third variables (e.g., fat intake, stress) as explanations for your correlation is to conduct a controlled experiment by randomly assigning participants to conditions.

Commonly, an experiment would consist of two random groups: one that is assigned to a certain amount of exercise, and one that is not allowed to exercise. However, a more informative way of conducting the experiment would be to assign a different amount of exercise (including zero) to each participant, and then calculate a correlation between the amount of exercise and the reduction in SCL during the course of the experiment. Because the exercise levels were *randomly assigned,* a significant correlation in this case would imply a causal connection between exercise and SCL reduction (provided that we keep participants from making other lifestyle changes during the experiment). In this (rather rare) case, exercise is a true independent variable (IV) and SCL reduction is a dependent variable (DV).

On the other hand, when the level of exercise is controlled by the participant rather than the experimenter, both variables are DVs, and causation cannot be inferred from a significant correlation. Similarly, a *t* test between a group of people who regularly exercise (by their own choice) and a group of people who don't cannot lead to a causal conclusion. Such an experiment is sometimes referred to as a *quasi-experiment,* and sometimes it is called *correlational* to indicate that there is no random assignment of participants. The latter term is a bit misleading because, as we just mentioned, a correlation can be the result of a true experiment, just as a *t* test can. We prefer to say that research is *observational* when participants are not randomly assigned to conditions and *experimental* when they are. Various uses for Pearson's *r* are summarized in Rapid Reference 4.1.

Graphing Correlations

A high Pearson's *r* may not demonstrate causation, but it does tell you that a z score on one variable is paired with a similar z score on the other variable, and that the two variables have a fairly linear relation, as will soon be described graphically. However, a low value for *r* is not very informative; there are a number of very different circumstances that can lead to a low *r*. Just as you should look at the distribution of scores for each of your variables to see if there is marked skewing, outliers, or other potential problems, you should look at a bivariate distribution

≡Rapid Reference 4.1

Some Major Uses for Pearson's Correlation Coefficient

1. Test-retest reliability
2. Internal reliability (e.g., split-half reliability)
3. Interrater reliability
4. Validity (e.g., correlating a subjective measure of a variable with a behavioral measure, or a more traditional, well-established subjective measure)
5. Assessing the relation between two different variables observed in the same group of people (e.g., generosity and self-esteem)
6. Assessing the relation between an experimental variable (IV) and some outcome variable (DV)

of any two variables whose correlation is of interest to you, especially when the correlation you have calculated is rather small.

The simplest way to display a bivariate distribution is with a *scatterplot* (also called a scatter diagram, or scattergram). The possible values of one variable are laid out along the horizontal (x) axis, and the other along the vertical (y) axis. If one variable is thought of as causing the other, it is customary to put the IV (the cause) on the x-axis and the DV (the effect) on the y-axis. Each person is represented by a dot on the graph at the intersection of his or her values on the two variables (if two or more people have the same x, y value, the dot can be replaced by a number or other symbol indicating how many people have landed at exactly that spot). The scatterplot for height and weight for a typical group of 30 people is shown in Figure 4.1 (weight is on the y-axis, because it is somewhat a function of height). Notice that as you move to the right in the graph, the points tend to get higher; that is how you can tell the two variables are positively correlated (the points would tend to get lower as you move to the right for a negative correlation).

It is particularly easy to spot perfect correlation on a scatterplot—all of the points fall on the same straight line. For instance, if you were to measure the high temperature of your town every day for a year on both the Fahrenheit and Celsius scales, the two sets of measurements would be perfectly correlated, and therefore all of the days of the year would fall on a straight line, as shown in Figure 4.2. The equation for the straight line, given that Fahrenheit is on the y-axis, is $F = 1.8C + 32$. The multiplier of C, 1.8, is the slope. When the temperature increases by one degree Celsius it increases by 1.8 degrees Fahrenheit. The number

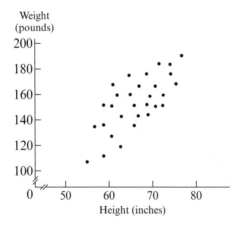

Figure 4.1 A scatterplot of height versus weight for a random sample of 30 people

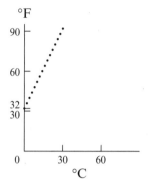

Figure 4.2 A scatterplot of daily high temperatures: Fahrenheit versus Celsius scales

added, 32, is called the y-intercept; it is the value of the y variable when the x variable is at zero (0° Celsius corresponds to 32° Fahrenheit). The straight-line scatterplot tells you that Fahrenheit temperature is just a linear transformation of Celsius temperature. Now you can see why it's called a *linear* transformation.

Degrees of Freedom for Correlations
The scatterplot gives us an easy way to explain why the df equals $N-2$ for correlation. Think of the df as how many pieces of information a sample gives you about the magnitude of the population correlation. If your two variables have been measured for only two people you will have only two dots on your scatterplot. Because the two dots will always fall on one straight line you can see that the sample r you calculate will always be either $+1$ or -1, regardless of the value for ρ. Thus, a sample size of two yields a zero amount of information about the magnitude of ρ; you need a sample of three just to have one piece of information about the size of ρ (df $= N-2 = 3-2 = 1$).

Curvilinear Correlations
You can get a low r because there is simply no relation between your two variables; the points will be scattered almost randomly across the scatterplot. However, the two variables in Figure 4.3 have a very obvious relationship (as age goes up, running speed goes up until some optimal age is reached, and then it goes down with increasing age), and yet Pearson's r would be near zero. The problem is that the relationship is curvilinear and Pearson's r captures only linear relationships. If you looked at age only from birth to the optimal age, the correlation would be high and positive; above the optimal age it would be highly negative. These two parts average out to yield an r near zero. If your scatterplot shows the

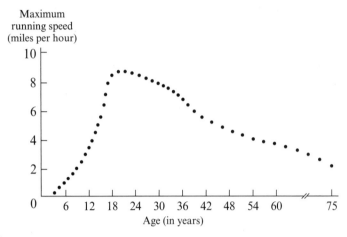

Figure 4.3 A scatterplot of a curvilinear relation: Age versus running speed

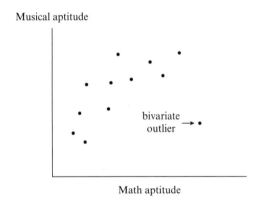

Figure 4.4 A scatterplot that includes one outlier: Mathematical versus musical ability

kind of pattern in Figure 4.3, you should use some kind of curvilinear correlation coefficient or limit your range to one side or the other.

Bivariate Outliers

Figure 4.4 depicts a very different way to get a low value for Pearson's *r*. In this example math and music ability are highly correlated, except for the presence of one person who is very mathematical but has little musical ability. This person is called a *bivariate outlier;* he or she needn't be an outlier on either variable separately but has an unusual combination of the two variables. Just as one univariate outlier can have a large effect on the mean or SD of a variable, one bivariate outlier can greatly lower or raise a correlation (raising a correlation will be discussed in the next section). Further investigation may show that the outlying person misunderstood the directions for the musical ability test, was wearing faulty headphones, or should be disregarded for some other reason. Removing an outlier can greatly improve a correlation, but outliers should not be removed merely for being outliers; there must be some independent reason for removing that data point if your statistical tests on the data are to remain accurate. Legitimate outliers may cause you to rethink your theory to try to accommodate them.

Restricted or Truncated Range

Figure 4.5 demonstrates yet another way to obtain a surprisingly low r. You might think that selecting a group of people all of whom scored highly on a math phobia questionnaire, and then giving them a speeded math test, would be a good way to obtain a high correlation between math fear and number of math errors. You can see that in Figure 4.5 all of the participants did indeed commit a lot of math errors, so why is the sample r near zero? The reason is that r is based on z scores with respect to your *sample;* the person with the lowest math anxiety in your sample will get a low (in fact, negative) z score for anxiety even though he or she is high on the scale in an absolute sense. So the people in your sample will not all have high z scores for both variables. In fact, if you look at the data points in Figure 4.5 you will see that they are scattered almost randomly and do not come close to falling on one straight line. However, if you were to add one score in the lower left corner of Figure 4.5 (low anxiety, low errors) it could shift the mean on both variables enough to make the z score positive on both variables for all of the par-

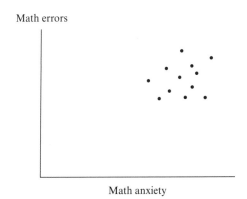

Math errors

Math anxiety

Figure 4.5 A scatterplot with a restricted range: Math errors versus math anxiety

CAUTION

Some Reasons for a Low Pearson's *r*

1. The true relation between the two variables may be curvilinear.
2. Most of the sample follows a fairly linear relationship, but the sample contains one or more bivariate outliers.
3. One or both of the variables may have a restricted (truncated) range in your sample.
4. There is very little relation between the two variables; the points in the scatterplot do not exhibit any clear trend.

ticipants except the new one. In this case a bivariate outlier could greatly increase the magnitude of the correlation.

The problem depicted in Figure 4.5 is called a truncated or *restricted range*. If you erect a vertical line three quarters of the way to the right in Figure 4.1, the points to the right of that line will not exhibit a strong trend and therefore will yield a rather small *r*. In general, the trend of the points has to outweigh the scatter of the points to attain a decent sample *r*. Because in social science research there is usually a good deal of scattering of points, you generally want to include a large range on both variables so the trend, if any, will be prominent. Of course, you don't want the range to be so large that the trend becomes curvilinear as in Figure 4.3. You can often use past research as your guide in deciding on the optimum range of your variables. Unfortunately, sometimes a researcher can be stuck with a sample of convenience that has a restricted range on a variable of interest (e.g., all of the available participants are well educated). In that case you may need to sample a large number of participants: The larger sample won't make *r* any higher, but it can increase your chances of getting statistical significance with a fairly small *r*.

REGRESSION

When two variables are highly correlated (whether positively or negatively), knowing a person's value on one variable allows you to make a fairly accurate prediction concerning his or her value on the other variable. Even with a moderate degree of correlation, useful predictions can be made. This is the logic behind using standardized aptitude tests (like the Scholastic Aptitude Test [SAT] or American College Test [ACT]) as one of the criteria for selecting applicants to a college (such tests yield a moderate *r* when correlated with a student's college GPA upon graduation). Although social scientists rarely make predictions, the most common method that is used for making them, *linear regression,* has other uses, as you will see. In this chapter we will deal only with simple (i.e., bivariate) linear regression: the prediction of one variable by only one other based on the linear relation between them. (Multiple regression is an important extension of bivariate regression, but it is beyond the scope of this book.)

The Standardized Regression Equation

If you recall the definition of perfect correlation, it should come as no surprise that when $r = 1.0$, the z score that is predicted for one variable is exactly the same as the z score of the other variable: $z_{y'} = z_x$ (the prime next to the y in the subscript indicates that this is a prediction). Similarly, when $r = -1.0$, $z_{y'} = -z_x$. When correlation is less than perfect the prediction rule is almost as simple:

$$z_{y'} = rz_x \qquad (4.5)$$

Because this formula is presented in terms of z scores, it is called a standardized regression equation. According to this equation, the lower the correlation, the more cautious you are in your prediction. Assuming the correlation between height and weight is $+.5$, if you know that someone is 2 standard deviations above the mean for height (i.e., $z = +2$), you would predict that person to be only 1 standard deviation above the mean on weight ($z_{y'} = rz_x = .5 \cdot +2 = +1$). Notice what happens when the correlation is zero. Regardless of the value of one variable you would always predict zero for the z score of the other variable. Remember that a z score of zero is always at the mean of a variable, so if, for instance, height and weight were not correlated at all, you would predict the average weight for everyone regardless of his or her height.

You can see then that as the correlation goes from perfect to zero, the prediction of the y variable goes from the same z score as the x variable through smaller and smaller portions of that z score, until it goes down to the mean of the y variable. The phenomenon, in which predictions involving a moderate correlation are a compromise between the same z score as the predictor and the mean of the variable being predicted, is known as *regression toward the mean*. Galton noticed this with height. Tall fathers tended to have tall sons, but not quite as tall as themselves. This tendency has led to a kind of gambler's fallacy wherein people think that nature is moving to even things out by making the son not as tall as his father. Actually, it's just that being tall is rather unlikely, so the odds are somewhat against the son being tall, even if his father is.

The Raw-Score Regression Formula

The expression "y has been regressed on x" means that y is being predicted from x. The variable being predicted is often referred to as the *criterion,* and the other variable is called the *predictor.* If it is sensible to think of one variable as causing a change in the other, then the causal variable is called the independent variable (x) and is used to make predictions about the other, the dependent variable (y). Because it is not convenient to convert all of one's data to z scores, it is more common to make predictions in terms of the scores themselves using a *raw-score* regression or prediction formula. If we start with Formula 4.5 and insert the appropriate z score formulas for the X and Y variables and then rearrange the terms algebraically, we will arrive at the following raw-score formula:

$$Y' = r\left(\frac{s_y}{s_x}\right)X + \overline{Y} - \left[r\left\{\frac{s_y}{s_x}\right\}\overline{X}\right]$$

This formula can be simplified by creating the following terms:

$$b_{yx} = r\left(\frac{s_y}{s_x}\right) \tag{4.6}$$

$$a_{yx} = \overline{Y} - b_{yx}\overline{X} \tag{4.7}$$

Now the raw-score regression formula can be written as

$$Y' = b_{yx}X + a_{yx} \tag{4.8}$$

Note that Formula 4.8 is the equation for a straight line in which b_{yx} is the slope and a_{yx} is the Y-intercept. When $r = +1$ or -1, all of the points in the scatterplot will fall on this line. When correlation is less than perfect the line represented by the formula is the best line that can be drawn through the points in the scatterplot—best in terms of the way it minimizes the distances from the points to the line (actually, squared vertical distances, as will be explained shortly). The procedure for finding the least-squares regression line is summarized in Rapid Reference 4.2.

When r equals zero, b_{yx} also equals zero, and a_{yx} reduces to $\overline{Y}$. Therefore, the regression line becomes $Y' = \overline{Y}$—that is, a horizontal line whose height is the mean of the Y variable. For any value of X, the predicted Y is the point on the regression line directly above that value of X. If you want to predict X from Y the regres-

Rapid Reference 4.2

Steps for Finding the Regression Line

1. Calculate Pearson's r for the two variables.
2. The slope, b_{yx}, is r times the ratio of the SDs for the two variables, with the SD for the criterion (Y) on top.
3. The Y intercept (a_{yx}) is the mean of the criterion (Y) minus b_{yx} times the mean of the predictor (X) variable.
4. The final equation is $Y' = b_{yx}X + a_{yx}$.

sion line will be different—$b_{xy} = r(s_x/s_y)$ and $a_{xy} = \overline{X} - b_{xy}\overline{Y}$—but it is rare to want to predict Y from X *and* X from Y, so it is customary to label the criterion Y and the predictor X. Note that whereas b_{yx} and a_{yx} are usually not the same as b_{xy} and a_{xy} (unless the means and SDs of two variables are the same), r_{yx} is the same as r_{xy}, so if we are dealing only with two variables we can refer to *r* without subscripts.

Making Predictions

It is time now to discuss using a regression line to make specific predictions. Suppose you have a group of 30 men who have been measured for height (X) and weight (Y), and $r = .4$. If $\overline{X} = 69$ inches, $s_x = 2.5$ inches, $\overline{Y} = 160$ pounds, and $s_y = 25$ pounds, then $b_{yx} = .4(25/2.5) = .4 \cdot 10 = 4$, and $a_{yx} = 160 - 4(69) = 160 - 276 = -116$. So the prediction equation is $Y' = 4X - 116$ (obviously the Y-intercept is not interpretable in this case). If in the place of X you put some (reasonable) height in inches, and solve, you will get the best prediction you can make for weight. For instance, a man who is 75 inches tall would be predicted to weigh $Y' = 4(75) - 116 = 300 - 116 = 184$ pounds, whereas a man who is only 60 inches tall would be predicted to weigh $Y' = 4(60) - 116 = 240 - 116 = 124$ pounds. Note that in simple linear regression the mean of one variable always leads to a prediction of the mean for the other variable (in our example, $Y' = 4(69) - 116 = 276 - 116 = 160$).

Of course, you are not just trying to predict values in the sample you already have. The purpose of creating a prediction equation is to make predictions for people not in your sample and often for values not yet known (e.g., predicting the length of someone's life span from their current health habits). The predictions can be thought of as point estimates of some true value, and they have the same problem as point estimates of the population mean. The problem is that predictions are much better when *r* is high than low, and better when they come from large rather than small samples. We hope that you remember from Chapter 2 that the solution to this problem is interval estimation. You can create a 95% confidence interval, for instance, around your prediction. The precise computations for such intervals are beyond the scope of this book (see B. Cohen, 2000); the important point is that you know when and why to use them.

Interpreting the Slope and Intercept of the Regression Line

Whereas *r* is unaffected by a change in measurement units, the slope is not. If weight is measured in pounds s_y could be about 30, and if height is measured in inches s_x could be about 3. With a height/weight correlation of .5 the slope would be $.5 \cdot (30/3)$, which equals 5. This means that if person A is 1 inch taller than

CAUTION

The Y-intercept of a regression line is not always interpretable. It does not always make sense to extend the regression line down to X = 0.

person B, person A is expected to be 5 pounds heavier than person B. However, if height is measured in centimeters and weight in kilograms, the slope would only be about .9. Although the sign of the slope must match the sign of r, the magnitude of the slope tells us nothing by itself about the magnitude of r.

The Y-intercept is, of course, also affected by a change in units, but unlike the slope it is not always meaningful. We will begin with a case in which it is. Imagine that you are predicting scores on a statistics exam from the number of hours studied. Hours of study would be on the x-axis of the scatterplot, and exam scores on the y-axis. The slope of the regression line tells you how many additional points you can expect to score on the exam for each hour that you study. The regression line could pass through the *origin* (0,0 point) of the graph, but more likely it will hit the y-axis at some positive value. That value (the value of Y when X = 0) is the Y-intercept, and it tells you, in this case, what exam score you can expect if you don't study at all for the test. However, it doesn't always make sense to extend the regression line all the way down to a zero value for X. The height/weight scatterplot is an example of this. As another example, consider predicting income or happiness or any other variable from IQ. It is not meaningful to make predictions for an IQ of zero because it is not clear what it would mean for a person to have an IQ of zero. Usually, linear regression makes sense only within a limited range of the X variable. Beyond that range the relation with other variables may not remain linear—if those extreme X values can be interpreted at all.

Variance around the Regression Line

The way error is measured in linear regression is important; in fact, sometimes the errors are the most important part of the regression, as you will soon see. In Figure 4.6 we have redrawn Figure 4.1 to illustrate how error is measured. Notice that the point representing Mr. Y in Figure 4.6 shows that Mr. Y is very tall. He is also very heavy; indeed, he is considerably heavier than expected for his height. The difference between his actual weight and his predicted weight (i.e., the vertical distance from the point to the regression line) is considered error. If we were really trying to predict his weight, this amount is how many pounds we'd be off. Subtracting his predicted weight from his actual weight yields Mr. Y's *residual* score, which is positive in this case. People whose weights fall below their predictions have negative residuals. It is an important property of the regression line

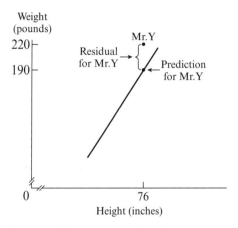

Figure 4.6 Measuring error from a regression line

that if you add up all of the residuals (i.e., errors from the line), the positives will exactly cancel out the negatives to yield a sum of zero.

The total amount of error around a regression line is determined by squaring all of the residuals and adding them up. The resulting sum of squares (SS) is called variously SS_{error}, $SS_{residual}$, or $SS_{unexplained}$. Another important property of the regression line is that it minimizes SS_{error}; it is the best possible line in the scatterplot, because no other line would produce a smaller SS_{error}. Therefore, the regression line has what is called the *least squares property*. The regression line may remind you of the mean; that's because it is a running mean of sorts. It is approximately the mean of the Y values at each X value (the larger the sample the better the approximation at each X value). Dividing $SS_{residual}$ by N (the sample size) gives you $\sigma^2_{residual}$, the variance of the residuals, which is also the variance of the data points from the regression line (in the vertical direction).

As the correlation gets closer to zero, $\sigma^2_{residual}$ gets larger, but until the correlation actually equals zero, $\sigma^2_{residual}$ remains less than the variance of the errors you would make without using regression at all. How much is the variance of your errors without regression? Recall that when r equals zero your best strategy is to guess the mean of Y as the Y value, regardless of X. Using $\overline{Y}$ as your prediction for everybody is the same as drawing a horizontal line through the scatterplot and using it as your regression line. The variance of the Y values around the mean of Y is just the ordinary variance of Y. In the context of regression it is called the *total variance*. To the extent that the points tend to rise or fall as you move to the right in the graph, a line that is angled to follow the points will get closer to the points, and the $\sigma^2_{residual}$ around that line will be less than the $\sigma^2_{residual}$ around the horizontal line (i.e., σ^2_{total}). The difference between σ^2_{total} and $\sigma^2_{residual}$ is the variance that has been accounted for by the regression—it is the amount by which the error variance has been reduced by having a predictor ($\sigma^2_{regression} = \sigma^2_{total} - \sigma^2_{residual}$).

That amount of variance—let's call it $\sigma^2_{regression}$—is not by itself a meaningful quantity (for instance, it depends on your measurement units), but divided by the total variance it is the *proportion of (the total) variance accounted for* by the regression. This proportion is directly related to the degree of correlation; the greater the magnitude of r, the greater the reduction in error variance and the larger the proportion of variance accounted for. In fact, the relationship is simpler than you might guess, as shown in Formula 4.9:

$$r^2 = \frac{\sigma^2_{regression}}{\sigma^2_{total}} \qquad (4.9)$$

The quantity r^2 is sometimes referred to as the *coefficient of determination*. Notice that it is the magnitude and not the sign of the correlation that determines the proportion of variance accounted for; an r of $-.5$ is just as good as $+.5$, in that both allow you to reduce error variance by 25% (i.e., $-.5^2 = .25$). Also note that the squaring of r results in less variance accounted for than you might expect. A moderate correlation of .3 reduces error variance by only 9%, and a small correlation of .1 reduces it by only 1% ($\sigma^2_{residual}$ is 99% as large as σ^2_{total} when $r = .1$). The complement of r^2 is the *coefficient of nondetermination,* sometimes symbolized as k^2, and it is the proportion of the total variance that still needs to be explained.

$$k^2 = \frac{\sigma^2_{residual}}{\sigma^2_{total}} \qquad (4.10)$$

Because $r^2 + k^2 = 1$, another way to define k^2 is as $1 - r^2$, so $1 - r^2 = \sigma^2_{residual}/\sigma^2_{total}$. This leads to a formula whereby the variance around the regression line does not have to be calculated directly if r has been found.

$$\sigma^2_{residual} = (1 - r^2)\sigma^2_{total} \qquad (4.11)$$

The Assumptions of Linear Regression

Ideally, the joint distribution of your two variables in the population will be a *bivariate normal distribution* (e.g., not only will extreme values of height and weight become increasingly unlikely, but extreme *combinations* of the two variables will drop off accordingly). Moreover, to make valid CIs for your predictions, the data points should become scarcer as you move up or down from the regression line; in fact, the density of the points should follow a normal distribution vertically at every value for X. Finally, all of these NDs should have the same σ^2 (their means are on the regression line), which is $\sigma^2_{residual}$ as defined earlier. This last condition is called *homoscedasticity*, but you can think of it as homogeneity of variance around the regression line. Having much more scatter around, say, the left half as compared to the right half of the line is called *heteroscedasticity*, and this condition threatens the validity of your predictions.

DON'T FORGET

The Assumptions of Linear Regression

1. Interval/ratio data
2. Independent observations
3. Bivariate normal distribution (bivariate outliers threaten this assumption)
4. Homoscedasticity (equal amount of scatter all along the regression line)

Other Uses for Regression

Prediction is not the only common use for linear regression. Regression can be used in conjunction with an experiment in which the independent variable has quantifiable levels. For instance, the IV could be dosage of caffeine, and the DV could be the score on a video game that simulates driving a truck (perhaps the participants are sleep deprived). Although the IV will usually have just a few discrete values (i.e., dosages), you could still display your data on a scatterplot and find the best regression line. The slope of that line will tell you how much scores improve when you increase caffeine dosage by one unit (the Y-intercept would indicate how well participants perform when deprived of both sleep *and* caffeine). If the change in scores with caffeine dosage is not linear (e.g., an optimum dosage is reached after which scores actually decrease), a more complex form of regression, like polynomial regression, should be used.

Another even more common use for regression is to focus not on the predictions but on the residuals. Suppose a researcher thinks there's a connection between a man's weight and his cholesterol level (CL). She is surprised to see that the correlation between weight and CL is rather low. Then she realizes that it is really obesity that should be related to CL. A man who weighs 200 pounds may be obese, or slim and just very tall. If she uses height to predict weight, the residual will be like an obesity score (how many pounds someone is above or below the average weight for his height). If she is right about the obesity-CL connection these residuals will correlate more highly with CL than the original weights of the men. In this way regression can be used to clean up a variable by adjusting it for some other variable that is not of interest (there is no reason to think that height is related to CL, so to the extent that height affects weight it is a nuisance variable). If you are studying the relation between memory and amount of exercise in the elderly you would probably want to correct or adjust your memory scores for age by using linear regression and finding the residual memory score.

The Point-Biserial Correlation

We don't want to end this chapter without talking about a special case of correlation in which one of the variables has only two possible values, and these values represent different groups. For instance, it is possible to find the correlation between height and gender. At first, this may seem impossible, because gender is not quantifiable, and you need numbers for both variables to calculate r. However, you can arbitrarily assign two different numbers to the two different groups and then calculate the correlation. Surprisingly, it doesn't matter what two numbers you assign: You will get the same r if you use 1 and 2, or 3 and 17. Perhaps even more surprising is the fact that the r you get, which is called the point-biserial r (symbolized r_{pb}), is meaningful. Suppose you assign 1 to females and 2 to males and correlate these gender numbers with their heights. In this case, r will measure the tendency for the heights to get larger as the gender number gets larger (i.e., goes from 1 to 2). The more consistently the men are taller than the women, the closer r will get to $+1$. Of course, if we assign the larger gender number to females, the sign of r will reverse, which is why the sign of r_{pb} is usually ignored. But in either case, the *magnitude* (i.e., absolute value) of r_{pb} will be the same, and it will tell us the degree to which one gender is consistently taller than the other.

Like any r, we can test r_{pb} for significance with a t test by employing Formula 4.4. Let us say we have calculated r_{pb} for the gender/height example, and then calculated its t value. We can also calculate a t value directly to compare the males and females on height using Formula 3.6. It should not be shocking that these two t values will always be exactly the same, because they are testing the same thing: the tendency for one gender to have more height than the other. Knowing that the two t values will be the same, we can take the t from any t test of two independent groups, plug it into Formula 4.4′, and solve for r to see what we would have gotten if we had calculated a correlation with arbitrary group numbers instead. Solving Formula 4.4 for r (which we label r_{pb}), we get

$$r_{pb} = \sqrt{\frac{t^2}{t^2 + df}} \qquad (4.12)$$

where df equals the combined number of participants from the two groups minus 2.

The Relation between r_{pb} and the t Test

What makes r_{pb} so useful in the two-group case is that the t value, which tells us only whether we can reject the null hypothesis, tells us nothing about how consistently the two groups differ on the dependent variable. Even a small, inconsistent difference between two groups can produce a very large t value if the samples are huge. But if a fairly large t, like 4.0, is associated with 240 df (121 people in each of the two groups) r_{pb} will be only

$$r_{pb} = \sqrt{\frac{4^2}{4^2 + 240}} = \sqrt{\frac{16}{256}} = \sqrt{\frac{1}{16}} = .25$$

If the same t is associated with only 16 df, r_{pb} will be

$$r_{pb} = \sqrt{\frac{4^2}{4^2 + 16}} = \sqrt{\frac{16}{32}} = \sqrt{.5} = .707$$

The larger r_{pb} indicates that there will be less overlap between the two groups, and that it will be easier to predict the DV from knowing which group someone is in.

Even more useful than r_{pb}, in many ways, is its squared value, r_{pb}^2; this value tells you the proportion of variance in your continuous variable that is accounted for by group membership. In terms of the gender/height example, r_{pb}^2 tells you how much height variance is reduced when measured within the two genders, rather than across all human beings. You may recall from the previous chapter that g also tells you about how well your two groups are separated. As you would guess, r_{pb}^2 increases as g increases. As g gets extremely large, r_{pb}^2 approaches 1.0.

If you were dealing with an entire population, r_{pb}^2 would be called *omega squared* (not rho squared, as you might expect) and is symbolized as ω^2 (the last letter of the Greek alphabet in lowercase). However, r_{pb}^2 from your data is a biased estimate of its corresponding ω^2. Fortunately, the bias can be corrected fairly well by the following formula:

$$\text{est } \omega^2 = \frac{t^2 - 1}{t^2 + df + 1} \tag{4.13}$$

Note that without the -1 and $+1$, this is just the square of Formula 4.12. Either r_{pb}^2 or the unbiased estimate of ω^2 from Formula 4.13 (or in some cases, g) should usually be reported along with a two-group t value, so that the reader is informed not only of the statistical significance of an experimental effect, but the actual size of that effect in the data. We will show you how to translate effect size measures into the probability of getting statistical significance (i.e., power) in Chapter 6.

Putting It Into Practice

1. As the correlation between two sets of scores becomes more positive, the RM t test comparing the means of the two sets gets larger. Reproduced below are the data from the second "Putting It Into Practice" problem in the previous chapter.

Participant No.	No Imagery	Imagery
1	8	14
2	11	15
3	7	5
4	10	16
5	9	9
6	15	16
7	7	8
8	16	20

(a) Calculate Pearson's r between the Imagery and No Imagery conditions. Is the correlation statistically significant at the level?

(b) The RM t value can be calculated in terms of the Pearson's r between the two sets of scores and the means and SDs of the two sets by using the following formula:

$$t = \frac{\overline{X}_1 - \overline{X}_2}{\sqrt{\dfrac{s_1^2 + s_2^2}{N} - \dfrac{2\,r\,s_1 s_2}{N}}}$$

Using this formula, calculate the RM t for the imagery data and compare it to the RM t you found for the same data in the previous chapter.

(c) Can the correlation be statistically significant if the RM t test is not (and vice versa)? Explain.

2. Students who have taken courses in both areas are asked to rate on a 10-point scale how much they like math and how much they like statistics. The ratings for 10 random students appear below.

Student No.	Math	Statistics
1	7	5
2	8	4
3	2	0
4	9	3
5	3	1
6	5	6
7	6	7
8	0	1
9	4	3
10	8	2

(a) Is there a tendency for those who like math to like statistics also? Determine the strength of the linear relationship by calculating the correlation coefficient between these two sets of ratings.

(b) Test the correlation in 2a for significance at the .05 level. Can you reject the null hypothesis that the two ratings have a zero correlation in the population?

(c) Draw the scatterplot for the data in this problem with the math ratings on the horizontal (x) axis. Is Pearson's r a good way to summarize the relation between the two variables? Explain.

(d) Find the regression equation for predicting the statistics rating from the math rating. What statistics rating would you predict for someone who gives a rating of 6 to math?

3. Calculate the point-biserial r corresponding to each of the p-v t values you found for the first "Putting It Into Practice" problem (1a) in the previous chapter. Compare these r's to the values you calculated for g in part b of that problem.

🐟 TEST YOURSELF 🐟

1. **If a variable, Y, is created by dividing all the values of another variable, X, by a constant and subtracting a constant from each value, what will the Pearson's r between X and Y be?**

   (a) 0

   (b) 100

   (c) $+1.0$ or -1

   (d) It depends on the means and SD's of x and y.

2. **If Pearson's r for a sample is found to be $-.9$, which of the following will be true of the scatterplot for those data?**

   (a) All of the points will be fairly close to one straight line.

   (b) The points will be almost randomly scattered.

   (c) The points will exhibit a strong relation, but not a linear one.

   (d) Nothing can be said about the scatterplot from the information given.

3. **If taking away one point from a sample causes Pearson's r to change dramatically, you are probably dealing with**

   (a) a bivariate outlier.

   (b) a curvilinear relation

   (c) a correlation near zero.

   (d) a correlation near ± 1.0.

4. **A truly random sample of the population (as compared to a convenient sample) will reduce the likelihood of which of the following?**

   (a) A curvilinear correlation

   (b) A near-zero correlation

   (c) A truncated range

   (d) Statistically significant results

(continued)

5. **If a journal article reports a small Pearson's r, and yet also reports that the r differs significantly from zero at the .05 level, which of the following must be true?**

   (a) The correlation was not a curvilinear one.

   (b) The sample size was not very small.

   (c) There must have been at least one bivariate outlier.

   (d) A large alpha must have been used.

6. **Find Pearson's r, given the following summary statistics: $N = 10$, $\Sigma XY = 2780$, $\mu_x = 3.2$, $\mu_y = 87.5$, $\sigma_x = .4$, $\sigma_y = 7.2$.**

   (a) $+.31$

   (b) $-.31$

   (c) $-.69$

   (d) $-.77$

7. **For a sample, r^2 is equal to**

   (a) the ratio of the explained variance to the unexplained variance.

   (b) the coefficient of nondetermination.

   (c) the proportion of the variance accounted for.

   (d) all of the above.

8. **A large positive slope means that**

   (a) the correlation will be large and positive.

   (b) the Y-intercept will be large and positive.

   (c) the value of Y will increase by (at least) several units when the X value increases by one unit.

   (d) all of the above are true.

9. **Suppose that the calculated t value for a two-group experiment with 43 participants per group is 4.0. What is the value of the point-biserial r?**

   (a) .16

   (b) .19

   (c) .4

   (d) .44

10. **Suppose that there is a .45 correlation between IQ ($\mu = 100$, $\sigma = 15$) and verbal SAT score ($\mu = 500$, $\sigma = 100$). What verbal SAT score would you predict for someone who has an IQ of 90?**

   (a) 433

   (b) 470

   (c) 490

   (d) 510

Answers: 1. c; 2. a; 3. a; 4. c; 5. b; 6. c; 7. c; 8. c; 9. c; 10. b.

Five

ONE-WAY ANOVA AND MULTIPLE COMPARISONS

ONE-WAY ANOVA

Don't let the name fool you. The procedure known as *analysis of variance,* or ANOVA for short, is really like the *t* test in that it helps you determine whether your sample means differ enough to conclude that they do not differ just by chance—that there is some real difference among the populations they represent. The advantage of ANOVA is that it can be applied to any number of groups, rather than just two as in the case of the *t* test. In fact, because ANOVA can be applied when there are only two groups there is no need for the *t* test (we will show you how to get *t* from your ANOVA). The reason the procedure in this chapter is called analysis of *variance* is related to the description of the *t* test in terms of linear regression presented at the end of the previous chapter: The total variation of the DV is analyzed (i.e., broken into smaller parts) into a proportion of variance accounted for by the IV, and a proportion representing residual or error variance (i.e., within the different groups).

In this chapter we will deal only with *one-way* ANOVA, which means that all of the groups involved are considered to be different *levels* of a single *factor,* which is the IV. Two- and three-way ANOVAs, for instance, have two or three IVs, respectively. Also, we will be dealing only with one-way ANOVAs, in which each level involves a different, separate group of participants. If people are matched from one group to another, or the same participant is involved in more than one level of the ANOVA, a different type of ANOVA is required, which will be described in Chapter 8. ANOVAs with only one DV are called *univariate,* whereas ANOVAs that combine two or more DVs into a single analysis are called *multivariate ANOVAs,* or MANOVAs, for short. In this chapter we will discuss only one-way univariate ANOVAs—that is, ANOVAs with one IV and one DV.

Comparing ANOVA with the t Test

To show you just how similar ANOVA is to the t test, we will start with a t formula, square it so that we are working with variances, and then rearrange it algebraically until it looks like an ANOVA. We will start with Formula 3.6, but with $n_1 = n_2$.

$$t = \frac{\overline{X}_1 - \overline{X}_2}{\sqrt{s_p^2\left(\frac{1}{n} + \frac{1}{n}\right)}} = \frac{\overline{X}_1 - \overline{X}_2}{\sqrt{s_p^2\left(\frac{2}{n}\right)}}$$

Now we square both sides and rearrange terms.

$$t^2 = \frac{(\overline{X}_1 - \overline{X}_2)^2}{\frac{2s_p^2}{n}} = \frac{n(\overline{X}_1 - \overline{X}_2)^2}{2s_p^2}$$

This leads to

$$t^2 = \frac{\frac{n(\overline{X}_1 - \overline{X}_2)^2}{2}}{s_p^2} \tag{5.1}$$

Formula 5.1 does not look anything like a t formula, but take its square root and you will get the same t value as you would using Formula 3.6 (if the n's are equal). If you don't take its square root, you have performed an ANOVA on the two groups. Unfortunately, the numerator of this formula will not work if you have more than two groups. The denominator of the formula, however, does not need to change to accommodate more than two groups. If you look at Formula 3.5 for the pooled variance, it is easy to imagine how you could add groups. For instance, for three groups the formula would be

$$s^2_{pooled} = \frac{(n_1 - 1)\, s^2_1 + (n_2 - 1)\, s^2_2 + (n_3 - 1)\, s^2_3}{n_1 + n_2 + n_3 - 3}$$

Also, note that the groups can be different sizes. If all of the groups are the same size, the formula above simplifies to an ordinary average of the group variances:

$$s^2_p = \frac{\sum s^2}{k} \tag{5.2}$$

where k is the number of different groups. It is not obvious how groups can be added to the numerator of the squared t test formula, but we will show you how next.

The ANOVA Formula for Any Number of Equal-Sized Groups

If you want to know how far apart two sample means are, a simple difference score will suffice. But if you want to know how spread out three or more sample means are, what measure can you take? The answer is that for any set of numbers, their standard deviation will tell you how spread out they are. However, for ANOVA, taking the variance of the sample means will be more convenient. It may not look like it, but the following term is actually the unbiased variance of the two sample means (or any two numbers): $(\overline{X}_1 - \overline{X}_2)^2/2$ (i.e., you would get the same result from plugging the two numbers into a formula for s^2, such as Formula 2.4). The symbol for the unbiased variance of sample means is $s^2_{\overline{x}}$. If we exchange these two terms in the numerator of Formula 5.1, then we can write that numerator as $ns^2_{\overline{x}}$ (the unbiased variance of the sample means multiplied by the size of any one sample). We can now rewrite Formula 5.1 as $[n(s^2_{\overline{x}})]/s^2_p$, which can clearly accommodate any number of same-sized groups.

Just as Formula 3.6 follows the t distribution when the null hypothesis is true and the proper assumptions are met, the expression above follows a distribution referred to as F (in honor of the pioneering work of Sir Ronald Fisher), when the appropriate null hypothesis and assumptions are true. Plugging Formula 5.2 into the preceding expression, we get a simple formula for the one-way ANOVA that works when all of the k groups are the same size, n.

$$F = \frac{ns^2_{\overline{x}}}{\dfrac{\sum s^2}{k}} \tag{5.3}$$

Suppose the means and (unbiased) SDs of your three groups are as follows: $\overline{X}_1$ = 6, s_1 = 4; $\overline{X}_2$ = 9, s_2 = 3; $\overline{X}_3$ = 15; s_3 = 5, and that there are only four people in each group. Given that the (unbiased) variance of 6, 9, and 15 is 21, and squaring the s's to get the variances for each group, the F ratio for these data would be

$$F = \frac{4(21)}{\dfrac{16 + 9 + 25}{3}} = \frac{84}{\dfrac{50}{3}} = \frac{84}{16.67} = 5.04$$

Whereas the t distribution depends only on the df of the pooled variance, the F distribution depends on the df for both the numerator and denominator of the F ratio, as we will explain shortly.

The General Formula for ANOVA

Formula 5.3 is very convenient for calculation in the equal-n case, and for making the concept of ANOVA clear (we will return to it for that purpose), but the df's will be easier to see in the more general formula for F. The following formula is needed when the groups are different sizes:

$$F = \frac{\dfrac{\sum n_i(\overline{X}_i - \overline{X}_G)^2}{k - 1}}{\dfrac{\sum[(n_i - 1)s_i^2]}{\sum(n_i - 1)}} \tag{5.4}$$

where n_i, $\overline{X}_i$, and s_i^2 are the size, mean, and variance of any one particular (i.e., the ith) group, k is the number of groups, and $\overline{X}_G$ is the *grand mean* (i.e., the mean of all the scores—it is the simple average of the group means only when all of the groups are the same size). Both the numerator and the denominator of the formula are variances; as we will explain shortly, these two variances are expected to be about the same when the null hypothesis is true.

Any unbiased variance can be written as SS/df, where SS stands for the sum of squared deviations from the mean, and df is the degrees of freedom; that is the case for both the numerator and the denominator of Formula 5.4. When an SS is divided by df it becomes a mean of squares instead of a sum of squares, so any variance can be symbolized as MS instead of s^2; this is a common notation when dealing with ANOVA. The numerator of Formula 5.4 is called the between-groups mean-square or $MS_{between}$, while the denominator is called the within-group mean-square or MS_{within}. This notation is often shortened even further as in the following formula:

$$F = \frac{MS_{bet}}{MS_w} \tag{5.5}$$

Let us look more closely at the numerator of Formula 5.4. It has the form of SS/df, where $\Sigma n_i(\overline{X}_i - \overline{X}_G)^2$ is $SS_{between}$ and $k-1$ is $df_{between}$ (the number of groups minus one). In the expression for SS_{bet}, the grand mean is subtracted from each mean and the difference squared before being multiplied by the sample size and summed. The squared deviations from the grand mean are being weighted by the sample size; hence, this method is called the *analysis of weighted means*. There is a variation of this formula that is known as the analysis of unweighted means, but it is used so rarely in the one-way ANOVA that we will not mention it again in this chapter. (The analysis of unweighted means is mentioned in "Putting it into Practice" in Chapter 7, and is described thoroughly in the two-way ANOVA chapter in B. Cohen [2000].)

The denominator of Formula 5.4 is a way of writing Formula 5.2 when the groups are different sizes. It too has the form of SS/df, where $\Sigma(n_i - 1)s_i^2$ is SS_{within} or SS_W, for short (each group variance is weighted by its sample size), and $\Sigma(n_i - 1)$ is df_w. Note that $\Sigma(n_i - 1)$ can be written as $\Sigma n_i - k$, which equals $N_T - k$ (the total number of participants minus the number of groups). In the two-group case df_{bet} equals one, and $df_w = n_1 + n_2 - 2$; the square root of F is just t with df equal to df_w. Also note that when all the n's are equal, n (without a subscript) can be moved in front of the summation sign in the numerator of Formula 5.4, and the denominator of that formula becomes the ordinary average of the sample variances. Thus, Formula 5.4 becomes the same as Formula 5.3.

There are several computational raw-score formulas for SS_{bet} and SS_w that were needed to reduce computational effort in the days before statistical software and hand-held statistical calculators. They are no longer useful, and because they are not informative to look at we will not bother to present them here. Now that we have defined both df_{bet} and df_w, we can discuss the F distribution and how it can be used to determine statistical significance for ANOVA.

CAUTION

If your IV (i.e., factor) in a one-way ANOVA has quantitative levels (e.g., different dosages of the same drug), the ordinary ANOVA approach will very likely not be optimal. You should consider using trend analysis, as described at the end of this chapter.

The F Distribution

Just as the *t* test helps us to make a decision about whether two populations have the same mean, one-way ANOVA uses an F test to decide about the equality of any number of population means. In the three-group case, the null hypothesis can be written as H_0: $\mu_1 = \mu_2 = \mu_3$, but H_0 easily can be expanded for any number of groups. When H_0 is true, the F ratio (as in Formula 5.5) should follow an F distribution, which is therefore the appropriate NHD. But there is a whole family of F distributions, which vary in shape whenever the df changes for the numerator ($df_{bet} = k - 1$) or the denominator ($df_w = N_T - k$) of the F ratio. Because F is a ratio of variances and therefore can never be less than zero, F distributions tend to be positively skewed, like the typical example depicted in Figure 5.1. Only when the sample sizes are extremely large does the F distribution begin to resemble the normal distribution (which it becomes as df_{bet} and df_w become infinite).

To find a critical value for F, with alpha at .05, go to Table A.3 in Appendix A. For the example with three groups of 4 participants each, df for the numerator (i.e., df_{bet}) equals $k - 1 = 3 - 1 = 2$, and df for the denominator (i.e., df_w) equals $N_T - k = 12 - 3 = 9$. F_{crit} from that table is 4.26, which means that 5% of the area of the F (2, 9) distribution is beyond 4.26 (see Figure 5.1). Because the F calculated for our example (5.04) is larger than 4.26 we can reject the null hypothesis (our result is too large to come up frequently by accident when the experiment doesn't work at all).

Note that we only use one tail (the positive, or right, tail) of the F distribution for ANOVA. The more that the sample means differ from each other, regardless of the order or the pattern of the means, the greater is the variance of the means and therefore the calculated F ratio. A very tiny F ratio (i.e., in the smaller, left tail) can only imply that the sample means are unusually similar to each other (con-

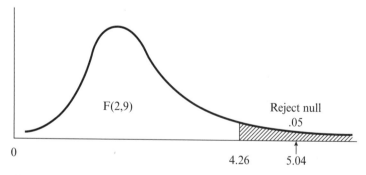

Figure 5.1 The F distribution with 2 and 9 degrees of freedom

sidering the possibilities for accidental variations), which cannot count against the null hypothesis.

The simplest way to wind up with an F distribution is to draw two samples from the same population and divide the variance of the first by the variance of the second. If you do this very many times (ideally, an infinite number of times), these F ratios will form an F distribution with dfs of $n_1 - 1$ and $n_2 - 1$. An F test can be used to decide if the two variances are significantly different, but there are more robust tests for HOV, as mentioned in Chapter 3. The reason that the same F test works for ANOVA is that both the numerator and denominator of Formula 5.5 are estimates of the same population variance. Explaining how this can be so will give you a deeper understanding of the logic of ANOVA, so we turn to this task next.

Both Parts of the F Ratio Estimate Population Variance

The denominator of Formula 5.5 rests on the HOV assumption, as did the use of s^2_{pooled} in Chapter 3. If HOV can be assumed, then all the sample variances are estimates of the same σ^2, and taking a weighted average of them is the best way to estimate the population variance (we will discuss what to do when HOV cannot be assumed in the next section). That the numerator of Formula 5.5 is also an estimate of this same σ^2 is much less obvious. It will be easier to explain in the equal-n case, when MS_{bet} equals $n(s^2_{\bar{X}})$, fortunately the same explanation is valid for the more general case.

If we square both sides of Formula 2.1 (the standard error of the mean), we get a formula that tells you what the variance of sample means will be when the samples are of size n and the population has a variance of σ^2: $\sigma^2_{\bar{X}} = \sigma^2/n$. If we multiply both sides of the preceding formula by n and reverse the equation, we get $\sigma^2 = n\sigma^2_{\bar{X}}$. This formula tells us that the population variance of individuals is equal to the variance of sample means (based on those individuals) multiplied by the size of those samples. Therefore, if you have several samples in your study, and you calculate $ns^2_{\bar{X}}$), that quantity is actually an estimate of σ^2, the variance of the population from which you drew your samples. This is only the case when H_0 is true, as we will explain shortly. Thus, when the null hypothesis is true, the denominator of Formula 5.5 estimates σ^2 from the sample variances, and the numerator estimates σ^2 independently from the variance of the sample means, and so the F ratios follow an F distribution with an expected value of about 1.0 (actually, the average F is $df_w/(df_w - 2)$, which becomes very close to 1.0 for large sample sizes).

In ANOVA the denominator of the F ratio is an estimate of σ^2, regardless of whether the null hypothesis is true. This is the person-to-person variation within each group of a study—the variation due to individual differences, measurement error, and minor random variations in experimental conditions—all of which is unexplained and considered error. That is why the denominator of an F ratio in an ANOVA is called the *error term,* and may be symbolized as MS_{error} (it is also common to write SS_{error} and df_{error}). The numerator in a one-way ANOVA is based on differences among the sample means, which may or may not be influenced by the different treatments given to the groups. When the population means are all the same (i.e., H_0 is true), we do not expect the sample means to all be the same; we expect them to show some variation based on sampling error that can get larger (as σ^2 gets larger or n gets smaller), or smaller (as n gets larger or σ^2 gets smaller). When H_0 is *not* true, we expect the variation of the sample means to depend on the size of the effects (i.e., population differences), *in addition to* sampling error. So, in the general case, the F ratio for one-way ANOVA looks like this: F = (treatment effects + sampling error)/sampling error.

When H_0 is true, the treatment effects are zero, so the F ratio consists of one estimate of sampling error divided by a different estimate of sampling error; therefore, it can be somewhat smaller or larger than 1.0, but it is usually not far from 1.0. When H_0 is *not* true, F is usually greater than 1.0 (although by accident it can still be less than 1.0), but unless it is larger than the critical value we must be cautious and not reject the H_0 (a large F could be due to the estimated sampling error in the numerator being much larger than in the denominator), even though we may be committing a Type II error. The assumptions required for the validity of the F test in ANOVA are the same as for the *t* test. However, the HOV assumption is a bit more problematic, as described next.

Homogeneity of Variance in ANOVA

When all of the samples in a one-way ANOVA are the same size, the Type I error rate is not affected much by differences in the variances of the populations represented. However, the more discrepant the sample sizes become, the more likely it is that differences in population variances can impact the one-way ANOVA. A test such as Levene's test (as introduced in Chapter 3) can evaluate the HOV assumption with any number of groups. If HOV is rejected by such a test, there are separate-variance versions of ANOVA that can be employed, but none of these solutions are as simple and universally accepted as in the case of the usual solution for the separate-variances *t* test. Consequently, data transformations are often recommended to bring the variances closer together, especially when the sample data are very far from following a normal distribution. In extreme cases, especially if the sample sizes are small as well as discrepant, a nonparametric version of the one-way ANOVA (e.g., the Kruskal-Wallis test) is recommended (see Chapter 9). The main assumptions of ANOVA are listed in Rapid Reference 5.1.

═Rapid Reference 5.1

Assumptions of ANOVA

• Interval or ratio scale of measurement for the DV
• Independent random sampling
• Normal distribution of the DV in each population sampled
• Homogeneity of variance—each population sampled has the same variance

Describing ANOVA results

Summary Table

The results of the one-way ANOVA are presented in a standard way in psychological journals (APA, 2001). Returning to the example we used to illustrate the use of Formula 5.3, the results of the ANOVA could be reported in the following way: "The means of the three groups (M's equal 6, 9, and 15) differed significantly, $F(2, 9) = 5.04, p < .05$." The numbers in parentheses after F indicate the dfs used to find the critical F, but the F given is the calculated, not the critical F. The notation $p < .05$ tells us that given the F distribution with 2 and 9 df, 5.04 has a p value (area beyond) less than .05. A practice that was more common in the past than it is now is to present a full summary table for the ANOVA. For the example just mentioned the summary table is shown in Table 5.1.

Each SS is divided by its df to yield its MS, except that no one bothers to do this for the total SS, because the total MS is not used for anything (note that $MS_{between}$ and MS_w would *not* add up to MS_{total} if it were calculated). If you calculate the two MSs directly, using Formula 5.4 for instance, you can find the SSs by multiplying each MS by the df to its left. The column of SSs provides important information to supplement the test of F for significance, as we will explain next.

Table 5.1

Source	SS	df	MS	F	p
Between groups	168	2	84	5.04	< .05
Within groups	150	9	16.67		
Total	318	11			

The Effect Size of ANOVA

As is true for the t test, F can be statistically significant even when there is very little difference among the sample means, whether in an absolute sense or relative to the variances within groups: All that is needed is very large sample sizes. To supplement a test of significance it can be very helpful to provide an estimate of effect size. At the end of the previous chapter we explained how r_{pb}^2 or an estimate of its population value, ω^2, could serve this purpose for a t test. A very similar statistic can be used for the one-way ANOVA. Unfortunately, you cannot calculate a simple correlation coefficient as in the case of r_{pb} for the two-group case, but you can find the proportion of variance accounted for in the DV by group membership by simply dividing $SS_{between}$ by SS_{total} (of course, this quantity is always equal to r_{pb}^2 when there are only two groups in your one-way ANOVA). Because SS_{bet}/SS_{total} can be calculated with more than two groups (and r_{pb} cannot), it is given a new symbol in the context of ANOVA; it is called *eta squared,* and it is symbolized by the lower-case Greek letter eta being squared (η^2). (The use of η^2 in this context is an unfortunate exception to the usual practice of reserving Greek letters for population quantities.) The corresponding population value is called *omega squared,* just as it is in the context of the t test, and once again η^2 is a biased estimator of ω^2. The bias can be (nearly) corrected by the following formula:

$$\text{est. } \omega^2 = \frac{SS_{bet} - (k - 1)\, MS_W}{SS_{tot} + MS_W} \qquad (5.6)$$

Fortunately, it is becoming fairly common to report either η^2 or ω^2 as a supplement to reporting an F ratio. However, if you are reading a journal article and see an F reported along with its df's, but no effect size measure is given, you do not need to have the raw data (or even the SS's) to calculate η^2. You can calculate η^2 with the following formula:

$$\eta^2 = \frac{df_{bet}F}{df_{bet}F + df_W} \qquad (5.7)$$

For instance, if you read $F(2, 9) = 5.04$, then

$$\eta^2 = \frac{2(5.04)}{2(5.04) + 9} = \frac{10.08}{19.08} = .528$$

This is the same value that you would obtain from dividing $SS_{between}$ by SS_{total} in Table 5.1, because that is where we got F and the df's to put into Formula 5.7. The value calculated above for η^2 represents a very large effect size. Although F is not extremely large, this F was obtained with very small sample sizes. The same F found for three groups of 100 participants each would yield an η^2 of only .033. We will describe an additional measure of effect size for ANOVA and demonstrate its use for estimating power in the next chapter.

MULTIPLE COMPARISONS

Let us say that your three-group ANOVA results in a significant F ratio. By rejecting H_0 you might be tempted to think that you can say that all three population means differ from each other, but that is not the case. You can only say that the three are not all the same. For instance, suppose you had tested two new teaching methods against the traditional method and rejected H_0. This could mean that both of the new methods are better than the traditional one but that the new methods are identical to each other; that one of the new methods is better than the traditional one, but the other is not; or that all three methods are different. Pairwise significance tests (called *pairwise comparisons*) are needed to determine which of the above choices is true (and there are other possibilities if one or both of the new methods are *worse* than the traditional one). These pairwise tests can be performed as two-group ANOVAs, but more commonly they are conducted as *t* tests. With three groups, three *t* tests are possible (each new method compared to the traditional, and the two new methods compared to each other).

At this point you may be wondering why you should bother performing a one-way ANOVA at all when you will almost certainly want to follow a significant ANOVA with a series of *t* tests. Why not skip the ANOVA and proceed directly to the *t* tests? Actually, if you perform specially modified *t* tests, as described shortly, you can do just that. There is a problem, however, with performing ordinary *t* tests in place of ANOVA, as we will explain next.

Protected t Tests

Imagine an experiment with seven groups for which the null hypothesis is likely to be true. Perhaps you have divided your participants based on the day of the week on which each was born and measured each person's IQ. You could proceed to test every possible pair of days for significance, but that would amount to a lot of *t* tests. The formula for the number of different unordered pairs is

> ### CAUTION
>
> Don't confuse η^2 and ω^2:
>
> η^2 refers to the effect size in your samples;
>
> ω^2 refers to the effect size in the population.
>
> Because η^2 is a biased estimator of ω^2, a corrected version of η^2 is often used as a measure of effect size to accompany the report of an F ratio.

$$\# \text{ pairs} = \frac{k(k-1)}{2} \tag{5.8}$$

where k is the number of groups. For the days of the week example the number of possible t tests is $(7 \cdot 6)/2 = 42/2 = 21$. If each of the possible 21 t tests is performed with an alpha of .05, there is a good chance that at least one of the pairwise comparisons will be significant, because an alpha of .05 implies that, on the average, one out of every 20 tests of a true null will yield significant results, and we are dealing with 21 such tests (assuming that IQ is not affected by one's day of birth).

The probability of making one or more Type I errors in a group of tests that are all part of the same experiment is called the *experiment-wise alpha,* symbolized as α_{EW}. In contrast, the alpha used for each particular test is called the *alpha per comparison,* or α_{pc}. For the days/IQ example, α_{pc} was .05, but α_{EW} was larger than .5. (For c independent comparisons, $\alpha_{EW} = 1 - (1 - \alpha_{pc})^c$; the 21 t tests are not all mutually independent, but the formula gives a reasonable approximation in this case.) Clearly there is a need to control Type I errors, not just for individual t tests, but for whole experiments; an α_{EW} of .5 or more is just unacceptably large. This is where the one-way ANOVA comes in. If all multigroup experiments must produce a significant F before t tests can be performed, then only .05 (or whatever alpha is used) of null experiments (like the days/IQ example) will reach significance and be followed by t tests; 95% of null experiments will fail the ANOVA test and not be followed up.

The two-step system just described, in which the significance of the ANOVA determines whether you can perform all the possible t tests, was created by Fisher. He called the follow-up t tests *protected t tests,* because the researcher was protected from testing an entire series of pairwise null hypotheses; a significant ANOVA virtually guaranteed that there was at least one pair of conditions for which H_0 was not true. Moreover, Fisher reasoned that when HOV could be assumed, the error term from the original ANOVA (i.e., MS_W) could be used in place of s^2_{pooled} for every t test following the ANOVA, thus providing more df and a lower critical value for each test. (If HOV cannot be assumed for the ANOVA, each follow-up t test should be a separate-variances t test.) The formula for Fisher's protected t tests is

$$t = \frac{\overline{X}_i - \overline{X}_j}{\sqrt{MS_W \left(\dfrac{1}{n_i} + \dfrac{1}{n_j} \right)}} \tag{5.9}$$

where i and j represent any two different groups in the ANOVA. The df for the critical t is df_w from the ANOVA.

Fisher's Least Significant Difference Test

When all of the samples are the same size, Formula 5.9 can be simplified as follows:

$$t = \frac{\overline{X}_i - \overline{X}_j}{\sqrt{\dfrac{2MS_W}{n}}} \qquad (5.10)$$

Notice that the denominator of the formula above is the same regardless of which pair of treatments is being compared. Also, the critical t is the same for every pair. Therefore there must be some difference in the numerator of Formula 5.10 that, when divided by the constant denominator, will produce a value exactly equal to the critical t for all pairs. Fisher called that difference the Least Significant Difference (its abbreviation, LSD, became popular long before the drug did), because any two groups differing by more than that amount would produce a t greater than the critical t. This is shown in the following formula:

$$t_{crit} = \frac{LSD}{\sqrt{\dfrac{2MS_W}{n}}}$$

If the above formula is solved for LSD, a great deal of labor can be saved when comparing groups that are all the same size. Instead of performing 21 t tests in the seven-group case, one need only find the 21 numerators of those t tests (i.e., all of the possible differences between pairs of means) and check to see which of them are larger than LSD; those differences are significant at whatever alpha is used to find critical t in the following formula for LSD:

$$LSD = t_{crit}\sqrt{\frac{2MS_W}{n}} \qquad (5.11)$$

When you are dealing with three groups it is highly recommended to begin with a one-way ANOVA and then follow it with Fisher's protected t tests. If you skip the ANOVA and perform the three t tests at the .05 level, your α_{EW} will be greater than .05 (it's quite possible one of the t tests will be significant even when the ANOVA is not). However, when you are dealing with more than three groups, Fisher's system does not give you all the protection you need to keep α_{EW} down to .05. We will present an alternative test next.

Tukey's Honestly Significant Difference Test

The statistician J. W. Tukey devised a new statistic, called a *range statistic,* that takes into account the fact that when you take, say, seven samples from the same population, the chance that the largest and smallest sample means will differ significantly by accident will be considerably greater than when you take only two samples. Like Student's *t* distribution, the range statistic also depends on the size of the samples, so it is called the *Studentized range statistic,* and it is symbolized by q. Because Tukey's test requires that the n's be equal, it is structured just like the LSD test with a critical q substituted for critical t. Tukey called his minimum difference score the "honestly significant difference" (HSD for short), undoubtedly to reflect the fact that his test keeps α_{EW} at whatever alpha is used to look up the critical value of q.

$$\text{HSD} = q_{crit}\sqrt{\frac{\text{MS}_{w}}{n}} \tag{5.12}$$

If you look at the table for q (we have included the table for q at the .05 level; see Table A.4) you will see that q gets larger as the number of groups increases (moving to the right in any row) because it gets easier to find a large accidental difference between the two most extreme groups. But q gets smaller as the sample size increases (moving down in any column), because MS_{w} becomes a better estimate of the population variance. You may have noticed that the factor of 2, which was under the square root sign in the LSD formula, is missing from the HSD formula. This does not represent an actual structural difference between the formulas; Tukey just multiplied his original q values by $\sqrt{2}$ so he could simplify his formula a bit.

You may have also noticed that the HSD formula requires that all of your samples be the same size. If your groups differ only slightly due to random fluctuations (e.g., a few more equipment failures in one group than another), you can take the harmonic mean of your sample sizes (average the reciprocals of your sample sizes and then find the reciprocal of that average), and use that mean as n in Formula 5.12. If your sample sizes are very different (e.g., there are many more patients with some diagnoses than others), you should not use HSD or any test based on the studentized range statistic. As an alternative, you can always use the Bonferroni test, which will be described presently.

Because the HSD test will not allow α_{EW} to creep above the alpha you set for q, regardless of the number of groups, HSD is called a *conservative* test—that is, a test that is good at controlling Type I errors. In contrast, Fisher's system is more *liberal* in that it is less strict about Type I error control, and with more than three groups it allows α_{EW} to climb well above the alpha used for critical *t*. Because Fisher's system is more liberal it is also more powerful; allowing more Type I errors means that fewer Type II errors are made. Of course, you can always gain power by using a larger alpha, but this is not considered acceptable in general practice. However, HSD is a bit more conservative than necessary, so since this test was devised statisticians have been looking for alternatives that have a bit more power without allowing α_{EW} to creep above .05 (it is so rare to shoot for any value of α_{EW} other than .05 that we will just assume that .05 is the desired level).

Alternatives to LSD and HSD

The Newman-Keuls (N-K) test is a more powerful version of the HSD test; the means are placed in order, and means closer together are tested with a smaller q (from Table A.4) than means further apart. Because it was thought that the N-K test was acceptably conservative, while being more powerful than HSD, it became for many years the most popular pairwise comparisons test. Recently, statisticians have made it clear that the N-K test gains its extra power by letting α_{EW} climb above .05, so its popularity is declining (the Duncan test is similar to N-K in structure, but it is so liberal that you are not likely to encounter it in recent research articles). Dunnett (1964) created a test just for the case when only one group is being tested against each of the others (e.g., each of six antidepressant drugs is tested against a placebo). In this case, the Dunnett test is more powerful than HSD, while keeping α_{EW} to .05.

Recently, several generally usable tests have been devised that are acceptably conservative and more powerful than HSD. For example, the REGW test (named for the initials of the statisticians whose work led to the test: Ryan, Einot, Gabriel, and Welsch) works well, but would be hard to perform without a computer; because this test is now available from software packages like SPSS its popularity is likely to increase. Another test that works about as well as REGW, but does not require a computer, is the *modified LSD test* devised by Hayter (1986). This test requires that the ANOVA be significant but follows it not with the LSD test, but rather the HSD test with q based on $k - 1$ (one less than the number of groups in your ANOVA) rather than k.

Some post hoc pairwise tests are called two-stage systems because they require an initial omnibus ANOVA (e.g., Fisher's LSD), and some are called simultaneous (e.g., Tukey's HSD), but they are all post hoc in the sense that you are not specifying particular pairs of means to test before seeing the data (except for Dunnett's test). These tests assume that you are going to test all the pairs, or that you are going to look for and test the largest difference of means (which has the same effect on α_{EW} as testing all the means against each other). However, you can gain extra power by picking only a few pairs to test before you see the results, just as you could increase power by predicting the direction of a two-group experiment and performing a one-tailed test. Although one-tailed tests are often frowned upon, planned pairwise comparisons are considered reasonable. They are fairly rare, because you have to make a strong case for testing just some of the pairs but not all. If you can select a few specific pairs to test on theoretical grounds, you still have to increase your critical value compared to ordinary t tests, but the adjustment can be considerably smaller than an acceptably conservative post hoc test. The logic of this adjustment is explained next.

Planned Pairwise Comparisons and the Bonferroni Adjustment

In the 1930s, the mathematician Carlo Bonferroni discovered that if you know the probabilities for each of several independent events, the probability that one or more will occur cannot be more than the sum of their probabilities. Therefore, if you're testing c comparisons, and the probability of a Type I error is set at α_{pc} for each, then α_{EW} cannot be more than c $\cdot$ α_{pc} (i.e., $\alpha_{EW} \leq c\alpha_{pc}$). This means that if you use α_{EW}/c for each comparison, than α_{EW} will not be more than c $\cdot$ α_{EW}/c, which is α_{EW}—and that is what you want. For instance, if you are studying five drugs and a placebo, and you are planning to compare each drug to the placebo but not to any other drugs, you have a total of five planned comparisons. According to the Bonferroni test you would use .05/5 or .01 as the alpha for each t test (using Formula 5.9 or 5.10 for each test if HOV can be assumed), in order to keep α_{EW} at or below .05. Assuming very large sample sizes, $t_{.01}$ is about 2.58. By comparison, q (from the bottom row of the column for six groups) when divided by the square root of 2 has a larger value of 2.85. Therefore, the Bonferroni test is more powerful than Tukey's HSD in this case, while maintaining good control over α_{EW} (the Dunnett test is even a bit more powerful in this particular case, but the Bonferroni test is much more flexible). However, if you planned all 15 possible tests, your Bonferroni α would be .0033, and the critical t would result in less power compared to the HSD test.

The Bonferroni test is too conservative to be used routinely for post hoc tests of all possible pairs, but it may be required if the various sample sizes are very different. The fewer tests that are planned, the greater the power of the Bonferroni test. The major drawback of the Bonferroni test when it was first used for social science research is that it was hard to find a t table with all possible alphas (e.g., .0033 in the preceding example). Because Olivia Dunn (1961) created a table that made it easy to use the Bonferroni test, the test came to be called the *Bonferroni-Dunn* test, or just the *Dunn* test. Of course, statistical software now makes it easy to run this test without the need for special tables. Aware that the Bonferroni test tends to be quite conservative—it usually keeps α_{EW} well below the value set for it—some researchers have recently proposed more powerful alternatives that use the same basic principle (Hochberg, 1988; Shaffer, 1986) and that are likely to increase in popularity as statistical software packages become more comprehensive.

Planned Complex Comparisons

An even more powerful (i.e., more likely to detect significance when H_0 is not true) way to conduct planned comparisons is to focus not on pairwise tests, but rather on *complex comparisons,* which involve the means of more than two groups at a time. With only two groups, all you can predict about the pattern of the means is which one will be larger. Beginning with three groups you can predict the relative spacing of the groups. Given that three conditions are ordered A, B, and C, the middle condition (B) can be midway between A and C, or it can be much closer to one than the other. One generally does not get credit for predicting the order of the means in ANOVA, but if the middle group is much closer to one of the outer groups than the other, *and* you predict the pattern correctly by planning the appropriate complex comparison, you can gain a great deal of power. First we will use an example to explain what a complex comparison is, and then we will show how one can be tested.

Suppose you plan to test both a conventional antidepressant drug (D) and an herbal (H) alternative (e.g., St. John's Wort) against a placebo (P). The three possible complex comparisons are (1) the average of P and H compared to D; (2) the average of H and D compared to P; and (3) the average of P and D compared to H. Although more than two means are involved, a complex comparison results in a single difference score, which can serve as the numerator of a t test. More commonly, the complex comparison is tested by way of an F ratio, but in this case, that just means a squared t test. We will use the letter L to represent the difference score created by the complex comparison. Suppose the sample means for the three conditions are as follows: $\overline{X}_P = 60, \overline{X}_H = 50, \overline{X}_D = 20$ (these could be based on a measure of depression at the end of the experiment). L for the first comparison listed above would be $[(60 + 50)/2] - 20 = 55 - 20 = 35$ (i.e., the average of P and H minus D). You can verify for yourself that L is 25 for comparison 2, and 10 for comparison 3.

Not surprisingly, the best comparison (i.e., the one with the best chance for statistical significance) is the one with the largest L (assuming that all of the groups are the same size and have essentially the same variance). For this example, comparison 1 is the best, because comparing the average of P and H to D makes the most sense when H is much closer to P than it is to D, as in this example. If comparison 1 were planned before the data had been seen, because you expected that H would not be much better than a placebo but D would be, you would have predicted the pattern well in this example, and therefore your L would be relatively large. Now we can show you how to test L for significance.

Calculating Linear Contrasts
Complex comparisons can get *quite* complex, so we will need a notational system to describe them. Comparison 1 can be rewritten as $L = + \frac{1}{2}\overline{X}_P + \frac{1}{2}\overline{X}_H - 1\overline{X}_D$. The numbers multiplying the means $(+ \frac{1}{2}, + \frac{1}{2}, - 1)$, are called coefficients, symbolized as c_1, c_2, and so on. Note that we get the same answer as before: $L = \frac{1}{2}(60) + \frac{1}{2}(50) - 1(20) = 30 + 25 - 20 = 35$. If the coefficients add up to zero, it is common to call the comparison a *linear contrast* (a pairwise comparison is a linear contrast with coefficients of $+1$ and -1). To find the SS for a linear contrast you can use the following formula, but only if all of the groups are the same size (the corresponding formula for unequal group sizes is given in B. Cohen, 2000).

$$SS_{contrast} = \frac{nL^2}{\sum c_i^2} \quad (5.13)$$

If the groups in our example have ten participants each, the SS for comparison 1 is $(10 \cdot 35^2)/(1/2^2 + 1/2^2 + 1^2) = (10 \cdot 1225)/(.25 + .25 + 1) = 12,250/1.5 = 8166.7$. Because linear contrasts result in a single number they involve only one df, so $MS_{contrast}$ always equals $SS_{contrast}$.

Assuming homogeneity of variance, the error term for $MS_{contrast}$ is MS_W based on all of the groups, regardless of which groups are involved in the particular contrast being tested. Therefore, to test the significance of a linear contrast, the following F ratio can be used (if all groups are the same size):

$$F = \frac{nL^2 / \sum c_i^2}{MS_W} \quad (5.14)$$

Note that when your contrast contains only two groups, L is $\overline{X}_1 - \overline{X}_2$, $\sum c_i^2$ is 2 (i.e., $1^2 + 1^2$), and MS_W can be written as s^2_{pooled}, so Formula 5.14 becomes Formula 5.1.

Comparing Contrasts to ANOVA

To make clear the advantage of planning the right linear contrast we need to calculate the ordinary ANOVA for our example. First, $MS_{between}$ equals $n \cdot s_{\bar{X}}^2$. The unbiased variance of 60, 50, and 20 is 433.33, and n equals 10, so $MS_{bet} = 4333.3$. If MS_W equals 1,800, the F ratio equals $4333.3/1800 = 2.41$, which is less than the critical F of 3.35 at the .05 level (the numerator df equals 2 because there are three groups, and the denominator df equals 27, because the number of groups is subtracted from the total N of 30). However, the $MS_{contrast}$ for comparison 1 divided by the same error term yields an F ratio of $8166.67/1800 = 4.54$.

Unfortunately, we cannot compare this F to the same critical value as the ANOVA, because the numerator df for the contrast is only one; $F_{.05}(1, 27)$ is 4.21. Although the critical value for the contrast is somewhat larger than for the ANOVA (4.21 rather than 3.35), the calculated F is much larger for the contrast than the ANOVA (4.54 rather than 2.41); in this example the F for the contrast is significant, even though the ANOVA is not. Had we planned comparison 2 instead, our F ratio would have been 2.315 (you should verify this for yourself), even less than the ANOVA, and certainly not significant. As with a one-tailed test, you get extra power if you predict the pattern of means correctly, but you can also lose the gamble (it wouldn't be fair otherwise).

Orthogonal Contrasts

A particularly neat way to plan comparisons is to plan a complete set of *orthogonal comparisons* (or *contrasts*), so that $SS_{between}$ from the ANOVA is completely accounted for. If one comparison is orthogonal to another, you can change the size of either one of them without affecting the other. If you start with comparison 1 (P & H – D), the only comparison that is orthogonal to it is a simple pairwise comparison of P and H. (In this context we will refer to comparison 1 as comparison 1a and to the P/H comparison as comparison 1b.) Notice that you can change comparison 1b (e.g., move P to 70 and H to 40) without affecting comparison 1a (if P = 70 and H = 40, their average is still 55, so comparison 1a is unaffected). L for comparison 1b is 10 (i.e., 60 – 50), so $SS_{contrast}$ is 500 in this case ($\Sigma c^2 = 2$). Note that $500 + 8166.67$ (the SS for comparison 1a) equals 8666.67, which is the $SS_{between}$ for the overall ANOVA ($8666.67/2 = 4333.33 = MS_{between}$). A set of orthogonal comparisons will divide $SS_{between}$ into non-overlapping pieces, so the SSs for these comparisons will always sum to $SS_{between}$. The degrees of freedom must add up, as well. Because $df_{between}$ equals $k-1$, and each of the orthogonal contrasts has one degree of freedom, there cannot be more than $k-1$ contrasts in a mutually orthogonal set (i.e., each contrast is orthogonal to every other).

Testing a set of orthogonal contrasts, each at the .05 level, is generally consid-

DON'T FORGET

Planned contrasts can be much more likely to reach significance than an ordinary one-way ANOVA (even though the critical value will be somewhat higher) if the pattern of means was predicted correctly. However, your chances of significance can be much lower if the pattern tested by your contrast turns out not to match your data very well.

ered a legitimate and often desirable alternative to performing a one-way ANOVA, assuming there is a strong theoretical justification for your choice of contrasts. In some cases a researcher may want to test several complex (and possibly pairwise) comparisons that are not mutually orthogonal. Such testing is considered reasonable if the desired α_{EW} (usually .05) is divided by the number of planned comparisons, and that fractional probability is used as the alpha for each comparison. If four comparisons are planned then the p value for each (as given by statistical software) is compared to .0125 (i.e., .05/4).

Post Hoc Complex Comparisons: Scheffé's Test

If a one-way ANOVA is not significant, it is often possible to find a reasonable complex comparison that will be significant, but if it was not literally planned in advance the comparison had better be so obvious that it should have been planned. Otherwise, it will be hard to convince a journal editor (or reviewer) to accept a test of such a comparison as a planned test. On the other hand, if a one-way ANOVA is significant, it is considered reasonable to test particular complex comparisons to specify the effect further, but one is required to use a post hoc test that is so stringent that no complex comparison will reach significance if the omnibus (i.e., overall) ANOVA did not. This test is called the Scheffé test, and it is remarkably simple and flexible. The critical F for testing a post hoc complex comparison is just $k - 1$ times the critical F for the omnibus ANOVA. According to Scheffé's test the critical F for testing any of the comparisons in our preceding example at the .05 level would be 6.7 (i.e., $2 \cdot 3.35$) if the comparison were not planned.

The largest F you can get when testing a comparison occurs when all of $SS_{between}$ fits into one contrast. Then $SS_{between}$ is divided by 1 instead of $k - 1$, making the F for the contrast $k - 1$ times the F for the omnibus ANOVA. If the critical value is also multiplied by $k - 1$, as in Scheffé's test, the largest possible contrast won't be significant unless the omnibus ANOVA is significant. That is the logic behind Scheffé's test. Because it is so easy to use and stringent about keeping α_{EW} to the value set for it, Scheffé's test has sometimes been used by re-

≡ *Rapid Reference 5.2*

Which Post Hoc Test or Planned Comparison Method Should I Use?

Only pairwise comparisons: If you have three groups, use Fisher's protected *t* tests (you can use the LSD version of the test if the three groups are the same size). If you have more than three groups that are all the same size (or have small random differences in size), you can use Tukey's HSD or the modified LSD test. If you have more than three groups that are very different in size, you can use ordinary *t* tests with some form of Bonferroni adjustment (separate-variances *t* tests should be used if homogeneity of variance cannot be assumed). If you are testing any number of groups against one particular group (e.g., a control group), use Dunnett's test.

Complex comparisons are included: Use Scheffé's test for all your comparisons.

Which Planned Comparison Test Should I Use?

If it is convenient to come up with a set of orthogonal contrasts, you can use the usual alpha of .05 for each test. If your tests are not orthogonal, you can use a Bonferroni adjustment to determine the alpha for each of your comparisons.

searchers who are only testing pairwise comparisons. In such cases Scheffé's test is not a good choice; it is so conservative about keeping α_{EW} constant for any type of comparison tested that its power is unnecessarily low when dealing only with pairwise comparisons. Tukey's HSD test or one of the newer options would be a better choice when complex comparisons are not being considered. The major options for post hoc tests, as well as planned comparisons, are summarized in Rapid Reference 5.2.

Trend Analysis

When the levels of the independent variable in a one-way ANOVA are quantitative (e.g., five different dosages of the same drug), you can calculate a linear correlation coefficient (as described in the previous chapter) between the IV and DV; the test of Pearson's *r* will likely lead to a smaller *p* value than the one-way ANOVA, assuming there is a fair amount of linear trend in the sample means. Consider the following experiment. Fifty participants are randomly assigned to exercise for an hour, either one, two, three, four, or five times a week (10 participants per level). After 6 months, everyone's resting heart rate is measured. The means (beats per minute) for the five groups are given in the following table.

Table 5.2

One	Two	Three	Four	Five
70	60	55	53	52

The trend isn't perfectly linear—it levels off as exercise increases—but it has a strong linear component. In this case, Pearson's r has a much better chance of reaching significance than the ANOVA, as we will explain below. However, an even more powerful way to analyze these data is to use specialized complex comparisons called trend components; the simplest of which is the linear trend. In the five-group case, the degree of linear trend is assessed by applying the following coefficients to the sample means: $-2, -1, 0, +1, +2$. For this example the L for linear trend equals $-2(70) - 1(60) + 0(55) + 1(53) + 2(52) = -140 - 60 + 0 + 53 + 104 = -200 + 157 = -43$. The SS for this contrast is found by Formula 5.13:

$$SS_{linear} = \frac{nL^2}{\sum c_i^2} = \frac{10(-43)^2}{-2^2 + (-1)^2 + 0^2 + 1^2 + 2^2} = \frac{10(1,849)}{10} = 1849 \qquad (5.13)$$

This is a single-df contrast, so $MS_{linear} = 1849$. Compare this to $MS_{between}$ for the one-way ANOVA, which equals $ns_{\bar{x}}^2 = 10 \cdot 54.5 = 545$. Most of $SS_{between}$ (dfbet · MS_{bet} = 4 · 545 = 2,180) is being captured by SS_{linear} (1845). If MS_w equals 400, the F for the ANOVA (545/400 = 1.36) would not be significant at the .05 level, but the F for the linear trend (1,849/400 = 4.62) would be.

If in our example the mean heart rate actually rose to 54 for the 5 times per week condition, this reversal in trend would indicate a quadratic component. Even the leveling off of the linear trend in our example indicates some quadratic component. In cases such as this you may want to consider using *polynomial trend components* to investigate the variance not captured by the linear trend analysis. A detailed discussion of polynomial trend analysis is beyond the scope of this book, but we refer you to B. H. Cohen (2000) for a more complete description of this approach.

Putting It Into Practice

1. Participants are measured on a 10-point depression scale after taking one or another of the following drugs for six months: a placebo, a natural herb (St. John's Wort), a tricyclic antidepressant (Elavil), and an SSRI drug (Prozac). The mean depression rating for each group is shown in the following table.

	Placebo	St. John's Wort	Elavil	Prozac
Mean	9	8	4	3
SD	6	7	6	6

(a) Given that there are 11 participants in each group, calculate the F ratio to test the null hypothesis (H_0).
(b) What is the critical F for a test at the .05 level? What is your decision with respect to H_0?
(c) Calculate Fisher's LSD for the data in this problem. Which pairs of conditions are significantly different at the .05 level?
(d) Calculate Tukey's HSD for the same data. Which pairs of drugs are significantly different at the .05 level?
(e) If the results of the HSD test differ from the results of the LSD test, explain why this discrepancy can occur. Which of these two tests is preferable when dealing with four groups? Why?
(f) If you were to use the Bonferroni adjustment for all the possible t tests in the drug experiment, what alpha level would you have to use for each t test?
(g) What proportion of the variance in depression is accounted for by the drug conditions?

2. Suppose that you believe that St. John's Wort is basically a placebo and that Prozac and Elavil are both very effective, but about equal to each other. Then you might plan a complex contrast that tests the average of the first two drug conditions against the average of the second two. Using the data from problem 1, calculate the F ratio for this contrast and test it for significance at the .05 level as a planned contrast. How does this result compare to the original ANOVA? Explain the advantage of this contrast. Would your F ratio for the contrast be significant at the .05 level with Scheffé's test? Explain the advantage of planning contrasts in advance.

3. Twenty-four different depressed patients are randomly assigned to each of five therapy conditions (a total of 120 patients in all), which differ according to the number of days per week the patient must attend a psychoanalytic therapy session. After 6 months of treatment, the patients are rated for positive mood. The means and standard deviations of the ratings for each condition are shown in the following table.

	One	Two	Three	Four	Five
Mean	50	70	82	86	85
SD	40	53	55	45	47

(continued)

(a) Calculate the one-way ANOVA, and test for significance at the .05 level.
(b) Suppose that you had planned to compare the classical analysis conditions (three sessions per week or more) to the briefer therapy conditions (one or two sessions per week). Calculate the contrast just described, and test for significance at the .05 level, assuming that the comparison was planned.
(c) Test the significance of the linear trend in the foregoing data. Test the residual for significance (in this case, $SS_{residual} = SS_{between} - SS_{linear}$, and $df_{residual} = k - 2$). Is there evidence that there may be a significant trend in the data that is of higher order than linear, such as the quadratic?

🐟 TEST YOURSELF 🐟

1. **In the two-group case, the F ratio for the one-way ANOVA equals**
   (a) the square root of the t value.
   (b) the square of the t value.
   (c) one half of the t vale.
   (d) twice the t value.

2. **Which is the weighted average of all the sample variances?**
   (a) MS_w
   (b) MS_{bet}
   (c) SS_{total}
   (d) The F ratio

3. **If the null hypothesis is true, MS_{bet} is expected to be approximately equal to**
   (a) 0
   (b) 1
   (c) MS_w
   (d) F

4. **Suppose that the F ratio calculated for a particular experiment is equal to .04. Which of the following can be concluded?**
   (a) A calculation error must have been made.
   (b) The null hypothesis cannot be rejected.
   (c) The null hypothesis can be rejected at the .05 level.
   (d) Nothing can be concluded without knowing the degrees of freedom.

5. **Which of the following will lead to a larger calculated F ratio (all else remaining constant)?**
   (a) Larger variances within each of the samples
   (b) Reduced separation of the population means
   (c) Larger sample sizes
   (d) A larger alpha level

6. **Which of the following is assumed when performing the ordinary one-way ANOVA?**
   (a) All of the population means are the same.
   (b) All of the population variances are the same.
   (c) All of the sample sizes are the same.
   (d) All of the sample variances are the same.

7. **Tukey's HSD test assumes that**
   (a) all of the samples have the same mean.
   (b) all of the samples have the same variance.
   (c) all of the samples have the same size.
   (d) all of the above.

8. **If two of the pairwise comparisons following an ANOVA exceed Fisher's LSD, how many would exceed Tukey's HSD?**
   (a) One or none
   (b) Two
   (c) At least two
   (d) No more than two

9. **Compared to Fisher's protected t tests, Tukey's HSD test**
   (a) involves a smaller alpha per comparison.
   (b) leads to a lower rate of Type II errors.
   (c) maintains less control over experiment-wise alpha.
   (d) is more liberal.

10. **Which of the following procedures is recommended when you are performing not only pairwise comparisons but complex comparisons as well?**
    (a) Scheffé's test
    (b) Dunnett's test
    (c) The Newman-Keuls test
    (d) Tukey's HSD test

Answers: 1. b; 2. a; 3. c; 4. b; 5. c; 6. b; 7. c; 8. d; 9. a; 10. a.

Six

POWER ANALYSIS

U p until this point most of this book has been devoted to describing tests of statistical significance, the purpose of which is to control Type I errors. To remind you, a Type I error occurs when the populations that underlie a study show no effect, but the samples in the study accidentally show an effect large enough that a statistical test yields a (falsely) significant result. Without statistical tests any result in the desired direction might be mistaken as a sign of a real population effect. Using an alpha of .05, statistical tests are so strict that 95% of experiments in which there is no population effect (what we call *null experiments*) fail to pass the test, and therefore do not create a misleading false alarm. However, it has been argued that null experiments are rare in the social sciences—so rare, in fact, that null hypothesis significance testing (NHST) does not serve an important purpose. Furthermore, it is argued that NHST is so often misunderstood that the widespread use of this procedure actually does more harm than good. We will argue that screening out null experiments is not the only function served by NHST and that NHST is very helpful under some circumstances. However, we agree that NHST is widely misunderstood and misinterpreted. We hope this chapter can make a small contribution in the direction of improving the situation.

Fisher's original conception of NHST did not include the Type II error. His position was that if the data do not allow you to reject the null hypothesis, then you cannot make any conclusion at all, and therefore you cannot make an error. He was not happy when Jerzy Neyman and Egon Pearson (Karl's son) reformulated NHST in such a way that not rejecting the null hypothesis was seen to be a decision to retain the null hypothesis—and could therefore be considered an error (of the second kind) when the null hypothesis is not true. In spite of Fisher's wishes, the Neyman-Pearson version of NHST (Neyman & Pearson, 1928) became widely accepted, and the focus on Type II errors has in fact grown over the years.

However, unlike the Type I error rate, which is fixed by choosing alpha, the

---

DON'T FORGET
....

When Will I Use the Statistics in This Chapter?

In this chapter you will learn how to estimate your chances of attaining statistically significant results as a function of the size of the effect you expect, and the number of participants you plan to use (or you can determine the best number of participants to use), when

- comparing the means of two groups that are either independent or matched.
- comparing the means of three or more groups.
- measuring the linear correlation of two variables.

You will also gain a deeper understanding of null hypothesis testing, including the interpretation of negative results and the combining of several studies into a larger one.

Type II error rate is not fixed and is in fact hard to measure, because it depends on (among other things) how far the experiment deviates from being a null experiment. Nonetheless it is often useful to estimate the probability of making a Type II error, especially *before* an experiment is conducted. For reasons that will soon be made clear, this is called *power analysis.* An explanation of power analysis will have the added benefit of giving you a deeper understanding of NHST in its everyday applications. For instance, failing to reach statistical significance is more informative when you are using large rather than small samples, for the same reason that a point estimate grows more accurate as your sample size increases. This will become clearer as we explain the complement of the NHD next.

POWER IN THE TWO-GROUP CASE

It will be easiest to begin our discussion of power analysis in the context of the two-group t test. If the two populations underlying our two-group study have the same mean and variance, we know what values to expect from our study. The NHD in this case is the t distribution with $n_1 + n_2 - 2$ degrees of freedom (assuming we perform pooled t tests). Although the t values over many studies will average to zero in this case (because H_0 is true), there will be a considerable range of possible t values. If the populations have the same variances but do *not* have the same mean, the variability of possible t values will be similar, but they will not average to zero. Because, in this case, H_0 is not true, the distribution is not the NHD. Rather, some alternative hypothesis (H_1) is true, so this distribution can be called the *alternative hypothesis distribution* (AHD). The AHD is related to the t distribution in this case, but because it is not centered on zero it is called a noncentral t distribution.

The Alternative Hypothesis Distribution

The value at the center of the AHD is called the *noncentrality parameter* and it is usually symbolized by the Greek letter delta (δ). Delta depends, in part, on just which H_1 is true (there are an infinite number of possibilities). The larger delta is, the more likely it is that your study will lead to a statistically significant result, so it is important to look at all of the elements that contribute to delta, as we do next.

Delta can be understood in a very concrete way. If you repeat the same two-group experiment over and over again, using new samples (from the same population) each time, and calculating t each time, the average of these t values should be about equal to delta, which can be defined as the expected t value (the average of the t values if you repeat the experiment an infinite number of times). Let's look at the t formula and see what can be expected in the long run. Our purpose will be best suited by beginning with a t formula that requires equal sample sizes and homogeneity of variance, and is based on Formula 3.6:

$$t = \sqrt{\frac{n}{2}} \cdot \frac{\overline{X}_1 - \overline{X}_2}{s_p} \tag{6.1}$$

where s_p is the square root of the pooled-variance. If the t test is repeated infinitely, $\overline{X}_1$ will average out to μ_1, $\overline{X}_2$ will average out to μ_2, and s_p will average out to σ. So the average of all the possible t's, the expected t (or delta), is given by the following formula:

$$\delta = \sqrt{\frac{n}{2}} \cdot \frac{(\mu_1 - \mu_2)}{\sigma} \tag{6.2}$$

Population Effect Size

The sample size is not changing, of course, so what Formula 6.2 is really showing us is that g, the sample effect size, $(\overline{X}_1 - \overline{X}_2)/s_p$, averages out to $(\mu_1 - \mu_2)/\sigma$, which is the population effect size and is symbolized by **d**:

$$\mathbf{d} = \frac{(\mu_1 - \mu_2)}{\sigma} \tag{6.3}$$

We would prefer to use a Greek letter to symbolize the effect size in a population, but the use of **d** was popularized by Jacob Cohen (1988), who did a great deal to make effect size measures and power analysis known and accessible to researchers in the social sciences. Like delta, **d** can be thought of in very concrete terms: **d** tells you how many standard deviations apart two population means are. Often the populations you are interested in are theoretical ones (e.g., all of the adults in the world after they have taken some drug), but the example of gender differences is much more concrete, because the two populations exist right now. For any dependent variable on which you might want to compare the two genders, there is some value for **d**. If the null hypothesis is true (i.e., $\mu_1 = \mu_2$), then **d** $= \mu_1 - \mu_2/\sigma = 0/\sigma = 0$. By contrast, for height **d** is rather large. Assuming average population heights of 69 and 64.5 inches for men and women respectively, and a common σ of 3 inches, $\mathbf{d}_{height} = (69 - 64.5)/3 = 4.5/3 = 1.5$. Although NHST is directed at determining whether **d** equals zero, it would be far more informative to determine just how large **d** is for a particular DV. We will discuss this approach later in this chapter.

You may have noticed that **d** looks like a z score; it measures the difference in populations in standardized units. Therefore, a given value of **d** has the same meaning regardless of the DV. A particularly useful way to understand **d** is in terms of the overlap of the two population distributions. Assuming that both distributions are normally distributed, a **d** of 1.0 can be represented as in panel A of Figure 6.1. There is a fair amount of overlap, but notice that only about 16% of the distribution on the left is above the mean of the distribution on the right. A **d** of 2.0 involves less overlap (panel B of Figure 6.1); now less than 3% of the left distribution exceeds the mean of the right one. However, with a **d** of 0.2 (panel C of Figure 6.1), there is a great deal of overlap. In the context of social sciences research, J. Cohen (1988) felt that a **d** of .2 represents a small effect size, .5 represents a medium effect size, and .8 represents a large effect size. With these popular guidelines in mind the gender difference in height (**d** = 1.5) can be thought of as a very large effect size, which is consistent with how noticeable the difference is to casual observation. All else being equal, a larger **d** means a larger delta, which means greater power. Next we define power and show how it is dependent on delta.

An Example of a Power Calculation

Suppose for the moment that aliens from outer space really are abducting earthlings to study them. They suspect that adult male earthlings are taller than adult females, but they have only eight people of each gender available for measurement. If we knew the heights of the 16 abductees we could calculate the aliens' *t* test and see if it is significant. Without the data we can nonetheless calculate the

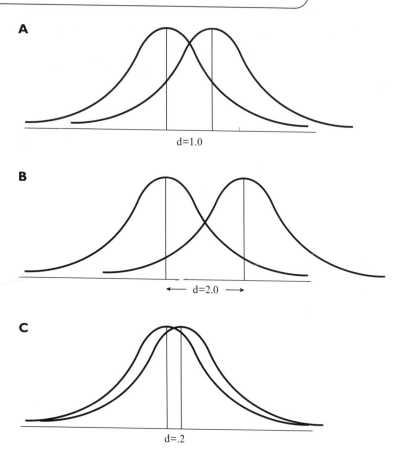

Figure 6.1 The overlap of populations as a function of effect size (d)

probability of the aliens' obtaining a significant *t* based on what we know about the height difference between the male and female populations on earth (and assuming that the aliens have selected a random sample of each gender). We need to calculate delta for this hypothetical study. Combining Formulas 6.2 and 6.3, we can obtain a formula for delta in terms of *n* and **d**.

$$\delta = \sqrt{\frac{n}{2}} \cdot \mathbf{d} \qquad (6.4)$$

Formula 6.4 is convenient for our purposes because we have already calculated **d** for the gender difference in height; it is 1.5. If eight females are to be compared to eight males, *n* equals 8, and delta is given by the following:

$$\delta = \sqrt{\frac{8}{2}}1.5 = 2 \cdot 1.5 = 3$$

So, without knowing which humans the aliens have abducted, we know that given their sample sizes, their expected t (i.e., delta) is 3.0. Depending on their actual abductees, they may get a t above 3 or below 3, but it is not likely they will get a t that is very far from 3. The distribution of the possible t's that the aliens could get is the AHD, and we know that it is a noncentral t distribution centered on 3.0. A rough approximation of the AHD for this kind of test, which is much easier to work with, is a normal distribution with a mean of 3.0 and a standard deviation of 1.0. This approximate AHD is shown in Figure 6.2.

Not all the t's in the aliens' AHD will be statistically significant. Only t's larger than the critical t will be significant. A crude approximation of the critical t for the .05 level (two-tailed test), in keeping with the use of the normal distribution as the AHD, is 2.0. Therefore, only the proportion of the AHD that is above 2.0 will be significant (the population below −2.0 would also be significant, but the probability that the women will come out significantly taller than the men in this study is too small to worry about). You can see in Figure 6.2 that the critical t (2.0) is 1 standard deviation below the mean of the AHD (3.0), and in the normal distribution, about .16 of the area would be below (i.e., to the left of) the spot where the critical value falls, in this case. Thus, 16% of the possible alien studies will produce a t less than 2.0 and therefore fail to achieve significant results. All of these nonsignificant results will be Type II errors because we know that the AHD is the true distribution in this case. The symbol for the Type II error rate is β (the lowercase Greek letter beta), so in this example β equals .16. The proportion of the AHD that is significant is $1 - \beta$, which equals .84 for this example. This propor-

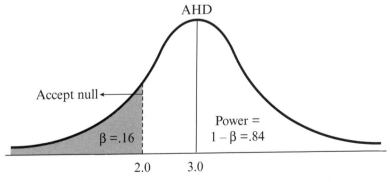

Figure 6.2 Type II error rate (β) and power when delta (γ) = 3.0

tion, which is the probability of getting a significant result when the null hypothesis is *not* true (because some AHD is true), is called the power of the statistical test.

Alpha, Delta, and Power

Figure 6.2 allows you to see graphically what happens if we try to reduce Type I errors by reducing alpha. The critical value would move to the right (it would be only about half a standard deviation below the mean for the .01 level), which increases β and decreases power. The normal approximation also allows us to present the relationship between delta, alpha, and power in a simple table, as we have done in Table A.5. Note that for any particular delta, power decreases as alpha decreases (i.e., moving to the right in any row of the table). The conventional alpha of .05 can be seen as a compromise between the need to minimize Type I errors and the desire to maximize power.

You can also see from Table A.5 that as delta gets larger, so does power. If delta is 2.0, power is about 50% because about half the *t* values will be larger than 2.0 and therefore larger than the critical value, which is also about 2.0 (actually the power for a delta equal to 2.0 is .52, because the .05 critical value for the normal distribution is actually 1.96 rather than 2.0). When delta is as high as 3.6, an alpha of .05 corresponds to an equally low β (β = 1 – power = 1 – .95 = .05), and when delta reaches 4.2, power is at .99. If you know delta, it is easy to find the approximate power (Table A.5 becomes less accurate as the sample size decreases). However, to know delta you would have to know **d**, and that is almost always what you would like to know but don't. Power analysis is usually a matter of translating guesses about **d** into guesses about power; it is a system that can help you decide whether to increase your sample size or, if that is not feasible, whether it is worth conducting the planned study at all. We will discuss how to guess about **d** next.

Estimating Effect Size

For a given type of statistical test (e.g., two-group *t* test) and a fixed alpha, power is a function of delta, which means that power is a function of **d** and the sample size. Because power is based on multiplying **d** by a function of the sample size, increasing either **d** or *n* will increase power. Although it is impossible to increase **d** when dealing with existing populations (e.g., the gender difference in height), increasing **d** is possible in some experimental situations. For instance, if you are testing the effectiveness of a drug you may be able to increase the dosage; for other treatments you may be able to increase the amount of time devoted to the treatment, or intensify the treatment in some other way. However, there are usually constraints based on safety and economics that fix the intensity of the treatment and therefore the size of **d**. If you can estimate **d** for your study you can determine the power for any possible sample size, and then make an informal decision about how (and if) to run the study.

Looking at Formula 6.3 you can see that if you can estimate the means of the two populations that underlie your study and the common standard deviation you can estimate **d**. If you have preliminary data from a pilot study or if you are dealing in such familiar territory that you can estimate the needed values from the data of previous studies, you can make a pretty good guess at **d** and proceed with the power analysis. Sometimes a previous study is relevant, but it is based on a different DV, or the published report does not contain the means and SDs you need. In such cases you can still obtain g from the previous study—$g = t\sqrt{(2/n)}$—and the g from a similar study can serve as a reasonable estimate of **d** for the planned study. For example, you want to compare self-esteem between science and humanities majors at a college. A previous study compared these groups with a different measure of self-esteem and reported $t(18) = 1.7, p > .05$. Assuming equal-sized groups, n equals 10 for that study, and $g = 1.7\sqrt{(2/10)} = 1.7\sqrt{.2} = 1.7 \cdot .447 = .76$. If you were planning to have 18 participants per group and use g from the previous study to estimate your **d**, delta for your study would be as follows: $\delta = \mathbf{d}\sqrt{(18/2)} = \sqrt{9} \cdot .76 = 3 \cdot .76 = 2.28$.

Looking in Table A.5, the power for this study is about .62. Is that value for power high enough to inspire you to conduct the study as planned? (We will assume that alpha is set to .05 in all of our remaining examples.) If your estimate for **d** is right, you stand a .38 chance of failing to reach statistical significance and therefore committing a Type II error. Of course, it depends on how much money, effort, and time the planned study will consume, but most researchers would like power to be at least about .7. From Table A.5, you can see that delta must be about 2.48 to attain that power.

In many cases the planned study is so novel in its design that there are no previous studies that can provide an estimate of **d** (pilot studies that are large enough to yield useful estimates are not always feasible). In such cases it is common to estimate the sample size for small, medium, and large effects (.2, .5, and .8, respectively, ac-

CAUTION

Don't confuse **d** and g:

d refers to the effect size in the population;

g refers to the effect size in your samples.

cording to the guidelines of J. Cohen) at the desired level of power (a power of .8 is often considered optimal). Then one looks at the feasibility of the required sample sizes, judges the likelihood of the true effect size being small, medium, or large, and makes a decision. Either some reasonable sample size is chosen or the study is redesigned.

The Power of Replication

One important insight power analysis can give you concerns the power involved in exactly replicating a previous experiment. If a previous experiment just barely attained statistical significance—calculated *t* was just slightly greater than the critical *t*—an exact replication would only have about a .5 chance of reaching significance as well. Without an understanding of power we might have the tendency to think that any significant result has a good chance of being replicated. However, just as our best guess for **d** in a replication is the *g* from the study being replicated, our best guess for delta for an *exact* replication (same number of participants) is the *t* from the previous study. If *t* from the previous study is just slightly larger than the critical *t*, then our delta is only slightly larger than the critical *t*, making power just slightly larger than 50%.

Thinking about power and effect size is the antidote to all-or-none thinking. The power for exactly replicating an experiment that just barely reached significance is only slightly better than the power for replicating one that just missed statistical significance. In general, a smaller *p* value means greater power for an exact replication. A very small *p* like .001 doesn't tell you that the effect size is large (you might be dealing with a small effect size coupled with very large sample sizes), but it does tell you that an exact replication will have a good chance of significance at the .05 level (and about a .5 chance of attaining significance at the .001 level). We will have more to say about the insights you can gain from an understanding of power toward the end of this chapter.

Determining Sample Size

Once you have an estimate for **d** and you know the delta you are shooting for, you can use Formula 6.4 to solve for *n*. Alternatively, Formula 6.4 can be solved for *n* beforehand to create a convenient formula for estimating the needed sample size, given an estimate of **d** and a desired level of power (i.e., delta).

$$n = 2\left(\frac{\delta}{d}\right)^2 \tag{6.5}$$

To attain a power of .7 in our example the size of *each* sample would have to be

$$n = 2\left(\frac{2.48}{.76}\right)^2 = 2\,(3.26)^2 = 2\cdot 10.6 = 21.2$$

To be safe, the answer is rounded up, so the power analysis suggests that 22 people need to be sampled in each group to have adequate power. If the answer for *n* were to come out higher than the sample size you were willing to deal with, you would have to decide whether it was feasible to try increasing **d** (not possible for the self-esteem study), or it was reasonable to use a smaller *n* and have less than the desired power, or it was desirable to just plan a different, more powerful study.

Fixed Sample Sizes

In some cases the sizes of the samples are fixed. Suppose that you are comparing two methods for teaching algebra, and students have already been assigned to two classes (randomly, we hope) of 32 students each. If you plan to use the classes as your samples you can then determine the power you have for different possible effect sizes. For this example, $\delta = \mathbf{d}\sqrt{(n/2)} = \mathbf{d}\sqrt{16} = 4\mathbf{d}$. For a medium effect size, delta $= 4\cdot.5 = 2.0$, so power would be only .52. If you do not expect any more than a medium effect size you would probably not bother to do the study as designed. (You could, however, increase your power without increasing your sample sizes by matching participants across groups, as we will demonstrate in the next section.) If you want .8 power, delta has to be 2.8, so **d** would have to be .7 ($4\mathbf{d} = 4\cdot.7 = 2.8$). The power analysis would tell you that if the effect size is less than .7 you will have less than the desired level of power.

Unequal Sample Sizes

So far we have assumed that your two samples will be the same size. This is the likely case when you are assigning participants randomly to groups. However, if you are dealing with preexisting groups, you may be stuck with groups of different sizes. Suppose that you want to compare patients with injuries to the left side of their brains with patients that are injured on the right side of the brain. As a researcher at a hospital you may have available 15 right-injured patients and only 10 left-injured patients. You could use only 10 of your 15 right-injured patients in order to make your calculations easier, but you would be reducing your power unnecessarily. You can use the power formulas of this chapter by taking the *harmonic* mean of your two sample sizes and using that value for *n*. The harmonic mean (n_h) involves averaging the reciprocals of the two numbers and then taking the reciprocal of that average. For two numbers the harmonic mean is given by the following simple formula:

$$n_h = \frac{2n_1 n_2}{n_1 + n_2} \qquad (6.6)$$

The harmonic mean of 10 and 15 is $2 \cdot 10 \cdot 15/(10 + 15) = 300/25 = 12$. For a large effect size of .8, delta $= \sqrt{(12/2)} \cdot .8 = 1.96$. If you don't expect the effect size to be larger than .8 you can either perform the study knowing that you have no better than a 50% chance of obtaining significant results, or try to find more patients appropriate for the study, or a more discriminating dependent variable that would show a greater effect (combining several DVs in a multivariate analysis could produce greater power).

> **CAUTION**
>
> Don't confuse **d** and δ:
>
> **d** refers to the effect size in the population;
>
> δ (delta) refers to your expected t value—it is a function of both **d** and your sample sizes.

THE POWER OF REPEATED-MEASURES DESIGNS

In Chapter 3 we discussed the main advantage of the repeated measures (RM) or matched-pairs design, which is an increase in power. Using power formulas we can now show how to quantify the power advantage of the RM design. Although Formula 3.12 is much more convenient for calculating a matched t test, the following equivalent formula allows for a simpler comparison with the independent-groups t test.

$$t = \frac{(\overline{X}_1 - \overline{X}_2)}{\sqrt{\frac{s_1^2 + s_2^2}{n} - \frac{2rs_1 s_2}{n}}} \qquad (6.7)$$

Notice that if the scores are not matched at all, then r equals zero, and the second term in the denominator drops out. Therefore, when $r = 0$, Formula 6.7 becomes a convenient formula for the independent-groups t test when the two groups are the same size. To find the expected t for the RM test we can use the same device we used at the beginning of this chapter—that is, we can substitute population values for sample statistics in Formula 6.7. With some algebraic rearranging we can create the following convenient power formula:

$$\delta = \sqrt{\frac{1}{1 - \rho}} \cdot \sqrt{\frac{n}{2}} \cdot \frac{\mu_1 - \mu_2}{\sigma} \qquad (6.8)$$

Note that Formula 6.8 is the same as Formula 6.2 except for the additional multiplying factor of $\sqrt{[1/(1-\rho)]}$. Therefore, $\delta_{RM} = \delta_{independent} \sqrt{[1/(1-\rho)]}$. When $\rho = 0$, there is no power advantage to the RM test, and, in fact, the RM test actually hurts you because of the loss in degrees of freedom. As ρ approaches 1.0, the power of the RM test approaches infinity. For a moderate value, such as $\rho = .5$, the delta for the RM test is about 1.4 times the delta for the independent test: $\sqrt{[1/(1-.5)]} = \sqrt{(1/.5)} = \sqrt{2} = 1.414$.

Let us return to the example of teaching two classes ($n = 32$) with different methods. With $d = .5$, delta was only 2.0, and power only about .52. However, if students could be matched in pairs based on previous relevant grades, and then randomly assigned to the two classes, this matching could result in a ρ as high as .5. The delta for the matched t test would be

$$\delta_{matched} = \sqrt{\frac{1}{1-\rho}} \, \delta_{ind} = \sqrt{2}(2) = 2.83$$

This yields power that is a bit over .8 and, therefore, very likely to be acceptable. Even when sample sizes are not strictly limited by circumstances, the costs of large sample sizes make the matching of participants a very desirable alternative for attaining adequate power. Of course, when it is reasonable for the same person to serve in both conditions the matching is almost always better, resulting in even greater power. The various factors that affect power in the two-group case are summarized in Rapid Reference 6.1.

THE POWER OF A TEST OF CORRELATION

Sometimes the result of a study comes in the form of a correlation coefficient (e.g., Pearson's r between tests of musical and mathematical ability). As you saw in Chapter 4, a t value can be used to test r for significance. A crude approximation of the expected t when testing a Pearson correlation coefficient can be obtained from the following simple formula:

Rapid Reference 6.1

Factors That Increase Power in the Two-Group Case

1. Increasing alpha (e.g., from .05 to .1). However, this increases the rate of Type I errors.
2. Increasing the size of the sample(s).
3. Increasing the size of the effect in the population (e.g., d for a two-group test).
4. Increasing the population correlation between the sets of scores, ρ, in a matched or repeated-measures t test. This principle can be extended to multigroup designs, as will be shown in Chapter 8.

$$\delta = \sqrt{N-1} \cdot \rho \tag{6.9}$$

where ρ is the actual correlation in the population. The value for delta can then be looked up in Table A.5 to find the power, just as in the case of the two-group t test. Note that ρ, like d, is considered a measure of effect size in the population, and r, like g, is a measure of that effect in the data you have collected. If you can use previous results to estimate ρ, you can calculate power for any sample size, or calculate the sample size needed for a particular amount of power. According to the guidelines of J. Cohen (1988), a value of .1 is a small effect for ρ; .3 is a medium effect size, and .5 is considered large. If you are expecting the effect size in the population to be of medium size and you want power to be at least .7 for a .05 two-tailed significance test, you can calculate the necessary sample size with Formula 6.9:

$$2.48 = \sqrt{N-1}\,(.3)$$

$$\text{therefore } \sqrt{N-1} = 8.27$$

$$\text{therefore } N - 1 = 68.3$$

$$\text{so } N = 69.3$$

Thus, you need to use a sample of at least 70 participants if you want your power to be at least .7 with $\rho = .3$.

THE POWER OF ONE-WAY ANOVA

Power analysis can be easily extended to more complex situations, such as the design of a multigroup experiment as described in the previous chapter. Just as we found the expected t for a two-group study, we can find the expected F for a one-way ANOVA. We start with a variation of Formula 5.3 and then substitute population values, as follows:

$$F = \frac{ns_{\bar{x}}^2}{s_{pooled}^2} = \frac{n\sigma_{\bar{x}}^2}{\sigma^2} = n\frac{\sigma_{\bar{x}}^2}{\sigma^2} = n\left(\frac{\sigma_{\bar{x}}}{\sigma}\right)^2$$

where n is the size of *each* sample, σ is the standard deviation of each population (assuming HOV), and $\sigma_{\bar{x}}$ is the standard deviation of the population means from the grand mean. The ratio, $\sigma_{\bar{x}}/\sigma$, is a measure of effect size that J. Cohen (1988) labeled f (in bold to signify it is a population measure). It is similar to d in that it compares the separation of population means to the standard deviation of individuals within a population. In fact, in the two-group case, $f = .5d$ (the distance

of each population mean to the grand mean is half the distance of the two population means from each other). If the expected F is symbolized as ϕ^2 (phi-
squared), and $\mathbf{f}$ is substituted for $\sigma_{\bar{x}}/\sigma$ in the preceding equation, the following
power formula is obtained:

$$\phi^2 = n\mathbf{f}^2 \tag{6.10}$$

As it turns out, ϕ^2 is not literally the average F you would get for a given $\mathbf{f}$—
for large samples the expected F is about $1 + (k\phi^2)/(k-1)$—but ϕ^2 is a convenient quantity on which to base a power table. Actually, ϕ is the more convenient
value (it is similar to δ; in the two-group case, $\delta = \phi\sqrt{2}$), so it is useful to take
the square root of both sides of Formula 6.10.

$$\phi = \mathbf{f}\sqrt{n} \tag{6.10'}$$

For each value of k (the number of groups), a different table is required to re-
late ϕ to power. However, in each case a normal approximation could be used, as
in Table A.5. Although this approach would lead to a simpler table, it produces a
considerable amount of error when used with small samples. Therefore, we have
presented a table which finds power for a given combination of k, ϕ, and df_w (df_w
is the denominator degrees of freedom for the ANOVA; with equal-sized groups,
$df_w = nk - k$, so $n = [df_w/k] + 1$). Table A.6 is easy to use if you are stuck with
particular sample sizes, but first we must consider how $\mathbf{f}$ is estimated from a previous study. Although the sample version of $\mathbf{f}$, which is symbolized as f without
the bold face, equals $\sqrt{(F/n)}$, this is a biased estimate of $\mathbf{f}$. To estimate $\mathbf{f}$ from a
previous study with k equal-sized groups you can use the following formula:

$$\text{estimated } \mathbf{f} = \sqrt{\left(\frac{k-1}{k}\right)\frac{F-1}{n}} \tag{6.11}$$

where n is the number of participants in each group. Recalling that in the two-
group case $\mathbf{f} = .5\,\mathbf{d}$, it should not be surprising that for $\mathbf{f}$, .1, .25, and .4 are considered to be small, medium, and large effect sizes, respectively. Now we are ready
to illustrate the use of Table A.6.

Suppose that you are planning a study with four groups, and you are stuck with
16 participants per group. If your estimate of $\mathbf{f}$ is .4, ϕ equals $\sqrt{16} \cdot .4 = 4 \cdot .4 =$
1.6; $df_w = (4 \cdot 16) - 4 = 64 - 4 = 60$. Looking in the section of Table A.6 for $k =$
4, we see that the power for $\phi = 1.6$ and $df_w = 60$ is .74, which is probably acceptable. However, an f of .3 would lead to an unacceptably low estimate of
power that equals .47. A sample size of 25 would be required for power to be
about .7 for that $\mathbf{f}$ ($\phi = \sqrt{25} \cdot .3 = 1.5$; $df_w = 96$).

Revisiting the Two-Group Case

The $k = 2$ section of Table A.6 allows you to make more accurate power estimates in the two-group case than you can get with Table A.5. Imagine that you have only eight patients in one group and six in the other. You expect **d** to be very large (1.2) for your comparison. To use Formula 6.4 you need the harmonic mean of 6 and 8, which is 6.857. Therefore, $\delta = \sqrt{(6.857/2)} \cdot 1.2 = 1.85 \cdot 1.2 = 2.22$. Using Table A.5 you would estimate power to be about .61. However, we can increase our accuracy by using Table A.6 ($k = 2$), noting that $\phi = \delta/\sqrt{2}$, so $\phi = 2.22/1.414 = 1.57$, and $df_w = 6 + 8 - 2 = 12$. In Table A.6 the power estimate is only about .53. The Table A.5 estimate is higher because the normal distribution is being assumed along with a critical value of 1.96, when the critical t value for 12 df is really 2.179 (the expected t of 2.22 is only a little more than that).

Estimating Sample Size for ANOVA

Table A.6 is a bit harder to use when the sample size is not fixed and you are trying to estimate the needed sample size for a particular combination of **f** and power. We will begin by solving Formula 6.10 for n.

$$n = \frac{\phi^2}{f^2} = \left(\frac{\phi}{f}\right)^2 \tag{6.12}$$

Now let us say that we think **f** is small (.1) for a particular five-group ($k = 5$) experiment, and we want power to be at least .7. The next step is to look up ϕ in Table A.6 by seeing which column contains a value of .7. The problem is that more than one value of ϕ is possible depending on the df_w—which you don't know because the sample size has not been determined yet. If you expect the needed sample size to be very large (a good bet with **f** being only .1), then you would look along the bottom row of the $k = 5$ section of the table for a value near .7; you'll see that ϕ is about 1.4. Then n is found from Formula 6.12: $n = (1.4/.1)^2 = 14^2 = 196$. This estimate of n (about 200 participants in each of your five groups) is consistent with the guess you had to make to choose ϕ. Had you initially estimated df_w to be about 17 and therefore chose ϕ to be 1.6, your calculated n—$(1.6/.1)^2 = 16^2 = 256$—would have told you that your initial estimate was way off. On the other hand, were a very large **f** of .8 expected, a ϕ of 1.6 would be a reasonable choice, as confirmed by the calculated n: $n = (1.6/.8)^2 = 2^2 = 4$; with $n = 4$, $df_w = nk - k = (4 \cdot 5) 5 = 20 - 5 = 15$, which would be consistent with an initial estimate for df_w of 17, which led to the choice of 1.6 for ϕ. The

Rapid Reference 6.2

J. Cohen Guidelines for Effect Sizes

	Small	Medium	Large
Two-group comparison (**d**)	.2	.5	.8
Multigroup comparison (**f**)	.1	.25	.4
Linear Correlation (ρ)	.1	.3	.5

general guidelines established by J. Cohen for effect sizes are summarized in Rapid Reference 6.2.

GENERAL TOPICS RELATED TO POWER

Increasingly, power analyses are being requested by doctoral committees over-seeing social science research, as well as the reviewers of research grants. Until recently these power analyses were performed with tables more detailed than Table A.6 (J. Cohen, 1988), or power curves that allow one to avoid having to interpolate between values in a table (Keppel, 1991). Fortunately, several software packages have recently been marketed for the purpose of automating the tedious process of performing a power analysis.

Confidence Intervals for Effect Size

There is also an increased emphasis on reporting estimates of effect size when publishing in journals. For instance, the fifth edition of the Publication Manual of the American Psychological Association (2001) states: "For the reader to fully understand the importance of your findings it is almost always necessary to include some index of effect size or strength of relationship" (p. 25). For ANOVA, eta-squared is often reported, or an adjusted version (i.e., a less biased estimate of omega-squared, as in Formula 5.6), but **f**, which is useful for power analysis, is rarely used for such descriptive purposes. However, as useful as effect size estimates are, they suffer from the same drawback as any other point estimate: An effect-size estimate based on large samples is much more reliable than one based on small samples; and yet you cannot tell from looking at the estimate how seriously to take it. We discussed this problem first in the context of estimating the mean of a population. The solution was interval estimation—creating a confidence interval (CI) around our point estimate. In a similar fashion creating a CI around an effect-size estimate (ESCI) adds a great deal of information.

Admittedly, there are times when the CI for the difference of the population means is more meaningful than the corresponding ESCI. For instance, if some herbal supplement claims to shorten the duration of the average cold, we would want an estimate involving the number of hours or days we could expect to be spared the symptoms of a cold virus. Having a CI in units of time would be a great aid in deciding whether to use the product being tested. On the other hand, if some other supplement claims to improve memory and we test it with a list of words we just created, the CI will give us a range of how many additional words we are likely to remember after taking the supplement. But that is hardly meaningful, depending as it does on the number of words on the list, the commonness of those words, study time, and many other factors. An ESCI would be more meaningful. If the ESCI demonstrates that the effect size is likely to be large, at least we would know that few people in the control condition can be expected to show memory improvements as large as the average person taking the supplement.

Unfortunately, ESCIs are rarely reported in the scientific literature, and this is undoubtedly due in large part to the fact that they are somewhat difficult to construct. The CIs we described in earlier chapters were based on critical values from the normal or the ordinary (i.e., central) t distribution. ESCIs, however, require the use of critical values from a noncentral distribution (e.g., for a given number of degrees of freedom there are an infinite number of noncentral t distributions each based on a different value for delta, the noncentrality parameter), and these values are not available in standard tables. Only in recent years have major statistical packages (e.g., SPSS) included a procedure for obtaining these critical values, and even at the time of this writing there is no readily available computer program that will construct such CIs for you. Steiger and Fouladi (1997) and Cumming and Finch (2001) explain how to construct CIs for effect-size measures, but we don't expect to see their widespread use anytime soon.

Meta-Analysis

A common misconception can occur when, say, a dozen researchers perform essentially the same experiment, and half obtain significant results in the expected direction, while the other half do not. It can look like the various results are contradictory, but it is possible that all 12 researchers are dealing with a situation in which power equals .5. Then we would expect only half of the results to be significant. If each researcher supplies a measure of effect size, we can quickly see if they are all similar; if they are, the various results can be viewed as not being contradictory at all. In fact, if all 12 results were not significant but produced similar, nonzero estimates of effect size, the cumulative evidence of the 12 studies would not be consistent with the null hypothesis. There is actually a way to combine the 12 results in order to reject the null hypothesis; it is called *meta-analysis*. The basic principle behind meta-analysis is simple. The 12 similar studies mentioned above can all be thought of as pieces of a larger, or meta, study. Assuming that we are only dealing with two-group studies, the g for the metastudy would be a weighted average of the g's of the 12 studies (weighted by the sizes of the studies). The total N for the meta study would be a sum of the n's for the 12 smaller studies. The meta study could be tested for significance with a t test using the following general formula:

$$t_{meta} = \sqrt{\frac{N}{2}} \cdot g_{avg} \tag{6.13}$$

where N equals Σn_i (assuming that each of the 12 studies consists of two equal-sized groups of size n_i).

The much larger N, with about the same g as the smaller studies, greatly increases the power of the meta-analysis relative to the smaller studies. There are also tests of whether the g's of the smaller studies differ significantly among themselves and, perhaps, should not be combined (Rosenthal, 1993). There are debates about how to correct the bias in g and how best to combine these estimates (Hedges, 1982). But the trickiest part of meta-analysis, most likely, is knowing when studies are similar enough to be combined. If two studies have compared the same herbal supplement to a placebo, but used two different memory tests, whether these studies can be combined hinges on the similarity of these memory tests. For instance, are they testing the same kind of memory?

Meta-analysis is relatively new, and its methods are still being worked out, but its potential for improving the quality of social science research is enormous. Social science research often deals with small to moderate effect sizes, and due largely to economic limitations, large sample sizes are rarely used. Therefore, most studies do not have much power; estimates in the field of psychology suggest an average power that is no more than 50%. That translates into a large number of studies that lead to negative results which are really Type II errors. These negative results are rarely published, leading to what Rosenthal (1979) called the "file drawer" problem—the results never get out of the file drawer. Meta-analysis presents the opportunity to combine several negative or inconclusive studies into one study with clear-cut results, and perhaps a fairly narrow ESCI. Fortunately,

DON'T FORGET

1. A result for which $p = .051$ is not likely to be significantly different from a result for which $p = .049$, even though the latter is significant at the .05 level and the former is not.
2. If you perform an exact replication of a result for which $p = .049$, the power for the replication will only be about .5.
3. A study that uses small samples and does not produce significant results provides little evidence in favor of the null hypothesis, or even that the effect size is small.

the World Wide Web can now provide a convenient place to store and search for an enormous number of file-drawer studies that may later be combined by meta-analysis. A web-based journal for negative results is being established at the time of this writing.

When Null Hypothesis Testing is Useful

Almost since the use of NHST began there have been researchers strongly cautioning against simple significance testing without the complementary inclusion of confidence intervals or effect size estimates (e.g., J. Cohen, 1994; Rozeboom, 1960). More recently there has been a growing movement to abolish NHST completely in favor of the reporting of CIs and the use of meta-analysis (e.g., Schmidt, 1996). A common argument against NHST is based on the following set of premises: (1) The null hypothesis is almost never exactly true for studies in social science research, so there are very few opportunities to make a true Type I error; (2) power is usually low in social science research, so there is a high rate of Type II errors; and (3) because H_0 is almost never true, almost any experiment can produce positive results if the sample sizes are made large enough. The critics further argue that not only is there little to gain by using NHST, but the procedure leads to various fallacies and confusions. As the weaknesses of NHST are pointed out more clearly and more often, the critics have wondered aloud: Why is this procedure still so popular? The answer to this question, we feel, lies not in theoretical conceptions of science, but in more practical considerations. Let us look at the function NHST actually serves in research.

We agree that if one takes an exact view about it, the null hypothesis is very rarely true in social science research. Inevitably, any new treatment will work at least very slightly, or any two treatments will differ slightly, or any two variables will have at least some very slight and inconsequential relation with each other. It is rare that social scientists investigate paranormal phenomena, or treatments so truly irrelevant that they may indeed have absolutely no effect at all. However, the direction that results will take is not always obvious. When we are comparing two methods for teaching math, for instance, a statistically significant result favoring method A gives us some confidence that method B would not be better in the entire population. A lack of significant results would not convince us that the two methods are identical, but rather that additional research would be needed to settle the issue.

If the direction the results will take seems obvious (e.g., individual attention will improve math performance as compared to classroom instruction alone) and you can safely rule out the possibility that the null hypothesis is true (in the previous example, can you imagine that adding individual attention to classroom instruction will have absolutely no benefit whatsoever?), it can be argued that NHST is pointless. Use enough participants and the results will be significant; don't use enough participants and you will commit a Type II error by failing to reject H_0. However, although it is very rare that the null hypothesis is exactly true, it is not unusual for the true effect size to be so small that it is of no interest to us practically. For example, a researcher may want to know if the frequent playing of music composed by Mozart to an infant will produce a smarter child (the so-called Mozart effect). If the true effect size involved an increase of one IQ point (say, from 100 to 101) after much playing of Mozart, a study would be likely to produce negative results and therefore a Type II error, but we see this as a benefit, not a drawback, of NHST. A significant result in this case, though technically correct, would be a false alarm in a practical sense, because we are not dealing with an effect that is large enough to be of interest. NHST is useful in that it usually does not yield significant results with very small effect sizes that are really trivial in some cases. For instance, in addition to screening out 95% of null hypotheses, NHST will also screen out about 93% of experiments with small effect sizes when a sample size of 32 participants per group is used ($\delta = .1 \cdot \sqrt{32/2} = .4$, so power = .07).

Statistics texts and instructors often caution students not to confuse statistical significance with practical significance. Certainly, one does not guarantee the other. However, because social science researchers usually have low power for small effect sizes due to their use of relatively small samples (using repeated measures or matched designs tends to raise power, but researchers usually exploit that tendency by reducing their sample sizes), they know that statistical significance is unlikely when the effect size is too small to be of any practical significance. Therefore, knowing intuitively that their power is low for small effect sizes, researchers are understandably impressed with results that attain statistical significance and dismissive of those that do not.

If researchers routinely used very large samples, NHST would not be very useful, because even experiments for which **d** is too small to be interesting would often yield significant results (e.g., with 1,250 participants per group, power is over

.7 for $\mathbf{d} = .1$). In this situation, statistical significance would no longer be indicative of a fairly large effect size, and researchers would have to pay more attention to effect size estimates and think more about how large $\mathbf{d}$ must be for a particular experiment to be of value. We don't think this would be a bad situation, but we feel quite certain that the use of large samples is not likely to become widespread any time in the foreseeable future. It should also be noted that, for some experiments, demonstrating that $\mathbf{d}$ is anything but zero can be of great theoretical interest (e.g., showing that voluntary mental activity can have a tiny but direct effect on the function of some internal organ, such as the kidney); however, in most cases with practical implications, tiny effect sizes are just not worth paying attention to.

Finally, it can be argued that NHST is a haphazard way of screening out small effect sizes. Although there is widespread agreement on the use of .05 for alpha, sample sizes, and therefore power for a given effect size, fluctuate a good deal. This is indeed true; NHST is a crude system. But until researchers can come together and agree about the meaning and usefulness of various effect sizes in different research areas, you can expect to see a great deal of reliance on NHST in the literature of the social sciences. In the next chapter, we show how NHST can be applied to increasingly complex research designs.

Putting It Into Practice

1. If Antarcticans have a normal body temperature that is 1 degree lower than the rest of the human population, and the population standard deviation is 0.7 degree (assume homogeneity of variance):
   (a) How many participants would you need in each group if you wanted power to be .8 for a .05, two-tailed test comparing Antarcticans to other humans? (Answer by using Table A.5, and then Table A.6.)
   (b) If you had only four Antarcticans available, and you wanted to compare them to 8 control participants, how much power would you have? (Answer by using Table A.5, and then Table A.6.)
   (c) Given the sample sizes in 1b, how large would $\mathbf{d}$ have to be to have power of .9 for a .01, two-tailed test? (Answer by using Table A.5.)
   (d) To obtain the $\mathbf{d}$ you found in 1c, how much would Antarcticans have to differ from the rest of the population (the standard deviation still equals 0.7 degree)?

2. Participants study a list of words while listening to either happy music or sad music. If the mean number of words recalled is half a standard deviation higher for the happy than the sad condition (use Table A.5 for these exercises):
   (a) How many participants are needed in each of two equal-sized groups to have a power of .74 (.05, two-tailed test)?

(b) If the two groups are matched such that ρ equals .4, how many participants per group would be needed in 2a?

(c) If the groups contained 18 participants each, how high would the correlation in 2b have to be so that power would equal .7?

3. This exercise concerns the correlation between math ability and music ability.

(a) If the correlation is .35 in the population, how large a sample is needed for power to be .7 with a .01, two-tailed test?

(b) If you are testing this correlation in a class of 26 students, how high would the population correlation have to be for power to reach .8 in a .05, two-tailed test?

4. Three drugs are being compared to a placebo in a one-way ANOVA.

(a) If there are 9 participants in each group, and **f** equals .5, what is the power of your ANOVA test at the .05 level?

(b) If **f** equals .2, how many participants would you need in each of the four groups to have power of .65?

(c) Given the sample size in 4a, how large would **f** have to be to attain power of about .82?

🐟 TEST YOURSELF 🐟

1. Power is

(a) the probability of accepting the null hypothesis when it is true.

(b) the probability of accepting the null hypothesis when it is false.

(c) the probability of rejecting the null hypothesis when it is true.

(d) the probability of rejecting the null hypothesis when it is false.

2. Increasing the effect size (all else remaining equal) will

(a) increase delta (the expected t value).

(b) increase beta (the Type II error rate).

(c) decrease the critical value.

(d) decrease alpha (the Type I error rate).

3. If you perform a two-sample experiment and obtain a large t value (e.g., $t = 10$), which of the following can be concluded?

(a) **d** (the effect size) is probably large.

(b) Delta (the expected t value) is probably large.

(c) Alpha is probably small.

(d) The sample size is probably large.

4. How can the effect size of a two-sample experiment be increased?

(a) Increase alpha.

(b) Increase power.

(c) Increase the separation of the population means.

(d) Increase the variance of both populations.

(continued)

5. **A sometimes useful side effect of null hypothesis testing with small independent groups is that**

   (a) large effect sizes do not lead to Type I errors.

   (b) small effect sizes do not lead to significant results.

   (c) the direction of an effect can be reliably determined.

   (d) small confidence intervals can be found.

6. **Suppose that for a two-group experiment, in which there are 18 participants per group, the calculated t value is 2.1. How large is g (the sample estimate of d)?**

   (a) .5

   (b) .7

   (c) 1.4

   (d) 6.3

7. **If the population correlation is expected to be .4, approximately how many participants are needed to have power equal .7 ($\alpha = .05$, two-tailed)?**

   (a) 7

   (b) 14

   (c) 20

   (d) 40

8. **As the correlation between the two sets of scores in a matched t test increases (all else remaining the same),**

   (a) the denominator of the t test decreases.

   (b) the numerator of the t test increases.

   (c) the variance within each set of scores decreases.

   (d) all of the above.

9. **Which of the following would result in an increase in f?**

   (a) Increasing the separation of the population means

   (b) Increasing the sample sizes

   (c) Increasing alpha

   (d) All of the above

10. **For a given F value, which of the following would lead to a larger sample value for f?**

   (a) Larger sample sizes

   (b) Smaller sample sizes

   (c) Larger within-sample variances

   (d) Smaller separation among the sample means

Answers: 1. d; 2. a; 3. b; 4. c; 5. b; 6. b; 7. d; 8. a; 9. a; 10. b.

Seven

FACTORIAL ANOVA

TWO-WAY ANOVA

Interaction Contrasts

Suppose you are testing a completely new drug for depression. You are happy that a t test shows the drug group to be significantly lower in depression than the placebo group at the end of the study. To explore your results further you decide to rerun your t test just for the men in the study, and then again just for the women. Although you have equal numbers of men and women in both conditions, you find that the t test for men just misses significance at the .05 level, whereas the t test for women is easily significant. Does this mean that the female population is more responsive to the drug than the male population? As we pointed out in the previous chapter, you cannot conclude this. In fact, the true effect sizes for men and women could easily be identical with accidental differences in sampling explaining the difference in results. However, even if the t tests for both genders were significant (or both not significant), the effect sizes for men and women could be quite different, and it would be useful to know if this were the case. There should be a way to test this, and there is. One way is to test the difference in the male and female results by means of a contrast, as described in Chapter 5.

First, let us look at some possible means for the drug/placebo experiment broken down by gender (see Table 7.1). The relevant contrast is to take the female difference of 18 points (i.e., $40 - 22$) and subtract from it the male difference of 8 points (i.e., $36 - 28$); the difference of these two differences is 10 points, so L equals 10 for this contrast. More formally, the contrast can be written as follows $L = +1 \cdot \overline{X}_{male/placebo} - 1 \cdot \overline{X}_{male/drug} - (+1 \cdot \overline{X}_{female/placebo} - 1 \cdot \overline{X}_{female/drug})$. Notice that all four of the coefficients are $+1$ or -1, so $\Sigma c_i^2 = 4$. If there are 20 participants per group, $SS_{contrast} = nL^2/\Sigma c_i^2 = 20 \cdot 100/4 = 500$, which also equals $MS_{contrast}$. The error term for this contrast is MS_w, which in this case would be an average of the four group variances.

Table 7.1 An Example of an Interaction Contrast

	Placebo	Drug
Males	36	28
Females	40	22

DON'T FORGET

When Will I Use the Statistics in this Chapter?

You are measuring one outcome (i.e., dependent) variable on a quantitative scale (or looking at one such variable at a time), and you are comparing groups along two or more dimensions or factors (any of the factors can represent existing populations, or experimental treatments or conditions).

The contrast just tested is called an *interaction contrast*. If it is significant, we can say that the drug interacts with gender, in that the effect of the drug, relative to a placebo, changes from one gender to another. Depending on the nature and the size of the interaction we might recommend that the drug be used only with females. Interactions can be very interesting both practically and theoretically. The simplest kind of interaction is the two by two (symbolized as 2 × 2) interaction, as in the example above (two drug conditions and two genders). Interactions, however, can get more complicated (e.g., three drug conditions by two genders), and when they do, a simple linear contrast will not be sufficient. To handle these more complex cases you will need an extension of the ANOVA procedure you learned in Chapter 5. This extension, called *factorial ANOVA* (for reasons soon to be made clear) is the subject of this chapter.

THE FACTORIAL DESIGN

The one-way ANOVA is called one-way because there is only one independent variable, also called a *factor*, that distinguishes the groups. If the groups differed along two factors, a two-way ANOVA could probably be applied to the results. (The dependent variable should have been measured on an interval or ratio scale. If more than one dependent variable is to be used in the same analysis you would need a multivariate analysis of variance [MANOVA]. In this book we will only deal with univariate ANOVAs—i.e., one DV at a time.) To illustrate how two factors can be combined in one experiment we offer the following example.

Suppose you are the principal of a large school and you want to improve reading scores. In comparison to the traditional method for teaching reading, you want to test two new methods—we'll call them visual and phonics. Imagine that many of your classes in a given grade consist of 20 pupils randomly selected. To get the power you want, you assign three classes at random to each of the three teaching methods. Suppose also that there are four reasonably good reading texts available and you want to decide which is best. Again, your power analysis suggests that you assign three classes to each of the four texts. But if you are already using 9 classes for the teaching method experiment you may not have 12 more classes for the text experiment. However, you can run both experiments more efficiently, using fewer classes, if you combine them in a two-way design.

The simplest way of combining two factors is the *completely crossed factorial design*, which is usually called the *factorial design* for short. In this scheme every level of one factor is combined with every level of the other factor. For the teaching method and text experiments the combination would come out as shown in Table 7.2. Each combination of levels in the design is called a *cell*. There are a total of 12 cells (e.g., the visual method combined with text C). This design is often referred to as a 3 × 4 (read three by four), or 4 × 3 for reasons that should be obvious from looking at Table 7.2.

If you actually multiply the two numbers (e.g., 3 times 4), you get the number of cells. If you assign one 20-student class to each cell you can run both the teaching method and text experiments using a total of only 12 classes, without sacrificing any power. For the text experiment you can see that there are three classes assigned to each text, and for the teaching method experiment there are four classes for each method, even more than originally planned. If any of the cells were left empty (no classes or pupils assigned), this would not be a completely crossed design, and it would not be easy to analyze (we will not discuss such incomplete designs, which are uncommon).

If the classes were not all the same size the design would not be balanced. This would make the analysis a bit trickier, and is best dealt with by statistical software (fortunately, the necessary adjustment is simple in the 2 × 2 case—see the second exercise in "Putting It Into Practice"). However, if the design becomes unbalanced in a manner that is not due to random accidents, but rather to the nature

Table 7.2 Layout of 3 × 4 ANOVA with One Class (20 students) per Cell

	Text A	Text B	Text C	Text D
Traditional	20	20	20	20
Visual	20	20	20	20
Phonics	20	20	20	20

of the treatments themselves (e.g., poor readers are so challenged by a particular combination of text and method that they transfer to another school), your results can become biased in a way that is difficult to compensate for statistically (B. Cohen, 2000).

At this point, you may be looking for the catch—the downside of running both experiments simultaneously, and therefore using only 12 instead of a total of 21 classes. The economy comes, of course, from the fact that each student is in two experiments at once. The analysis of the two-way design begins with two one-way ANOVAs, each ignoring the presence of the other factor, except that the error term for both one-way ANOVAs (i.e., MS_w) is the average of the variances within each cell. The potential problem is that the interpretation of these two one-way ANOVAs can be greatly complicated if there is an interaction between the two factors.

It may have occurred to you that one text might work particularly well for the traditional method but not for either of the new methods, whereas some other text works well with the phonics method, and so on. If the relative effectiveness of the texts changes for different teaching methods (or vice versa), you will have some interaction between the factors, though it may not be large enough to be statistically significant or otherwise worrisome. Sometimes an interaction is what you were expecting (or hoping for) when you designed the study. But even if the interaction was not expected, if it is there, you should want to know about it.

Comparing the teaching methods with just one text can lead to results that will not generalize to other texts; another researcher replicating your experiment but using a different text may reach a different conclusion about the teaching methods. If you get essentially the same pattern among the teaching methods for all four texts (assuming these texts are a good representation of all available texts), you can feel confident about the generality of your conclusions with respect to the teaching methods. If you obtain a significant interaction this is also valuable information, leading to more specific recommendations—for example, use text A with the phonics method, but not with the other methods.

THE NESTED DESIGN

It could be the case that the texts are written so specifically for one method or another that it would not make sense to use, say, a phonics text with a visual teaching method. This situation would rule out a factorial design, but a two-factor design would still be possible. For each of the three teaching methods a different set of four appropriate texts could be chosen at random; thus there would be four different texts for each method for a total of 12 different texts. This design is

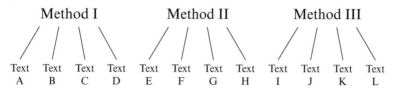

Figure 7.1 A diagram of a nested design: Texts are nested within methods

called a *nested* design; the different texts are nested in the different methods (see Figure 7.1). Because the design is not crossed you cannot look for an interaction. However, there are two one-way ANOVAs that can be performed. The first one-way ANOVA is calculated by first finding the mean for each text. The calculation proceeds as though the texts were the participants; the numerator of the F ratio is based on the variability of the means of the teaching methods (multiplied by the number of texts used for each method), and the error term is based on the variability from text to text within each method. The logic is that the variability from method to method should be large in comparison to the variability from text to text within each method (for more detail, see Myers & Well, 2003).

The second one-way ANOVA tests whether the texts differ significantly from each other within each method using person-to-person variability within each text condition as the error term. A significant F for this factor suggests that it really does matter which text is used. In such a nested design, the text factor is usually a random-effects factor, because the texts for each method would normally be picked at random from all available texts. In this chapter and Chapter 5, we deal only with fixed-effects factors; the levels of your factors (e.g., texts) are chosen specifically because you are interested in testing those particular levels. However, the main drawback to the nested design is that for the first one-way ANOVA there are usually not many participants (in this case, texts) for each condition, and therefore not much power. Generally, if the second ANOVA is not close to significance (e.g., choice of text makes little difference within each method), the nested factor is essentially ignored; in this example the analysis would revert to an ordinary one-way ANOVA of the teaching methods with person-to-person variability as the error term.

Technically speaking, a one-way ANOVA with three classes assigned to each of three teaching methods—all using the same text—is a *two-factor* nested design, because the *classes* are nested within each method. Often, this aspect of the design is ignored, and all of the participants in one method are considered one large group, because we don't expect the participants to differ from one class to another. However, when classes are coming from different schools or patients from different hospitals, ignoring the nesting can increase your chances of making a Type I error, so more attention should be paid to any clumping of participants within a single condition of the ANOVA.

Calculating the Main Effects of a Two-Way ANOVA

Deliberately nested designs (as opposed to obtaining your participants haphazardly in clumps) are quite rare, so we will not discuss them further in this text. We turn now to the practical matter of obtaining the three F ratios in a two-way factorial ANOVA. Table 7.3 displays possible *cell means* for the teaching methods/texts experiment. Each cell mean is the average of 20 scores. Notice that we have also filled in means for each row and column; these are called *marginal means*. Because this is a balanced design the error term for all three F ratios, MS_w, is just an ordinary average of the 12 cell variances.

The numerator for the one-way ANOVA for teaching method is given by $ns_{\bar{x}}^2$, where n is the number of participants in each teaching method ($4 \cdot 20 = 80$) and $s_{\bar{x}}^2$ is the (unbiased) variance of the row (i.e., teaching method) means. Therefore, $MS_{method} = 80 \cdot s^2 (5.725, 6.2, 5.95) = 80 \cdot .05646 = 4.52$. If MS_w turns out to be .5, then $F_{method} = 4.52/.5 = 9.04$. To find the critical F we must note that the numerator df is one less than the number of levels of the factor; in this case df_{num} equals 2 (3 methods minus 1). The denominator df is df_w, which is the total number of participants (N_T) minus the number of cells.

For this example df_w equals 228 (i.e., $240 - 12$), so $F_{crit} = F_{.05} (2,228) = 3.0$ (from Table A.3). Because F_{method} is greater than its critical F we can say that the *main effect* of method is significant (each of the two one-way ANOVAs is referred to as a main effect). Similarly, we can show that $MS_{text} = 60 \cdot s^2(5.77, 6.1, 6.03, 5.93) = 60 \cdot .0205 = 1.23$ (note that in this case, n is $3 \cdot 20$ because there are three cells or classes for each text). Therefore, $F_{text} = MS_{text}/MS_w = 1.23/.5 = 2.46$, which is less than $F_{.05} (3,228) = 2.6$, so the main effect of text is *not* significant (note that for the text effect, $df_{num} = 3$, because there are four texts).

Table 7.3 Layout of 3 × 4 ANOVA with One Class (20 students) per Cell

	Text A	Text B	Text C	Text D	Row Mean
Traditional	5.6	6.0	5.5	5.8	5.725
Visual	5.7	5.8	6.4	5.9	5.95
Phonics	6.0	6.5	6.2	6.1	6.2
Column mean	5.77	6.1	6.03	5.93	5.96

The SS Components of the Two-Way ANOVA

Finally, we want to test the F ratio for the interaction of the two factors. Because the design is larger than a 2 × 2, the interaction cannot be found from a simple linear contrast. In fact, the easiest way to find MS_{inter} is to deal with the SS components of the two-way ANOVA. We hope you recall that any MS can be expressed as SS/df. In the case of the one-way ANOVA, we showed (see Chapter 5) that $SS_{total} = SS_{between} + SS_w$ (note, however, that the corresponding MS components do not add up like that). In the two-way ANOVA the SSs add up as follows: $SS_{total} = SS_{rows} + SS_{columns} + SS_{interaction} + SS_w$; in our example SS_{rows} equals SS_{method}, which equals $df_{method} \cdot MS_{method} = 2 \cdot 4.52 = 9.04$. Similarly, $SS_{columns}$ equals $SS_{text} = 3 \cdot 1.23 = 3.69$, and $SS_w = df_w \cdot MS_w = 228 \cdot .5 = 114$. If you calculate SS_{total} (find the unbiased variance of all the scores as though they were one large group and multiply by df_{total}, which is $N_T - 1$), SS_{inter} can be found by subtracting SS_{rows}, $SS_{columns}$, and SS_w from SS_{total}.

Suppose, however, that you are given a table consisting of the means and standard deviations of each cell and you don't have access to the original scores. You cannot calculate SS_{total} directly, but you can still calculate the two-way ANOVA. Here's how: First you can square all of the SDs to get the cell variances and average them to get MS_w. Then you can treat the cell means like the group means of a one-way ANOVA and calculate the $SS_{between}$, which in this context we will call $SS_{between-cell}$. We have a little calculator trick to make this easy: Enter all of the cell means into your calculator, and then press the key for the *biased* SD (you have to have a scientific or statistical calculator that includes the biased as well as the unbiased SD, and know how to enter numbers in stats mode). Square the biased SD (of the cell means) and then multiply by the total N. This trick can be summarized in the following formula:

$$SS_{between} = N_T\sigma^2 \text{ (means)} \qquad (7.1)$$

SS_{rows} and $SS_{columns}$ can be found by using the same formula; just enter either the row means or the column means, and multiply the biased variance of these means by the total N. Then, $SS_{interaction}$ can be found by subtracting both SS_{rows} and $SS_{columns}$ from $SS_{between-cell}$. We will illustrate the use of Formula 7.1 on the data in Table 7.3.

$$SS_{between-cell} = 240 \cdot .08576 = 20.58$$

$$SS_{method} = 240 \cdot .03764 = 9.03$$

$$SS_{text} = 240 \cdot .01576 = 3.78$$

$$SS_{interaction} = SS_{between-cell} - SS_{method} - SS_{text} = 20.58 - 9.03 - 3.78 = 7.77.$$

Note that SS_{method} and SS_{text} agree with what we found when we obtained MS_{method} and MS_{text} directly and multiplied them by the corresponding df's; the slight discrepancy is due to different rounding off in the two calculation sequences. (Due to rounding, these hand calculations are not extremely accurate. When you need real precision, retain a large number of digits for intermediate results [including marginal means] or use a computer. These calculations are useful, however, for understanding the concepts of the two-way ANOVA.) The df for the interaction is always equal to df_{row} times df_{column}. For this example, $df_{inter} = 2 \cdot 3 = 6$; therefore, $MS_{inter} = 7.77/6 = 1.295$, and $F_{inter} = MS_{inter}/MS_w = 1.295/.5 = 2.59$. Because this F is larger than $F_{.05}$ (6,228) = 2.1, the null hypothesis for the interaction can be rejected at the .05 level. We will explain what this implies shortly.

You may be wondering why we explained how to calculate a two-way ANOVA from just a table of means and SDs, as though you don't have the original data. The fact is that tables of means and SDs are often published in journal articles, along with statistical tests, but the authors may not present all of the F ratios you would like to see. You can fill in the missing results with the procedure just described. The procedure is summarized in Rapid Reference 7.1. (For further details on this procedure see B. Cohen, 2002 or B. Cohen, 2000.) If you don't have a calculator that includes the biased standard deviation as a built-in function, you can obtain one very inexpensively, or you can use the computational ANOVA formulas presented in most introductory texts. Of course, most of the

---

≡ Rapid Reference 7.1

Calculation Procedure for Two-Way ANOVA

$SS_{total} = N_T\sigma^2$ (all scores) optional
$SS_{between-cell} = N_T\sigma^2$ (cell means)
$SS_{row} = N_T\sigma^2$ (row means)
$SS_{column} = N_T\sigma^2$ (column means)

$SS_{interaction}$ is obtained by subtracting SS_{row} and SS_{column} from $SS_{between-cell}$; SS_w can be obtained by subtracting $SS_{between-cell}$ from SS_{total}; or MS_W can be obtained directly by averaging the cell variances.

Then SS_{row}, SS_{column}, and $SS_{interaction}$ are divided by df_{row}, df_{column}, and $df_{interaction}$ respectively, to create MS_{row}, MS_{column}, and $MS_{interaction}$, each of which is divided by MS_W to create the three F ratios.

If r = number of rows, c = number of columns, and n = size of each cell, $df_{row} = r - 1$; $df_{column} = c - 1$; $df_{interaction} = (r - 1)(c - 1)$, and $df_W = rc(n - 1)$.

time you will have access to the original data and will analyze your data with statistical software.

Varieties of Interactions

When the interaction turns out to be statistically significant, as in the method/text example, you will probably want to draw a graph of the cell means to see what is going on. There are many ways that an interaction can combine with the main effects even in the simplest two-way ANOVA, the 2 × 2 design. Before we show you a graph of the cell means in Table 7.3, we will illustrate the major patterns that can occur in a 2 × 2 design. Imagine an experiment in which sleep-deprived participants are given two pills and then asked to perform a motor task (e.g., play a video game that simulates driving a truck). The first pill can be either caffeine or a placebo. The second pill can be either amphetamine or another placebo. There are four possible combinations, and therefore four groups of participants. The (hypothetical) average performance for three of the four groups is shown in Table 7.4.

The drug example is convenient because there has been a good deal of attention paid in recent years to the topic of drug interactions, and if, for instance, there is a drug interaction between caffeine and amphetamine, it is likely to be reflected in a statistical interaction in our experiment. The easiest way to understand an interaction is to first look at a case with absolutely no interaction whatsoever. In Table 7.4 you can see that taking caffeine improves performance by 10 points relative to a placebo, and amphetamine adds 20 points. If these two drugs do not interact, taking both of them will be additive—that is, performance will improve by 10 + 20 = 30 points, relative to taking two placebos. Imagine that the empty cell in Table 7.4 contains a 60, and you have the case of zero interaction. This case is graphed in panel A of Figure 7.2. Notice that the two lines (corresponding to the rows of Table 7.4) are parallel. This is an easy way to see that there is no interaction. With *no* caffeine, the amphetamine line is 20 points above the "no amphetamine" line, and *with* caffeine you get the same difference between the two lines.

Table 7.4 Hypothetical Cell Means for a Two-Way Interaction

	Placebo	Caffeine
Placebo	30	40
Amphetamine	50	

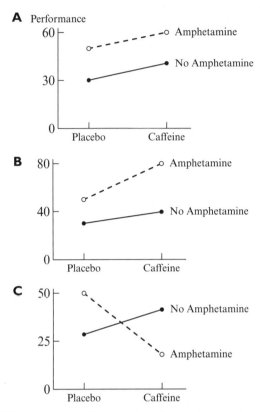

Figure 7.2 Different types of interaction. A, zero interaction (lines are parallel); B, ordinal interaction (lines slant in same direction but with different slopes); C, disordinal interaction (lines cross or slant in opposite directions)

There are several quite different types of interactions that are possible in the 2 × 2 case. For instance, the two drugs in our example may facilitate each other in such a way that the score in the empty cell of Table 7.4 comes out to 80. This case is graphed in panel B of Figure 7.2. The fact that the lines are not parallel tells us that the F ratio for the interaction will not be zero (whether the F is significant, or even greater than 1.0, depends on the relative size of the error term, MS_w). That the two lines slant in the same direction tells us that this is an *ordinal interaction*; the effect of amphetamine may be greater with caffeine than without, but it is in the same direction (or order). We next illustrate an interaction that involves a reversal of the order of the means.

Imagine that the combination of caffeine and amphetamine makes the participants so jittery that it interferes with performance on the video game and, therefore, leads to a mean score of only 20 (worse than the two placebos) in the empty cell of Table 7.4. This pattern of means, graphed in panel C of Figure 7.2, is indicative of a *disordinal* interaction; the effect of amphetamine in the presence of caffeine (i.e., to decrease performance) is opposite to its effect without caffeine. Whenever the interaction is significant (or even very close) in a two-way ANOVA you should be cautious in interpreting the significance or lack of significance of either of the main effects. If the interaction is significant and disordinal, it is unlikely that the main effects will be interpretable at all, so the significance (or lack of significance) of the main effects will usually be ignored in this case.

> ## CAUTION
> When the interaction in a two-way ANOVA is disordinal and significant (or even nearly significant), do not take the results of the main effects at face value.

The easiest way to see the direction of the main effects is to look at the marginal means; Table 7.5 shows the table of cell and marginal means for the case that was graphed in panel C of Figure 7.2. Notice that the two row means are the same, which implies that MS_{row} and therefore F_{row} will be zero. Looking only at the main effect of amphetamine, therefore, would suggest that taking amphetamines has no effect on performance, which is certainly not the case in this experiment (two opposite effects are balancing each other out). The marginal means for placebo/caffeine suggest a main effect in which caffeine hurts performance, but even if this effect were significant it would be ignored as misleading.

Simple Main Effects

When the interaction in a 2 × 2 ANOVA is significant, it is not likely that you will want to stop your analysis with that result. Imagine that your two-way ANOVA involves two types of boys—hyperactive and average—and two types of drugs—placebo and Ritalin (a form of amphetamine). The data (based on some measure of activity) as graphed in panel A of Figure 7.3, could lead to a significant

Table 7.5 The Cell Means Corresonding to Figure 7.2C

	Placebo	Caffeine	Row Means
Placebo	30	40	35
Amphetamine	50	20	35
Column Means	40	30	35

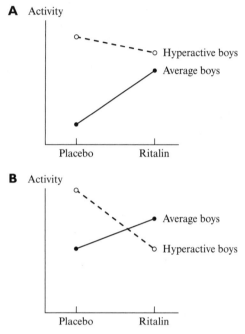

Figure 7.3 Disordinal interactions with different simple main effects. A, large simple main effect for average boys, but small simple main effect for hyperactive boys; B, small simple main effect for average boys, but large simple main effect for hyperactive boys

interaction, but you would then want to test the Ritalin-placebo difference separately for each type of boy (you could perform a simple *t* test in each case, or a one-way ANOVA, whose F would equal the square of the corresponding *t* value). Looking at panel A of Figure 7.3, it would not be surprising if the Ritalin group was significantly higher in activity than placebo for average boys, but not significantly lower for hyperactive boys. The significant disordinal interaction is still theoretically interesting—it demonstrates that the same drug has paradoxically opposite effects on the two types of boys—but if you are wondering whether to give Ritalin to hyperactive boys as a form of treatment, the follow-up results could be discouraging. Results as graphed in panel B of Figure 7.3 would be more encouraging, especially if the Ritalin-placebo difference turned out to be significant for the hyperactive boys alone.

The Ritalin/placebo comparison for each group of boys is called a *simple main effect*. You could also look at simple main effects by comparing the two groups of boys for each drug condition separately, but for this experiment those tests are less interesting. A main effect is always the average of the simple main effects that contribute to it. In this example the main effect of the drug is obtained by averaging the simple main effects of the drug for the two groups of boys. The more different the simple main effects are, the less sense it makes to average them. When the simple main effects are significantly different (that is what a significant interaction tells us), averaging them usually makes little sense, which is why we tend to ignore the main effects in such cases (especially when the simple main effects go in opposite directions, producing a disordinal interaction).

Post Hoc Tests When the Interaction Is Not Significant

If the interaction for a 2×2 ANOVA is not significant the focus shifts to the main effects. If a main effect is significant you can look at the direction of the effect (i.e., which level is higher), and interpret the effect accordingly. Because each main effect has only two levels, follow-up tests are not possible. However, whenever a significant main effect has more than two levels, follow-up tests are not only possible, but almost always desirable. Let us return to our 3 (methods) $\times$ 4 (texts) example and imagine that the interaction was *not* significant, in order to see how main effects are followed up. In the 3×4 example the main effect of methods was significant. We can look at the column means of Table 7.3 to see which method is best, which is worst, and so on, but we cannot tell from looking at the means, for example, whether the visual method is significantly better than the traditional method, or whether the phonics method is significantly better than the visual.

Fortunately, we can test this main effect further with pairwise comparisons, just as you would for a one-way ANOVA. With three conditions and a balanced design you can use Fisher's LSD test; MS_w is the error term from the two-way ANOVA. Just remember that n in Formula 5.11 is the number of participants that receive each method, not the cell size. For this example four classes are assigned to each method, so $n = 4 \cdot 20 = 80$. If the text factor had been significant, Tukey's HSD would be recommended (Formula 5.12) because there are more than three levels. In this case, n would be $3 \cdot 20 = 60$.

Post Hoc Tests When the Interaction Is Significant

When the interaction is significant in a 3×4 ANOVA (as in the method/text example), a test of simple main effects is often appropriate, but there are other options as well. First, we will look at the simple effects in our example. We can either run one-way ANOVAs comparing the four texts for each method, or compare the three methods for each text; sometimes it is interesting to look at both sets of simple main effects. For all of these tests the numerator is based on the three or four cell means we are comparing (n is the cell size), and the denominator is MS_w from the two-way ANOVA (the critical value is the same as the corresponding main effect). In our example the text factor is significant only for the visual method: $MS_{bet} = ns_{\bar{X}}^2 = 20 \cdot s^2 (5.7, 5.8, 6.4, 5.9) = 20 \cdot .0967 = 1.933$; F $= 1.933/.5 = 3.867 > F_{.05}(3,228) = 2.6$. Next we will want to further clarify this effect with pairwise comparisons. We can use Tukey's HSD to compare each pair of texts for the visual method only:

$$HSD = q_{crit} \sqrt{\frac{MS_w}{n}} = 3.63 \sqrt{\frac{.5}{20}} = 3.63 \cdot .158 = .574$$

Therefore, texts A and B both differ significantly from text C.

It is legitimate to skip the analysis of simple main effects and proceed directly to relevant cell-to-cell comparisons, but given the large number of possible pairs to test (there are 66 possible pairs in a 3 × 4 design, but 36 involve crossing both a row *and* a column, so only 30 pairs are reasonable to test) it is important to control for Type I errors (Tukey's test can be modified for this purpose according to Cicchetti, 1972).

Interaction Contrasts

A second option for looking more closely at a significant interaction is to look at 2 × 2 subsets of the original interaction; these subsets are called interaction contrasts, and are calculated exactly the same way as in our 2 × 2 example at the beginning of this chapter. Figure 7.4 is a graph of the cell means (Table 7.3) for the methods/text example. Looking at Figure 7.4 you can see that there is more interaction in some portions of the graph than others. For instance, looking only at

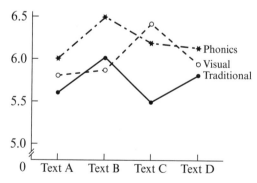

Figure 7.4 Graph of cell means from Table 7.3

texts B and C you can see that there is very little interaction involving just the traditional and phonics methods, but a good deal of interaction if you focus on the traditional and visual methods. For traditional/phonics, $L = (6 - 5.5) - (6.5 - 6.2)$ $= .5 - .3 = .2$, but for traditional/visual $L = (6 - 5.5) - (5.8 - 6.4) = .5 - (-.6) =$ 1.1. Therefore, MS_{cont} in the first case equals $nL^2/\Sigma c_i^2 = (20 \cdot .2^2)/4 = 20(.04)/4$ $= .2$; in the second case, $MS_{cont} = 6.05$. After dividing by MS_w, $F_{trad/phon} = .4$, whereas $F_{trad/vis} = 12.1$. As with any 2×2 interaction or contrast the numerator df is just one, so the critical F for these interaction contrasts is $F(1,228) = 3.84$. Not surprisingly, the contrast is significant for traditional/visual, but not for traditional/phonics for texts B and C.

In a 3×4 design there are eighteen possible 2×2 subsets. It is not reasonable to test them all without protecting against the build-up of Type I errors. If a few of the 2×2 contrasts are carefully planned before the data are seen, it is acceptable to test those contrasts as we did in the preceding section. If, however, you are looking for the best contrasts to test, these are considered post hoc (complex) comparisons, and Sheffé's test is recommended. For an interaction, $F_S =$ $df_{inter}F(df_{inter}, df_w)$; in other words, the critical F for Sheffé's test is just df_{inter} times the critical F for the overall interaction. For this example, $F_S = 6 \cdot 2.1 =$ 12.6. By this criterion the trad/visual by texts B/C contrast just misses significance. The Sheffé test is designed to be so strict that if the omnibus interaction is not significant, none of the 2×2 F's will be greater than F_S.

Partial Interactions

The preceding paragraph points to the advantage of planning comparisons in advance. One form of comparison that is more likely to be planned than discovered post hoc is the *partial interaction*. Typically, a complex comparison is used to reduce one of the factors to two levels, and then this comparison is crossed with the other factor. For example, the phonic and visual conditions can be averaged together to create a nontraditional level. Then a two-way ANOVA is created with one factor as traditional/nontraditional and the other factor as text. If the partial interactions you are testing were not planned, you should use an adjusted version of Sheffé's test as described by Boik (1979).

Finally, another system for planning interaction comparisons is to create a set of interaction contrasts that are all mutually orthogonal. For our example, df_{inter} equals 6, so there can be six orthogonal contrasts in a set. One possibility is to cross the traditional/nontraditional comparison just described with the following text comparisons: A versus B, B versus C, and C versus D. Then cross visual versus phonics (a comparison that is orthogonal to the traditional/nontraditional factor) with the same text comparisons. The resulting six 2×2 interactions are

≡ Rapid Reference 7.2

Follow-Up Tests for the Two-Way ANOVA

If the interaction is **not** *significant:* Perform pairwise comparisons for whichever main effects are significant and have more than two levels (LSD is acceptable for three levels, HSD for four or more).

If the interaction **is** *significant:* (1) Test the simple main effects (i.e., at each level of one factor, perform a one-way ANOVA on the other factor) for one or both factors. Perform pairwise (i.e., cell-to-cell) comparisons for whichever simple main effects are significant and have more than two levels, or (2) conduct (2 × 2) interaction contrasts, or partial interactions for ANOVAs that are larger than 2 × 2.

all orthogonal to each other. The possible follow-up tests for a two-way ANOVA are summarized in Rapid Reference 7.2.

The Two-Way ANOVA with Grouping Factor(s)

Our method/text example involves the combination of two experimental factors. It should be noted, however, that another important use of the two-way ANOVA involves combining an experimental factor with an individual differences (or grouping) factor. Suppose, for instance, that you are studying only the three teaching methods from our previous example (all students get the same text). You may notice that the girls have consistently higher reading scores than the boys in each class, regardless of the method used. This gender difference will contribute to the size of MS_w and therefore serve to reduce the size of your F ratio. If gender were added as a factor to create a two-way (gender × method) ANOVA, MS_w would be calculated separately for each method/gender combination and *then* pooled. Gender differences would then contribute to the main effect of gender, but *not* to MS_w; this reduces MS_w and therefore increases the F ratio for testing the method factor.

Another advantage of adding gender is that you can test whether boys and girls respond in a similar pattern to the three methods, or whether there is some interaction between gender and method. You pay a price for adding a grouping factor, in terms of losing degrees of freedom, so factors should not be added unless they are likely to be related to your dependent variable (as gender is related to reading scores among children) or to create an interesting interaction with your experimental factor.

Instead of a categorical factor like gender, you may discover that your DV is affected by a continuous individual-difference variable, like age. This kind of variable, often thought of as a nuisance variable, also can contribute to your error term and thus reduce the power of your one-way ANOVA. Age can be turned into a second factor in your ANOVA by dividing your participants into blocks according to ranges of age (e.g., 18 to 22, 23 to 27, etc.). If age affects your DV, your error term will be reduced by creating a two-way blocks by treatment ANOVA. If there is a simple linear

DON'T FORGET

If your participants fall into different categories (e.g., ethnic background) that differ on your DV, you can restrict your participants to a single category, but for greater generality you should consider adding a factor to your ANOVA. If your participants differ along some continuous measure that affects your DV (e.g., IQ), consider breaking the continuous measure into categories and adding it as a factor, or performing an ANCOVA.

relation between age and your DV, you can gain even more power by performing an *analysis of covariance (ANCOVA)*. The topic of ANCOVA goes beyond the scope of this book but is covered thoroughly in B. Cohen (2000).

THREE-WAY ANOVA

As we just mentioned, one way to get a two-way ANOVA is to start with a one-way ANOVA and add a grouping factor. Similarly, if you take our two-way method/text example and divide the children by gender, you would get a three-way ANOVA. Or if you divided the children by those who were above or below average in school performance before the method/text experiment, and added that as a factor, you would have a three-way ANOVA. Of course, you can also design an experiment with three factors—for instance, the method/text experiment could be run with weekly testing for half of the children and only before-and-after testing for the other half (the resulting three-way ANOVA might use only the last test as the dependent variable for all of the participating children).

A three-way ANOVA allows the testing of three main effects, and a three-way interaction—an effect not available in a two-way ANOVA. There are also three two-way interactions that can be (and usually should be) looked at, for a total of seven effects (and therefore seven F ratios) that can be tested for statistical significance. In general, a factorial ANOVA with N factors has $2^N - 1$ effects that can be tested (for a four-way ANOVA, $2^N - 1 = 2^4 - 1 = 16 - 1 = 15$), all of which involve the same error term, MS_w (in a balanced design, this is just the simple average of all of the cell variances). In this chapter we are only discussing experiments in which each cell contains a separate, independent group of participants, so experiments with many factors that have many levels become impractical. For example, a 2 × 3 × 4 × 5 (four-way) ANOVA requires 120 different groups of participants, and, if each cell is to have 5 participants, a total of 600 participants. Such experiments are not common, but 2 × 2 × 2 or 2 × 2 × 3 ANOVAs are fairly common in the social sciences, so we will consider such an example next.

A Simple Example of Three-Way Interaction

Let us return to our hyperactive/Ritalin example and add gender to create a three-way ANOVA. The cell means of a three-way design are easy to see if a two-way graph is created for each level of the third variable and these two-way plots are placed side by side, as in Figure 7.5. Of course, it is arbitrary which factor is chosen as the third, but choosing the factor with the fewest levels will minimize the number of plots. We chose gender as the third variable in Figure 7.5 for ease of interpretation. First, you can see that there is some main effect of gender. The average of the four means in the boy plot is 8, whereas the average is only 6 for the girls. You can also see a (not surprising) main effect for hyperactivity, which is the average of the simple main effect of hyperactivity for the boys and the same effect (which appears larger) for the girls. However, the main effect for drug is *zero*; notice that the two placebo means have the same average as the two Ritalin means for the boys (M = 8) and this is also true for the girls (M = 6).

You can also see a good deal of two-way interaction in the graph of the boys; this interaction is clearly less for the girls. The difference in these two-way interactions represents a three-way interaction of gender by drug (Ritalin vs. placebo) by activity type (hyperactive vs. normal). However, because both interactions are in the same direction, this is an *ordinal* three-way interaction. The two-way interaction of drug by activity type for the three-way ANOVA will be an average of

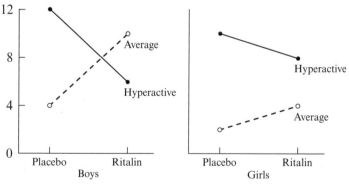

Figure 7.5 Graph of three-factor experiment: Gender X activity level X drug

the *simple interaction effects* at each gender, and will therefore be midway between those two simple effects. The fact that the two-way interaction is fairly similar for both boys and girls means that in this case the overall two-way interaction will be interpretable even if the three-way interaction is significant.

The 2 × 2 × 2 Interaction Contrast

Because all of the factors have only two levels, the three-way interaction can be tested as a contrast. This contrast is the difference of the amount of two-way interaction for the boys and the amount for the girls (you would get the same amount of three-way interaction no matter which factor is chosen as the third one). You can see from Figure 7.5 that for the boys, the 2 × 2 contrast is $(12 - 4) - (6 - 10) = 8 - (-4) = 12$. For the girls this contrast is $(10 - 2) - (8 - 4) = 8 - 4 = 4$. Therefore, L for the 2 × 2 × 2 contrast is $12 - 4 = 8$, and this value can be used to obtain $SS_{contrast}$ just as was shown at the beginning of this chapter.

In addition to the effects we have already pointed out, there are possible two-way interactions of gender by drug and gender by activity type to be tested. These effects would be easier to see if drug or activity type were selected as the third factor. In fact, for purposes of hand calculation of the three-way ANOVA you would have to create a total of three 2 × 2 tables of marginal means—for example, one of these tables would result from averaging the boys and girls as plotted in Figure 7.5 to create one 2 × 2 table of means. Further details concerning the calculation of a three-way ANOVA can be found in a pdf file available on the web (see the Preface).

Varieties of Three-Way Interaction

A significant three-way interaction can be defined as a significant difference among the simple interaction effects, just as a significant two-way interaction is a significant difference among the simple main effects of which it is composed. There are a variety of cell-mean patterns that can result in a significant three-way ANOVA. For instance, suppose that the girls in Figure 7.5 exhibited a two-way interaction as strong as the boys, but in the reverse direction (i.e., the hyperactive line slanting upwards from placebo to Ritalin, and the normal line slanting downwards). This would create a large, disordinal three-way interaction, and eliminate the two-way interaction of drug and activity type. When looking at the results of a three-way ANOVA, consider the three-way interaction first. If it is significant you need to be cautious in interpreting any of the three two-way interactions; if it is disordinal as well, none of the two-way interactions are likely to be interpretable.

CAUTION

When the three-way interaction is significant (especially if it is disordinal), all six of the other effects must be interpreted with extra care. If the three-way interaction is not significant but a two-way interaction is significant, the main effects for the two factors involved in that interaction should be interpreted cautiously. If more than one two-way interaction is significant, all three main effects must be interpreted with caution.

Another way to obtain a three-way interaction in a $2 \times 2 \times 2$ design is for one cell mean to be high, while the seven others are low. For instance, in a hypnosis study one factor might be hypnotic susceptibility (high or low), a second might be induction (hypnotic or relaxation control), and the third factor could be suggestion (numbness or control). It could occur that only the participant group (i.e., cell) that is highly susceptible, hypnotically induced, and given a numbness suggestion shows high pain tolerance. This could easily lead to the significance of all seven F ratios, but a significant three-way interaction would signal you to be cautious about the other effects (which would all be misleading in this case).

Post Hoc Tests for a Three-Way ANOVA

If the three-way interaction is not significant or nearly so, look next at the three two-way interactions. As usual, if a two-way interaction is significant be cautious in interpreting the main effects of the two factors involved. Look again at Figure 7.5, and imagine the drug by activity type interaction averaged for the two panels (i.e., across the boys and the girls). This interaction will be disordinal, and therefore likely to render the main effects of drug and activity as uninterpretable. However, the gender main effect is not affected by that interaction and appears to be unambiguous (a generally lower activity level for girls).

If the three-way interaction in a $2 \times 2 \times 2$ ANOVA were significant you would choose a factor and look at the two simple interaction effects (e.g., the boy and girl plots in Figure 7.5); there are three ways to do this, and, depending on your interests, you might look at it from all three perspectives. Significant simple interaction effects could be followed by cell-to-cell comparisons, as we discussed for the 2×2 ANOVA. If the three-way interaction is not significant, any significant two-way interaction would be followed up in the usual way (for the example in Figure 7.5, the boys and girls would be averaged together and if the drug by activity type interaction were significant it could be followed up with an analysis of simple main effects as though the gender factor never existed, except that the error term MS_w, from the three-way ANOVA, would be used).

In designs with more levels than $2 \times 2 \times 2$, follow-up is a bit more complicated. If no interactions (two-way or three-way) are significant, any main effect with more than two levels can be followed with pairwise comparisons as described in Chapter 5. A significant 2 × 3 interaction, when the three-way is not significant, can be analyzed in terms of simple main effects. A significant simple main effect with three levels, say, would then be subject to pairwise (i.e., cell-to-cell) comparisons. A significant three-way interaction can be followed with an analysis of simple interaction effects or a variety of partial interactions (for more detail, see Keppel, 1991). However, with complex ANOVA designs so many possible tests can be conducted that it is a good idea to plan your tests carefully when you are designing your study, before you have collected, or at least before you have seen, your data. Planned comparisons are more powerful and are easier to interpret than unexpected results from post hoc comparisons. The latter findings may require replication before other researchers take them seriously.

Higher-Order ANOVA Designs

Sometimes a three-way ANOVA is designed to test whether a two-way interaction is affected by some third variable (e.g., does gender affect the drug by activity type interaction?). A three-way factorial is said to be a *higher-order* design than a two-way factorial, and a four-way design is of a higher order still. Sometimes a four-way ANOVA is designed to test whether a three-way interaction is affected by a fourth variable (e.g., would the three-way interaction in Figure 7.5 be much larger or smaller if the study were conducted in a very different part of the world?). Or a grouping variable may be added to a study with three experimental factors. However, experiments with four or more factors are quite rare, unless one or more of the factors involves repeated measures on the same participants. Designs that include repeated measures are the subject of the next chapter.

THE GENERAL LINEAR MODEL

As we discussed at the end of Chapter 4, the results of a two-group experiment could be expressed as a correlation coefficient (r_{pb}). Therefore, the two-group results can also be expressed in terms of a regression equation. For instance, the regression equation for the height difference for male and female samples could be $Y' = 2X + 67$, where X is −1 for women and +1 for men—that is, the height prediction is $(2 \cdot -1) + 67 = 65$ inches for women and $2 \cdot +1 + 67 = 69$ inches for men. Using −1 and +1 as the values for X is an example of effect coding and has the convenient property that the intercept (in this case, 67 inches) is the grand mean. For this example −2 and +2 are the (height) effects of being female and male, respectively. Designs with more than two levels, and any number of factors can be expressed in terms of a very similar equation known as the General Linear Model (GLM).

The equation for Y' yields only the predicted value for each woman or man (the average in each case). If you want to write a general equation to give you each individual's actual height, it would have to look like this: $Y = bX + \overline{X}_G + e_{ij}$, where b is half the height difference of the two genders, $\overline{X}_G$ is the average of the two genders, and e_{ij} is an amount of error, the amount by which the "ij" person (i for gender group and j for person within that group) differs from the mean of his or her group (the e's can be positive or negative and average out to zero for each group).

For a one-way ANOVA with a quantitative factor (e.g., the IV is caffeine dosage in milligrams, and the DV is the score on a simulated truck driving task), a simple regression approach would be reasonable and could be used to represent the data (X would be the caffeine dosage and b the slope of the regression line predicting score from caffeine dosage). However, to represent a one-way ANOVA with three or more qualitative levels, the GLM is appropriate. The usual way of discussing the GLM is in terms of population parameters (the equation can always be expressed in terms of sample statistics to represent a particular set of data). The theoretical GLM for a one-way ANOVA looks like this: $Y_{ij} = \mu + \alpha_i + \varepsilon_{ij}$, where μ is the grand mean (across all conditions or levels) in the population, α_i is the effect of the ith treatment in the population (i.e., the difference between the mean of the ith group and the grand mean), and ε_{ij} is the error associated with a particular participant (i.e., that person's deviation from his or her group mean). If the population means are 30 for Prozac, 20 for St. John's Wort, and 16 for placebo, the grand mean (μ) is 22, and the α's are $+8, -2$, and -6, respectively (note that the α's will always sum to zero for a fixed-effects experiment). A participant in the Prozac group with a score of 26 has an ε of -4 ($Y = 22 + 8 - 4 = 26$).

Higher-Order General Linear Model

For a two-way ANOVA the GLM looks like this: $Y_{ijk} = \mu + \alpha_i + \beta_j + \alpha_i\beta_j + \varepsilon_{ijk}$. Any one woman's score is a sum of the grand mean, the effect of her level on the first factor, the effect of her level on the second factor, the interaction effect for her cell, and an error term (her deviation from the mean of her cell). Consider the text/method example. We don't know the actual α's and β's, and so on, but we do know the corresponding values for our data. From Table 7.3 the grand mean is 5.96. The value for a child in the visual method group using text C can be expressed as $Y = 5.96 - .01 + .07 + .38 + e_{ijk}$, where $-.01$ is the effect of the visual method (relative to the grand mean), $+.07$ is the effect of text C, and $+.38$ is the amount of interaction that results from combining the visual method with text C (apparently they go together well).

As you would imagine, the GLM becomes increasingly complex as factors are added to an ANOVA. For instance, the GLM for the three-way ANOVA is Y_{ijkl} $= \mu + \alpha_i + \beta_j + \gamma_k + \alpha_i\beta_j + \alpha_i\gamma_k + \beta_j\gamma_k + \alpha_i\beta_j\gamma_k + \varepsilon_{ijkl}$, where γ (the Greek letter gamma) represents the third variable. The GLM allows you to mix both qualitative and quantitative IVs in the same design. Among other uses, the GLM provides a straightforward way to understand how the effects of a quantitative nuisance variable can be removed from an ANOVA by means of a procedure mentioned earlier, known as ANCOVA. One way that ANCOVA can increase the power of your ANOVA is by reducing the error term. Another powerful way to reduce your error term involves repeated measures, or, alternatively, the matching of participants. These procedures will be discussed in the next chapter.

Putting It Into Practice

1. As in exercise 1 in chapter 5, participants were measured on a 10-point depression scale after taking one or another of the following drugs for six months: a placebo, a natural herb (St. John's Wort), a tricyclic antidepressant (Elavil), and an SSRI drug (Prozac). All of the participants in the previous exercise were men; an equal number of women participants has been added to this exercise. The mean depression rating for each group is shown in the following table.

	Placebo	St. John's Wort	Elavil	Prozac
Men	9	8	4	3
Women	8	2	5	1

   (a) Given that there are 11 participants in each group and that MS_W equals 32, calculate the F ratios to test all three null hypotheses.
   (b) Calculate and test the simple main effect of drug for each gender.
   (c) Calculate the interaction contrast for gender by St. John's Wort/Elavil, and test for significance. If this were a post hoc contrast, would it be significant by Scheffé's test?

2. The following table is being reprinted from Gist, Rosen, and Schwoerer (1988). Participants in this study were trained on a particular computer skill by one of two methods and were classified into one of two age groups. Mean performance (along with SD and **n**) on the computer task is given for each of the four subgroups (cells).

(continued)

	Younger		Older	
	Modeling	Tutorial	Modeling	Tutorial
Mean	36.74	32.14	29.63	26.04
SD	6.69	7.19	8.51	7.29
Cell n	52	45	20	30

(a) In Chapter 3, you performed t tests on these data. Now perform a two-way ANOVA as though the cells were balanced (add the cell sizes to get the total N, use Formula 7.1, and find MS_W as the weighted average of the squared SDs, as in the denominator of Formula 5.4).

(b) One can compensate for the lack of balance in the cell means by performing what is called an *analysis of unweighted means* on these data. You use Formula 7.1, but N_T is found by averaging the reciprocals of the cell means (e.g., the reciprocal of 52 is 1/52 or .01923), dividing that average by the number of cell means, and then taking the reciprocal of that result (MS_W is the same as in 2a). Compare these results to the results in 2a.

3. Imagine an experiment in which each participant is required to use his or her memories to create one emotion: either happiness, sadness, anger, or fear. Within each emotion group, half of the people participate in a relaxation exercise just before the emotion condition, and half do not. Finally, half the participants in each emotion/relaxation condition are run in a dark, soundproof chamber, and the other half are run in a normal room. The dependent variable is the participant's systolic blood pressure when the participant signals that the emotion is fully present. The design is balanced, with a total of 128 participants. The results of the three-way ANOVA for this hypothetical experiment are as follows: $SS_{emotion} = 223.1$; $SS_{relax} = 64.4$; $SS_{dark} = 31.6$; $SS_{emo \times rel} = 167.3$; $SS_{emo \times dark} = 51.5$; $SS_{rel \times dark} = 127.3$; $SS_{emo \times rel \times dark} = 77.2$. The total sum of squares is 2344.

(a) Calculate all seven F ratios, and test each for significance.

(b) Create a hypothetical graph of cell means that would be generally consistent with the results in 3a (do not try to come up with cell means that would give the exact F ratios found—just make the effects with large F ratios look large compared to those with small F ratios).

(c) What kinds of post hoc tests would be justified by the results in 3a?

4. Imagine an experiment in which each participant solves one of two types of problems (spatial or verbal) at one of three levels of difficulty (easy, moderate, or hard). Half of the 60 participants are given instructions to use visual imagery, and half are told to use subvocalization. The dependent variable is the number of eye movements per second that a participant makes while working on a problem.

	Subvocal Instructions		Imagery Instructions	
	Spatial	Verbal	Spatial	Verbal
Easy	1.5	1.6	1.9	2.2
Moderate	2.6	1.9	3.4	2.5
Hard	2.8	2.1	7.8	2.9

Draw a graph of the cell means for the three-way design. Does a three-way interaction appear to be present? Explain.

 TEST YOURSELF

1. **Under which of the following conditions will the critical F be the same for testing each of the three F ratios in a two-way ANOVA?**

   (a) When there is no interaction

   (b) When the design is balanced

   (c) When there are two levels of each factor

   (d) When the two factors have the same number of levels

2. **Suppose that you are conducting an experiment in which gender is one factor, and the other factor involves three degrees of competitiveness in a simulated industrial task. If the marginal means for the two genders are the same, this implies that**

   (a) the main effect of gender will not be significant.

   (b) the interaction will not be significant.

   (c) the F ratio for the main effect of competitiveness will be zero.

   (d) none of the above.

3. **When the lines on a graph of cell means are not perfectly parallel, you know that**

   (a) the interaction is disordinal.

   (b) there must be some interaction among the population means.

   (c) the F ratio for the interaction will be greater than 1.0.

   (d) the F ratio for the interaction will not be zero.

4. **In a balanced two-way independent-groups ANOVA, the error term (i.e., the denominator) for each of the three F ratios**

   (a) is the mean of all the cell variances.

   (b) is the variance of the cell means.

   (c) tends to get smaller as the sample size increases.

   (d) may differ depending on the degrees of freedom associated with each effect (i.e., all three error terms can be different).

(continued)

5. **In a particular two-way ANOVA, comparing low self-esteem people with high self-esteem people performing a cognitive task for either a small or large reward, a significant interaction was found. This implies that**
   (a) the different levels of reward affected performance in both groups of participants.
   (b) the different levels of reward affected performance for one group of participants but not the other.
   (c) the different levels of reward affected performance in opposite directions for the two groups of participants.
   (d) none of the above.

6. **If df_w for a 2 × 3 ANOVA is 90, how many participants were in each cell?**
   (a) 5
   (b) 15
   (c) 16
   (d) 17

7. **Averaging simple effects together to form a main effect is likely to be somewhat misleading when**
   (a) that main effect has more than two levels.
   (b) that main effect is significant.
   (c) the other main effect is significant.
   (d) the interaction is significant.

8. **Suppose that you are following up a significant interaction in a 3 × 4 ANOVA by computing various interaction contrasts. How does the critical F from Scheffé's test compare to the critical F that you would have used to test the entire 3 × 4 interaction?**
   (a) It is six times larger.
   (b) It is eleven times larger.
   (c) It is twelve times larger.
   (d) It is somewhat smaller.

9. **Suppose that a study finds a significant three-way interaction between gender, economic class, and religion. This implies that**
   (a) the simple interaction effect (class by religion) for men differs significantly from the one for women.
   (b) the two-way class by religion effect will also be significant.
   (c) all of the two-way interactions will be significant.
   (d) all of the simple main effects will be significant.

10. **For a 2 × 2 × 2 × 3 × 3 ANOVA, how many effects (i.e., different F ratios) are there to test?**
    (a) 5
    (b) 25
    (c) 31
    (d) 72

Answers: 1. c; 2. a; 3. d; 4. a; 5. d; 6. c; 7. d; 8. a; 9. a; 10. c.

Eight

REPEATED-MEASURES ANOVA

In Chapter 6 we showed you how power increases for a repeated-measures (RM) or matched-pairs design relative to using two independent groups. This advantage also can be gained if you have more than two conditions, and even if you have several factors in your study, but the analysis does get a bit complicated. This chapter will explain the analyses of one-way RM designs, as well as two-way designs with repeated measures on one or both factors. We will begin with the simplest case that requires an RM ANOVA: Participants are measured three times—for instance, before and after being monitored for 3 months on a new diet, and again 6 months after the experiment has ended (follow-up). You could, of course, perform three matched *t* tests, but let us see how you could perform a one-way ANOVA, while taking into account the fact that the measures are repeated.

THE ONE-WAY REPEATED-MEASURES DESIGN

In Table 8.1 we show hypothetical data for six participants who participated in a weight-loss study. We deliberately set up Table 8.1 (complete with marginal means) so that it looks like you are dealing with a two-way ANOVA. The key to understanding the one-way RM ANOVA is to see this analysis as a special case of two-way ANOVA. The factor of interest in Table 8.1 could be called time. The other factor, strange as it may seem, is the participant or subject factor. Each participant is a different level of the subject factor (note: Although we are following the recent custom of using the term *participant* in place of *subject* when describing the design of experiments, the term *subject* is still so ingrained in statistical notation that we will use that term when necessary to facilitate comparisons with other statistical texts). Although everyone's weight changes during the course of the experiment, some participants are, in general, at a heavier level than others. To continue the analogy with the two-way ANOVA we have graphed the values from the cells of Table 8.1 (see Figure 8.1). If each participant had followed the same weight loss pattern over the three measurements the lines would have all

Table 8.1 Weight in Pounds as a Function of Time

Participant #	Before	After	Follow-Up	Row Mean
1	200	185	195	193.33
2	170	160	158	162.67
3	220	195	230	215
4	190	178	192	186.67
5	180	173	170	174.33
6	210	190	187	195.67
Column mean	195	180.167	188.667	187.944

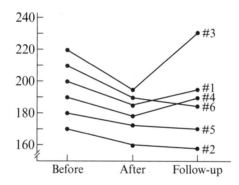

Figure 8.1 Graph of cell means (only one observation per cell) from Table 8.1

been parallel, indicating a total lack of subject by treatment interaction. Normally, there will be some amount of interaction, but for the sake of power you would prefer that it not be very large. If the diet is to be considered reliable in its effects, the lines in Figure 8.1 should be fairly close to being parallel.

Calculating the One-Way Repeated-Measures ANOVA

The calculation of the RM ANOVA begins like a two-way ANOVA of in-

DON'T FORGET

When Will I Use the Statistics in This Chapter?

You are measuring one outcome (i.e., dependent) variable on a quantitative scale, and one or more of your factors (i.e., independent variables) involves repeated measures (e.g., taking the same measurement at different points in time; measuring the same DV under different conditions on the same or matched participants).

dependent groups, as described in the previous chapter. However, a key difference is that the entries in Table 8.1 are *not* cell means: They are single observations. Therefore, MS_w cannot be calculated for this design. That turns out not to be a problem, and it serves in fact to simplify the procedure. The fact that there is only one entry per cell in Table 8.1 means that $SS_{between-cell}$ is the same as SS_{total}. Using Formula 7.1 on the data in Table 8.1, SS_{total} equals $N_T \cdot \sigma^2$ (data) $= 18 \cdot 348.108 = 6265.94$. The next step is to calculate SS_{row} and SS_{column} just as in a two-way ANOVA, except that in this context SS_{row} can be referred to as $SS_{subject}$, and SS_{column} as SS_{RM}, where RM stands for repeated measures. $SS_{subject} = 18 \cdot \sigma^2$ (193.33, 162.67, 215, 186.67, 174.33, 195.67) $= 18 \cdot 274.42 = 4936.6$; $SS_{RM} = 18 \cdot \sigma^2$ (195, 180.167, 188.667) $= 18 \cdot 36.932 = 664.78$. Finally, SS_{inter} is found by subtracting SS_{RM} and $SS_{subject}$ from $SS_{between-cell}$ (which is the same as SS_{total}). To be more specific, we will refer to the interaction in the one-way RM ANOVA as the subject by RM treatment interaction, or $SS_{sub \times RM}$ for short. For this example, $SS_{sub \times RM} = 6265.94 - 664.78 - 4936.6 = 664.56$.

The corresponding df's also follow the breakdown of the two-way ANOVA: $df_{subject} = n - 1$ (where n is the number of rows, or different participants, in this case), $df_{RM} = c - 1$ (where c is the number of columns, or conditions) and $df_{inter} = df_{sub \times RM} = df_{sub} \times df_{RM} = (n-1)(c-1)$. For this example, $df_{total} = nc - 1 = 18 - 1 = 17$; $df_{subject} = 6 - 1 = 5$; $df_{RM} = 3 - 1 = 2$; and $df_{sub \times RM} = 5 \cdot 2 = 10$. Therefore, the MSs are as follows: $MS_{subject} = SS_{subject}/df_{subject} = 4936.6/5 = 987.32$; $MS_{RM} = SS_{RM}/df_{RM} = 664.78/2 = 332.39$; and $MS_{sub \times RM} = SS_{sub \times RM}/df_{sub \times RM} = 664.56/10 = 66.46$.

Because this is a *one*-way RM ANOVA there is only one F ratio to calculate. We are interested in testing the dieting factor, *not* the subject factor (we know that people differ in general in terms of body weight). However, without MS_w as an error term, what do we divide MS_{RM} by to get our F ratio? We could divide by $MS_{subject}$ but $MS_{sub \times RM}$ is usually smaller (as it is in this example) and would give a larger F ratio. Fortunately, dividing by $MS_{sub \times RM}$ is easy to justify, so the formula for the F ratio in this case is: $F_{RM} = MS_{RM}/MS_{sub \times RM}$. For our example F $= 332.39/66.46 = 5.0$. The calculation steps for the one-way RM ANOVA are summarized in Rapid Reference 8.1.

Why is it reasonable to divide by $MS_{sub \times RM}$? Actually, a similar trick was used and explained in the context of the RM *t* test in Chapter 3. We will draw a connection with the RM *t* test next.

Comparison to the Repeated-Measures t Test

If you were studying only the before-and-after measurements in Figure 8.1 you could perform either an RM *t* test or a one-way RM ANOVA. As in the case of

≣Rapid Reference 8.1

Calculation Procedure for the One-Way RM ANOVA

$SS_{total} = SS_{between-cell} = N_T\sigma^2$ (all scores)

$SS_{subject} = N_T\sigma^2$ (subject means)

$SS_{RM} = N_T\sigma^2$ (treatment means)

$SS_{sub \times RM}$ is obtained by subtracting $SS_{subject}$ and SS_{RM} from SS_{total}; then SS_{RM} and $SS_{sub \times RM}$ are divided by df_{RM} and $df_{sub \times RM}$, respectively, to create MS_{RM} and $MS_{sub \times RM}$, which are divided to create the F ratio. If n = # of different participants and c = # of repeated treatments, $df_{RM} = c - 1$ and $df_{sub \times RM} = (n-1)(c-1)$.

the pooled-variance t test versus the one-way independent-groups ANOVA, the F is just the square of the corresponding t value, and you wind up with the same p value either way. The denominator of the RM t test is based on the variability of the difference scores. Looking at Figure 8.1 we can see that because all of the before-after differences are about the same, there is very little interaction in that part of the graph, leading to a large F for the before-after RM ANOVA, and a large RM t (due to a small SD of the difference scores). In fact, the variability of the difference scores (s_D^2) will always be exactly twice as large as $MS_{sub \times RM}$ in the two-condition case. Both the RM ANOVA and RM t test depend on the consistency of *changes* in scores from person to person, and ignore differences in overall level from person to person (that is why $MS_{subject}$ can be ignored). If the changes are fairly consistent, these RM procedures can yield a much better chance of statistical significance than their independent-group counterparts.

In the two-condition case you have your choice between working with difference scores or the interaction, but when you have three or more conditions you do not have a single difference score for each participant, so it makes sense to work with the interaction. In Figure 8.1 the amount of interaction in the entire graph is an average of the amount of interaction for each possible pair of conditions (before-after; after-follow-up; before-follow-up). Whether it is reasonable to take this average at all can be questioned under some conditions. We will return to this issue shortly in the "Assumptions" section.

Comparison to the One-Way Independent-Groups ANOVA

To see in dramatic fashion the advantage of the RM ANOVA we will compare it to an independent ANOVA on the same data set. The first step of the ordinary one-way ANOVA is to break SS_{total} into $SS_{between}$ and SS_{within}. For the data in

Table 8.1, SS_{total} is the same for both types of ANOVA, and $SS_{between}$ is the same as SS_{RM} (just as the numerator of the RM t is always the same as the numerator of an independent t test on the same data). However, SS_{within} is equal to 5601.16, which is the *sum* of $SS_{subject}$ and $SS_{sub \times RM}$. You can think of the RM ANOVA starting with SS_w as the basis of its error term, but then reducing that term by subtracting out $SS_{subject}$, leaving only $SS_{sub \times RM}$, before creating the MS components of the F ratio.

To be fair, we must point out that the df for the error term is also reduced in RM ANOVA, which *raises* the critical value. For instance, for the independent one-way ANOVA the critical F is based on df_{bet} and df_w, so for our example the critical F is $F_{.05}(2, 15) = 3.68$. For the RM ANOVA the critical F is based on df_{RM} and $df_{sub \times RM}$, so for this example $F_{.05}(2, 10) = 4.10$, which is higher than it is for the independent ANOVA. This is a disadvantage of the RM ANOVA, as it was for the RM t test. However, the F ratio for the independent ANOVA is only $332.39/5601.16/15 = 332.39/373.41 = .89$, which is much smaller than the F for the RM ANOVA (5.0). Whereas the independent groups' F is nowhere near significance, the RM of 5.0 is larger than the critical F for this test (4.10), so the RM ANOVA is significant by the usual standards. With a reasonable consistency of scores across participants, the reduced error term and therefore larger F of the RM ANOVA will more than compensate for the larger critical F due to reduced degrees of freedom.

Assumptions

To be valid the RM ANOVA requires the same basic assumptions as the independent ANOVA:

1. The DV is measured on an interval or ratio scale.
2. The DV has a normal distribution under each condition.
3. Although any particular participant is measured under all conditions, different participants must be chosen randomly and independently from the population of interest.

In addition, the usual homogeneity of variance assumption is modified for this design. Because the error term, $MS_{sub \times RM}$, is actually an average of all the possible pairwise interactions, it must be assumed that all of these pairwise interactions are equal in the population—this justifies averaging them into a single error term. This assumption is usually referred to as the *sphericity* assumption. When sphericity does not apply to the population, the F ratio from the one-way RM ANOVA can exceed the critical value too easily—the rate of Type I errors can exceed the value used for alpha. Understandably, statisticians have been concerned about this problem, and several reasonable solutions have been proposed.

Dealing with Violations of Sphericity

Like Levene's test for HOV, there is a test, known as Mauchly's W, for sphericity. Unfortunately, like Levene's test, it lacks power when it is needed most—with small samples. When Mauchly's W is significant you should correct the critical value for your RM ANOVA, but even when W falls short of significance many statisticians suggest a correction to be on the safe side. As with the separate-variance t test, the correction involves a reduction in degrees of freedom, which results in a larger critical value. Both df_{RM} and $df_{sub \times RM}$ are multiplied by a coefficient, called epsilon (ε), which equals its largest possible value, 1.0, only when the data from your sample indicate that sphericity is really true for the population (i.e., the interaction is the same for every pair of levels of your RM factor).

The lowest value that ε can attain (i.e., lower-bound epsilon), when your data exhibit the least amount of sphericity possible, is equal to $1/(c-1)$, where c is the number of conditions. Multiplying your dfs by $1/(c-1)$ and finding the corresponding critical F allows you to check whether your calculated F exceeds the critical F for the worst-case scenario. If your F beats this conservatively adjusted F you can declare your results statistically significant without worrying about the sphericity assumption. For our example, lower-bound ε is $1/(3 - 1)$ = .5, so the conservatively adjusted df would be $df_{RM} = .5 \cdot 2 = 1$; $df_{sub \times RM} = .5 \cdot 10 = 5$. Therefore, the conservative critical F would be $F_{.05}(1, 5) = 6.61$. By this strict criterion the results in our example would not be statistically significant.

Both Greenhouse and Geisser (1959) and Huynh and Feldt (1976) have come up with more precise procedures to estimate ε for your sample data. It is best to let your statistical software calculate these. For our example the Greenhouse-Geisser (G-G) value for ε is .63, leading to a p of .06, whereas the more liberal Huynh-Feldt (H-F) ε is .74, leading to a smaller and significant p of .049. An inspection of Figure 8.1 reveals why ε is so low for these data. You can see that the amount of interaction for before versus after is much less than it is for after versus follow-up. The data in our example do not look consistent with having sphericity in the population. Given how low both the G-G and H-F epsilons are, the cautious approach would be to use the more conservative G-G correction and not reject the null hypothesis for these data. The steps for dealing with the sphericity assumption are summarized in Rapid Reference 8.2.

≣Rapid Reference 8.2

What to Do about the Sphericity Assumption

1. If your results are not significant by the usual RM ANOVA test there are no further steps. Do not reject the null hypothesis (in which case there is no chance of making a Type I error).
2. If your F ratio exceeds the conservative (i.e., worst-case) critical F your results are significant. There is no need to worry about too easily committing a Type I error.
3. If your F lands between the usual critical value and the conservatively adjusted value, use statistical software to calculate Mauchly's W and the G-G and H-F epsilons. If Mauchly's test is not significant and ε is fairly close to 1.0, use the H-F correction (cautious approach), or the ordinary RM ANOVA. Otherwise, use the G-G correction.

The MANOVA Alternative to Repeated-Measures ANOVA

Yet another option for performing an RM ANOVA without worrying about the sphericity assumption is to perform a MANOVA instead. We are not covering multivariate tests in this volume, so we will only discuss this option briefly. A MANOVA treats the three possible sets of difference scores (i.e., before-after, after-follow-up; before-follow-up) as three different dependent variables to be combined into one analysis. Just as an RM t test compares the mean of the difference scores to zero, MANOVA in this case finds the weighted combination of the three sets of difference scores that differs most from zero. It is not assumed that the three sets of difference scores have the same variance, so the sphericity assumption does not apply. However, finding the best combination of the sets of difference scores costs degrees of freedom. The df for the error term in this form of MANOVA is $(n - c) + 1$, which for our example equals $(6 - 3) + 1 = 4$ (instead of 10 for the RM ANOVA). This MANOVA cannot be performed if there are more conditions than participants (e.g., 10 participants are measured every month for a year). However, for fairly large samples, MANOVA often has more power than an RM ANOVA that has df adjusted to be cautious about sphericity (Davidson, 1972).

A MANOVA usually has its greatest advantage when one or more of the RM t tests embedded in an RM ANOVA are much better than some others. If you look at Figure 8.1, you'll see that the before-after RM t test will yield a much larger value than the after-follow-up t test, mainly due to the obviously smaller error term of the former (less interaction). A MANOVA on this data set capitalizes on this situation and leads to an F ratio of 15.65. Even with df of only 2 and 4, the MANOVA yields a smaller p value than the corresponding RM ANOVA. On the other hand, when sphericity is true for the population, the RM ANOVA will have greater power than the corresponding MANOVA.

Post Hoc Comparisons for the Repeated-Measures ANOVA

So what can we conclude from our weight loss example? Although Mauchly's test would not be signifi-

> # DON'T FORGET
>
> ## When to Use MANOVA
>
> When your sample is not very small (the number of different participants is at least several times the number of different treatments), and it looks like you have a lot more interaction for some pairs of treatments as compared to other pairs, MANOVA is a good alternative to RM ANOVA. It has been suggested that you always perform both tests when possible and report the better result (Algina & Keselman, 1997). This is legitimate if you use an alpha of .025 for each test.

cant for the data in Table 8.1, the G-G and H-F epsilons are so low that the cautious approach would be to go by the G-G p value, and therefore fail to reject the null hypothesis. However, had we performed the MANOVA instead or decided not to be conservative and use the ordinary, uncorrected RM ANOVA, we would have rejected the null hypothesis. Our next step, as in the case of an independent-groups ANOVA, would have been to conduct post hoc comparisons to specify the source of our significant results. With only three conditions it is reasonable to use the LSD test with $MS_{sub \times RM}$ in the place of MS_w. Because LSD comes out to about 10.5 pounds, the before and after conditions differ significantly, but the other two pairs do not. However, sphericity is an even greater concern for post hoc pairwise comparisons than it is for the omnibus RM ANOVA. Note that whereas using the omnibus error term hurts the before-after comparison (an error term based only on these two conditions would be smaller), it helps the after-follow-up comparison relative to an error term based only on those two conditions.

When there is any doubt about the sphericity assumption, the cautious way to conduct post hoc pairwise comparisons is to perform separate RM t tests for each pair of conditions (even if your RM ANOVA was not adjusted for sphericity concerns). However, to avoid a buildup of Type I errors from multiple tests it is suggested that the alpha for each t test be reduced by a Bonferroni correction (e.g., for three tests the α_{pc} would be .05/3 = .0167). You can check for yourself as an exercise that an RM t test for before versus after yields a t of 5.44 with $p < .01$, so that this t test would be significant even with the Bonferroni correction. The other two t tests do not even approach significance.

Therefore, if we had planned the before-after comparison before seeing the weight loss data we could have used a Bonferroni adjustment and declared the results to be statistically significant. Should that give us confidence, then, that our diet really works? The problem with this experiment is that there is no control group; it is possible that a fake diet pill (i.e., a placebo), could have produced similar results. Adding a control group would convert the experiment into a two-way design. We will discuss two-way designs involving repeated measures later in this chapter. For now we will describe other types of one-factor experiments involving repeated measures.

Simple Order Effects and Counterbalancing

The easiest RM design to interpret is one in which all of the conditions are presented virtually *simultaneously*. For instance, three types of words are mixed together in a single list; the number of words recalled of each type is recorded. It is somewhat problematic when the three conditions must be presented *successively*. For instance, similar lists of words are studied while listening to either classical music, harsh noise, or silence. It is not reasonable to keep changing the background sound during a session. For any given participant you would pick an order and present a list to the person first, perhaps during harsh noise, then a similar list during silence, and finally a third list during classical music. A serious problem would occur if all of the participants received these conditions in the same order. In that case the results could be affected by *simple order effects,* such as practice and fatigue. Significantly higher recall during classical music could be due to the fact that participants have had some practice with the recall task by the time they get to this condition; perhaps any condition given consistently in third place would have the highest recall.

The way to prevent simple order effects from contributing to one condition yielding higher scores than another is to *counterbalance* the conditions. With three conditions there are six permutations (i.e., orders) in which they can be presented. If an equal number of participants is assigned to each of these six orders, no one condition will have an advantage due to order. However, order effects will contribute to the subject by treatment interaction, which increases the error term and reduces the F ratio for the RM analysis. To remove the order effects from the error term we can analyze the data with a two-way mixed ANOVA, as will be discussed later in this chapter.

When there are four conditions to be repeated (e.g., four types of distractions that can be administered while the participant solves problems), there are a total of 24 (i.e., $4 \cdot 3 \cdot 2 \cdot 1$) orders in which the conditions can be presented. It is very impractical to use *complete counterbalancing*—that is, to assign several participants to each of the 24 orders, and in the case of five conditions it is not likely that any researcher has balanced the 120 orders that are possible. Fortunately, complete counterbalancing is not necessary to neutralize simple order effects. For instance, using A, B, C, and D to represent the four conditions, assigning equal numbers of participants at random to the four orders ABCD, DCBA, BDAC, and CADB is sufficient to balance out order effects (notice that each letter appears once in each of the four positions). This set of orders is known as a *Latin Square* (L-S) design. In fact, the particular L-S design just listed is *digram-balanced,* as well. Note that any letter you choose is preceded by a different letter in each order, except when it appears first.

The aforementioned type of balancing is particularly important when there is a chance that the effects of one condition will carry over and therefore affect the next condition. When the number of conditions, k, is even, only k orders are necessary to create a digram-balanced L-S design. When k is odd you can counterbalance with k orders, but $2k$ orders are required for digram balancing. This means 10 orders when k is 5, but this is much less than the 120 orders required for complete counterbalancing. However, if you have a list of, say, 20 words and you want to vary the order from participant to participant, it is not likely that you would attempt to counterbalance the orders. In that case, you would simply pick an order at random (out of the astronomical number of possible orders) for each participant, relying on randomness to ensure that a consistent bias will not arise in your design.

Carryover Effects

We mentioned that digram balancing can help if one condition tends to affect the next. However, *carryover effects* can affect conditions beyond the very next one and can be somewhat unpredictable. It is best to minimize carryover effects as much as possible. Consider a two-condition experiment in which participants are put in both happy and sad moods while their performance on a task is measured. One half of the participants have the happy condition first, and let's suppose that there is no carryover into the subsequent sad condition, which is aided by a small practice effect. However, suppose that when participants have the sad condition first, the sadness lingers, and the happiness manipulation is therefore not very effective. If a happy mood actually improves performance, this experiment may fail to show it because half of the participants are not getting very happy in their happiness condition. This is an example of *differential carryover effects;* they can often be minimized by leaving sufficient time between conditions or by imposing some neutral distracting task (e.g., counting backwards by threes) between conditions.

It is important to realize, however, that there are circumstances in which carryover cannot be sufficiently reduced. Suppose one of the conditions in a problem-solving experiment involves giving participants helpful strategy hints. If hints are given for the first condition they certainly can't be removed for a subsequent condition. Or suppose you are comparing two fairly effective weight loss methods. After participants have lost considerable weight with one method, the second method cannot be tested fairly on the same set of participants. We have already discussed the solution to this problem at the end of Chapter 3. It involves matching participants, as we will describe next.

The Randomized Blocks Design

When you have two conditions to compare (e.g., diet vs. placebo), you can match your participants in pairs (based on initial weight, and other relevant characteristics), but if you have three conditions (e.g., two different diets and a placebo), you need to match your participants into triplets. The more general term for any number of participants matched together is a *block*. Because the participants within a block are randomly assigned to the different conditions, the experimental design we are describing is called a *randomized blocks design* (the matched-pairs design is a special case of this). The number of participants in a block does not have to equal the number of repeated conditions (c), but it does have to be some multiple of c to be balanced (e.g., with three conditions you can match participants into blocks of 6 or 9, etc.). When the number of participants in each block is equal to c, the randomized block (RB) design is calculated exactly like the RM design we described earlier: The scores of the participants in one particular block are treated as though they were all scores from the *same* participant measured under each condition (i.e., each block is treated like a single participant).

You might use larger blocks (i.e., multiples of c) when it is difficult or inconvenient to match participants precisely (e.g., you do not have all of your participants at the beginning of the experiment), but you can at least place your participants into a series of ordered categories (e.g., slightly phobic, moderately phobic, etc.). When the blocks are some multiple of c, the RB design is analyzed as an ordinary two-way ANOVA with the blocks being different levels of a blocking factor. However, if the blocking factor is measured on an interval or ratio scale (e.g., weight, age, etc.), an ANCOVA will often yield more power (if its assumptions are met) than an ordinary two-way ANOVA of the data from an RB design (Maxwell & Delaney, 2000).

Trend Analysis

Sometimes the independent variable in an RM ANOVA is itself measured on an interval or ratio scale. The most obvious example involves measurements over time (e.g., participants are measured every month during some treatment). Or one could present the same task at several levels of difficulty (e.g., solving anagrams involving five, six, or seven letters). In such cases a trend analysis is usually preferable to the ANOVA, as was de-

> ## CAUTION
>
> If you present repeated treatments successively in your study, it is important to employ some form of counterbalancing to neutralize order effects. However, order effects will increase your error term, so you need to consider a mixed design as described in the second half of this chapter. If you have asymmetrical carryover effects, you may have to match your participants in blocks instead of using repeated measures. If you can't get rid of your carryover effects *and* it is not convenient to match your participants (or you have no basis for doing so), you may have to resort to a study with independent groups (although an ANCOVA may still be possible).

scribed near the end of Chapter 5. However, instead of applying the trend coefficients to the means of the conditions, we apply these coefficients to the scores of each individual. Suppose, for example, that each participant performs the same task (and the number of errors is recorded) at four different levels of distracting noise. To test for a linear trend, you would multiply a participant's number of errors by −2 for the lowest level of noise, −1 for the next higher level, +1 for the next level, and +3 for the highest level; these four products would then be added together to create a single linear trend score for that participant. The trend scores of all the participants would then be treated exactly like the difference scores in an RM *t* test. The resulting *t* value could then be squared to obtain an F value for the linear trend component. The quadratic trend could be tested in the same way, except that the coefficients multiplying the scores would be different (see B. Cohen, 2000).

Although it is sometimes interesting to observe a participant's performance as a function, for instance, of the dosage of some drug, or the intensity of some treatment, a more conclusive experiment often requires the inclusion of a separate control group. Such experiments may lend themselves to an analysis by a two-way ANOVA, with one factor repeated (e.g., dosage, intensity), and one not (e.g., drug vs. placebo). A two-way ANOVA with one between-subjects factor and one within-subjects (i.e., RM) factor is usually referred to as a two-way *mixed-*

design ANOVA (sometimes this arrangement is referred to as a *split-plot design*, but this term, which reflects its roots in agriculture work, seems less popular these days). However, if the RM factor is quantitative and you are focusing on trends, the analysis can be reduced to a simple independent-groups *t* test or one-way ANOVA. For instance, in each group, linear trend scores can be calculated for each participant. The trend scores can be treated as your new DV, and if there are only two different groups, these trend scores can be compared by means of an ordinary *t* test; with more than two groups a one-way independent-groups ANOVA on the trend scores would be required. Of course, quadratic and higher trend components can be compared in the same way.

In the simplest mixed design, the 2×2, you might have two groups of participants measured before and after two different diets. In this case you don't need to create trend scores; the before-after difference scores (i.e., changes in weight) can be compared with an independent-groups *t* test. Squaring this *t* value would give you the F ratio for the interaction in the 2×2 mixed-design ANOVA. In this case, the interaction of the ANOVA is all you care about (actually, an ANCOVA using the before score as the covariate and the after score as the DV would normally be more powerful). The main effect of diet averages before and after scores together to create marginal means, and because there shouldn't be any "before" difference, this averaging tends to obscure the effects of the diets (Huck & McLean, 1975). Similarly, the main effect of time (before vs. after) involves averaging the two diets together, which is not likely to be of interest. However, sometimes the main effects of a mixed design are interesting, and sometimes with multilevel factors the interaction cannot be reduced to simple difference scores or trend components. In those cases you need to understand the complete mixed-design ANOVA, as will be described next.

THE TWO-WAY MIXED DESIGN

There are a number of situations in which a mixed design arises as the most appropriate way to conduct an experiment. For instance, it is often convenient to repeat the levels of one factor within participants, but not the other. Suppose a researcher is studying the impact of different sound environments and attitudes toward the sounds on the performance of routine office tasks. It is convenient to have the participants perform the same task during three (completely counterbalanced) sound conditions: classical music, popular music, and random noise. However, half the participants are told that the sounds piped into the experimental room are *expected* to affect task performance; the other half are told that the sound system is being tested for a future experiment, and that they should *ig-*

nore the sounds (it would not be reasonable to run the same participants with both explanations for the sounds). A possible set of data for this experiment (the DV is the number of errors made per minute) is shown in Table 8.2. The calculation proceeds with elements of a one-way ANOVA, a two-way ANOVA, and a one-way RM ANOVA.

Like any two-way ANOVA, the mixed design yields three F ratios: the main effect of the between-group factor (e.g., instruction), the main effect of the RM factor (e.g., type of sound), and the interaction of the two factors. The numerators of the three F ratios are calculated exactly as they are for the two-way independent-groups ANOVA (see Chapter 7). First, calculate $SS_{between-cells}$, and then use the appropriate marginal means to calculate SS_{row} and SS_{column} ($SS_{instruction}$ and SS_{sound}, in this case). Subtracting SS_{row} and SS_{column} from $SS_{between-cells}$ yields $SS_{interaction}$. Each SS is divided by its corresponding df to produce the MSs that are the numerators of the three F ratios. The SSs can be calculated using Formula 7.1, where N_T is the total number of observations or measurements, which equals 36 for this example (there are 12 participants times 3 measurements per participant).

Table 8.2 Errors per Minute as a Function of Sound Type and Instruction Group

Expect sound	Classical	Popular	Noise	Subject Means	Row Means
1	1	3	3	2.33	
2	0	0	1	0.33	
3	3	2	4	3.00	
4	0	2	2	1.33	
5	2	3	2	2.33	
6	1	1	0	0.67	
Cell means	1.167	1.833	2.000		1.6667
Ignore sound					
1	1	1	3	1.67	
2	2	4	5	3.67	
3	1	2	4	2.33	
4	0	3	6	3.00	
5	4	4	5	4.33	
6	2	1	6	3.00	
Cell means	1.667	2.500	4.833		3.0000
Column means	1.4167	2.1667	3.4167		

$$SS_{\text{between-cells}} = 36 \cdot \sigma^2 (1.167, 1.833, 2.0, 1.667, 2.5, 4.833) = 36 \cdot 1.4075$$
$$= 50.667;$$

$$SS_{\text{sound}} = 36 \cdot \sigma^2 (1.4167, 2.1667, 3.4167) = 24.5;$$

$$SS_{\text{instruction}} = 36 \cdot \sigma^2 (1.6667, 3.0) = 16; SS_{\text{inter}} = 50.667 - 24.5 - 16 = 10.167;$$
$$df_{\text{sound}} = 2; df_{\text{instruction}} = 1; df_{\text{inter}} = 2.$$

$$MS_{\text{sound}} = 24.5/2 = 12.25; MS_{\text{instruction}} = 16/1 = 16; MS_{\text{inter}} = 10.167/2$$
$$= 5.083.$$

The SS_w in a two-way ANOVA can be referred to more accurately as $SS_{\text{within-cells}}$, and we will do that here, because we want to use SS_w to represent just part of that error term, as you will soon see. As in any two-way ANOVA, we can calculate $SS_{\text{within-cells}}$ by subtracting $SS_{\text{between-cells}}$ from SS_{total} or by calculating the SS within each cell directly and adding these SSs together. Calculating SS_{total} is particularly easy because all you do is enter all of your observations (36 for this example) and then multiply the *biased* variance of those observations by how many you entered. For this example, $SS_{\text{total}} = 100$, so $SS_{\text{within cells}} = 100 - 50.667 = 49.333$. However, $SS_{\text{within-cells}}$ must then be divided into two very different error terms: one for the between-subjects part of the analysis, and one for the within-subjects (i.e., RM) part. First, we will describe the between-subjects error term, which we will call SS_w, because of its similarity to SS_w in the one-way ANOVA of Chapter 5.

The Between-Subjects Part

The between-subjects error term requires that you first average across the measurements for each participant (e.g., average across the three types of sounds) and then calculate the SS for these averages. This SS was called SS_{subject} in the one-way RM analysis, and after it was subtracted from SS_{total} it was ignored. However, in this design some of the person-to-person variability is due to the between-groups factor, so SS_{subject} can be broken down into two meaningful pieces: SS_{groups} and SS_w. For this example, SS_{subject} can be calculated by applying Formula 7.1 to the 12 subject means from Table 8.2. $SS_{\text{subject}} = 36 \cdot \sigma^2 (\text{subject means}) = 36 \cdot 1.2778 = 46$. We already calculated SS_{groups} when we calculated $SS_{\text{instruction}}$ above. Subtracting SS_{group} from SS_{subject} yields SS_w, so $SS_w = 46 - 16 = 30$. To find MS_w we must first find df_w, which in this design is the number of different participants (or blocks), not the number of measurements, minus the number of groups. For this example, df_w equals $12 - 2 = 10$, so $MS_w = 30/10 = 3.0$. Finally, we can calculate the F ratio for the between-subjects (instruction) main effect: $F_{instruction}$ = $MS_{instruction}/MS_w = 16/3 = 5.33$. We have actually averaged across the three types of sound and then ignored that factor completely, performing an ordinary one-way ANOVA (as in Chapter 5) on those averages (subject means). The critical F for this part is based on df_{group} and df_w; in this case, $F_{.05}(1, 10) = 4.96$, so the main effect of instruction is significant.

The Within-Subjects Part

If you subtract SS_w from $SS_{within-cells}$ ($49.333 - 30 = 19.333$) you get the SS for the RM error term. We will call this $SS_{sub \times RM}$, because it is the same as the subject by treatment interaction in the one-way RM ANOVA, except that it is equivalent to calculating that SS term separately for each group of participants and then adding, rather than calculating it across all participants from all groups. For some experiments, calculating $SS_{sub \times RM}$ separately for each group can bestow a considerable advantage, as we will see shortly. Finding $df_{sub \times RM}$ is easy because it always equals df_w times df_{RM}; for this example it is $10 \cdot 2 = 20$, so $MS_{sub \times RM}$ equals $19.333/20$ = .967. Now that we have found the error term for the main effect of the RM factor, we can calculate the main effect of sound type: $F_{sound} = MS_{sound}/MS_{sub \times RM}$ = $12.25/.967 = 12.67$. The rationale for this error term is the same as for the one-way RM ANOVA. The more consistently that participants respond to the several RM conditions, the smaller is $SS_{sub \times RM}$, regardless of overall differences in the level of participants (the latter contributes to SS_w). The critical F for this effect is based on df_{RM} and $df_{sub \times RM}$; in this case, $F_{.05}(2, 20) = 3.49$, so the main effect of sound type is significant.

What may be surprising is that $MS_{sub \times RM}$ is also used as the error term for the F ratio testing the interaction of the two factors. However, this arrangement makes sense when you look at a graph of data from a hypothetical mixed design (see Figure 8.2). The individual participants are shown, as well as the cell means (heavy lines). The more that the participants in a particular group are parallel to each other, the more they will be parallel to the heavy line for that group. The reliability of the interaction is a function of the extent to which participants within a group follow the same pattern, and this is measured by $MS_{sub \times RM}$. Note particularly that if $MS_{sub \times RM}$ were calculated across all participants it would be affected by the fact that participants in one group exhibit a generally different pattern from participants in the other group. When $MS_{sub \times RM}$ is in effect calculated separately for each group, MS_{inter} does not affect the error term.

Now we can calculate the third F ratio; $F_{inter} = MS_{inter}/MS_{sub \times RM} = 5.083/.967$

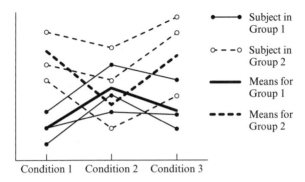

Condition 1   Condition 2   Condition 3

Figure 8.2 Graph of individual scores and cell means from a hypothetical mixed-design experiment

$= 5.26$. Because df_{inter} equals 2 for this example, the critical F is the same as for the main RM effect (this won't be true if you have more than two groups); $5.26 > 3.49$, so the interaction is significant, as well. The calculation steps for the mixed design are summarized in Rapid Reference 8.3.

≡ Rapid Reference 8.3

Calculation Procedure for the Two-Way Mixed-Design ANOVA

SS_{total}	$= N_T \sigma^2$ (all scores)	N_T	= total number of observations
$SS_{between-cells}$	$= N_T \sigma^2$ (cell means)	c	= number of repeated treatments
$SS_{subject}$	$= N_T \sigma^2$ (subject means)	k	= number of different groups
SS_{RM}	$= N_T \sigma^2$ (RM treatment means)	df_{RM}	$= c - 1$
SS_{groups}	$= N_T \sigma^2$ (group means)	df_{groups}	$= k - 1$
SS_{inter}	$= SS_{between-cells} - SS_{RM} - SS_{groups}$	df_{inte}	$= (c-1)(k-1)$
SS_w	$= SS_{subject} - SS_{groups}$	df_w	$= N_s - k$, where N_s = total number of different participants $(N_T = c \cdot N_s)$

$SS_{within-cells}$	$= SS_{total} - SS_{between-cells}$		
$SS_{sub \times RM}$	$= SS_{within-cells} - SS_w$	$df_{sub \times RM}$	$= (N_s - k)(c - 1)$
F_{group}	$= MS_{group} / MS_w$		
F_{RM}	$= MS_{RM} / MS_{sub \times RM}$		
F_{inter}	$= MS_{inter} / MS_{sub \times RM}$		

Assumptions

The mixed design follows the same assumptions as the one-way RM ANOVA, including sphericity with respect to the RM factor, as well as homogeneity of variance for the between-groups factor (SS_w should be the same for all of the populations represented by groups in the study). There is one additional assumption unique to the mixed design. The value for $SS_{S \times RM}$ should be the same for the populations represented by each group. Of course, the actual $SS_{S \times RM}$'s of the different groups will differ, but if you can assume that these differences are accidental and do not represent real differences in the population, you can justify adding the $SS_{S \times RM}$'s together to form the basis of the RM error term. There are tests for this assumption (SPSS gives you Box's M test), but the tests are not very accurate in some common situations (Huynh & Mandeville, 1979). Having equal numbers of participants in each group makes this assumption less critical. A more serious problem is having missing values within a particular participant. Dealing with unequal n's on the RM factor used to be so formidable that researchers would just replace the missing value with appropriate averages. Now, complex statistics can handle the problem in several ways with the help of recent statistical software.

As in the one-way RM case, lower-bound ε is $1/(c-1)$, and can be used to multiply the df's for both the RM main effect and interaction to create a test that makes no assumption about sphericity. For this example, $\varepsilon = 1/2$, and the conservative critical F for both effects is $F_{.05}(1, 10) = 4.96$. Both effects are still significant with this adjustment, so there is no need to calculate an exact ε for Table 8.2.

Post Hoc Comparisons

As with any two-way ANOVA, we look at the significance of the interaction first before deciding about more specific tests. If the interaction is significant, as in our example, you would be very careful about follow-up tests on the main effects, knowing that the interaction can render these effects misleading. For the moment, let's pretend our interaction is nowhere near significance. Our attention would turn to the RM main effect, which *is* significant. If we felt very comfortable about sphericity being true in the population, we could perform LSD tests (HSD for more than three groups) using $MS_{Sub \times RM}$ in place of MS_w. However, as we mentioned for the one-way RM ANOVA, the more conservative procedure is to do separate matched t tests, correcting the alpha with a Bonferroni adjustment (for the mixed design a matched t test is performed across all groups, and you simply pretend that all of your participants are in one big group).

Even if our between-groups factor were significant, there would be no follow-up tests to do, because it has only two levels. If the between-groups factor has more than two levels and proves to be significant, post hoc tests can be performed using MS_w from the omnibus ANOVA. However, if the interaction is significant this error term is not entirely appropriate. A significant interaction is often followed by tests of simple effects: one-way RM ANOVAs for each group, one-way ANOVAs across groups for each repeated condition, or both. The use of error terms from the omnibus ANOVA for testing simple effects is questionable in the presence of a significant interaction. A conservative alternative is to treat the simple effect (or whatever subset of the original ANOVA is being tested) as a new ANOVA, using its own error term, and not using error terms from the original mixed-design ANOVA. Follow-up tests for a significant interaction that involve interaction contrasts or partial interaction should be compared to a critical F based on Scheffé's test (multiply the critical F for the omnibus interaction by the df for the interaction), unless they were planned in advance.

Mixed Designs Involving a Grouping Factor

Two of the most common types of mixed designs have already been discussed: (1) two or more groups are given different treatments, and measured at several points in time; and (2) two experimental factors are involved, but for one of them it is not convenient to employ repeated measures. Next, we discuss two more types of mixed design: when one of the factors is a grouping variable, and when one of the factors is the order in which treatments are presented. Imagine an experiment comparing three methods for muscle building (e.g., light weights and many repetitions, heavy weights and few repetitions, etc.). Participants are matched into blocks of three based on initial muscle mass and then randomly assigned to the three methods; all are measured for muscle mass after 6 months of practice. A graph of 6 participants (i.e., blocks) in this experiment might look just like Figure 8.2. Notice that the dashed lines are far from being parallel to the solid lines, leading to a considerable amount of subject by treatment interaction.

Even though the use of randomized blocks allows us to calculate a one-way RM ANOVA for these data, we can see that the error term would be fairly large. Given that the body-building methods do not differ much on average, we would expect the RM ANOVA to fail to reach significance. However, suppose we tell you that the dashed lines represent blocks of men and the solid lines blocks of women. If we add gender as a factor, our one-way RM ANOVA becomes a mixed design. The subjects by treatment interaction would then be calculated separately for each gender, and then the two SSs would be added to create $SS_{S \times RM}$. This greatly reduces the error term for the body-building method comparison, increasing the chance that this effect will produce a significant F (this is because the dashed lines are fairly parallel to each other, as is the case for the solid lines as well). The $SS_{S\times RM}$ from the original RM ANOVA is divided into two parts in the mixed design: the new, smaller $SS_{S\times RM}$ and SS_{inter}. Thus, the gender by method interaction is removed from the error term, and it may prove to be significant and interesting on its own.

Any grouping variable (i.e., a variable based on preexisting individual differences among your participants) that interacts considerably with your RM factor can be helpful if added to your ANOVA. (Note that an experimental variable that interacts with your RM ANOVA can add variance to your error term, but a grouping variable just separates part of $SS_{S\times RM}$ that was already present.) Of course, exploring the interaction can be reason enough to add a grouping factor. In the example we gave it is useful to know that men and women respond differentially to different weight-lifting methods; this could lead to practical recommendations in a health club. On the other hand, if a grouping variable is shown not to interact with an RM factor, the generality of the RM effect has been demonstrated, at least in one domain. And, of course, a significant main effect of the grouping factor can be interesting when it is not as obvious as it is in the preceding example. Certainly, you can reduce error variance by restricting the variability of your participants (e.g., by using only one gender), but then you sacrifice the ability to generalize the results of your study to the larger population.

Mixed Designs Involving Order as a Factor

Our final example of the use of the mixed-design ANOVA begins with a one-way RM design in which the treatments are counterbalanced. If simple order effects are present (e.g., practice or fatigue), as they often are, they will contribute to the $SS_{S\times RM}$ error term and therefore reduce the power of your analysis. The solution is the same as in the preceding example, but first we will use the simplest type of RM design (two conditions) to show you why a counterbalanced design so often leads to an inflated error term. Suppose half the participants perform a clerical task for 30 minutes while listening to happy music and then, after a brief break, perform the same task for another 30 minutes while listening to sad music. The other half of the participants performs the same task with the music types reversed. Let us further suppose that, on average, happy music leads to a 5-point increase in performance compared to sad music, but that the second task period is always 10 points higher than the first due to a practice effect. The data could look something like those in Figure 8.3. Without a practice effect, all of the participants could be fairly parallel (we are assuming that all participants react alike,

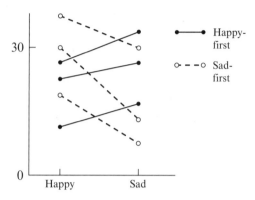

Figure 8.3 Graph of participants exposed to both happy and sad music in a counterbalanced order

for simplicity)—the slant in the lines would be due only to happiness being 5 points higher than sadness. Notice, however, that the practice effect causes the happy-first participants to slant differently from the sad-first participants, adding to the subject by treatment interaction.

If we add order as a between-groups factor and create a mixed design, the simple order effect shows up as a considerable order by music type interaction, but $SS_{S \times RM}$ is greatly reduced because it is now calculated separately for each order group. Of course, this approach can be used just as easily with a four-treatment experiment using an L-S design for counterbalancing. The larger the order effects, the greater the advantage of including order as a factor. However, if the order by treatment interaction is very small (indicating very small order effects), it can be better to leave order out of the analysis—otherwise, including order can hurt your analysis a bit by reducing degrees of freedom in your error term.

Although an order by treatment interaction is usually not cause for alarm, a main effect of order is a bad sign. Why should the happy-first participants perform better overall (averaging both types of music together), or worse? A likely cause for a significant main effect of order is a problem involving differential (i.e., asymmetrical) carryover effects, as discussed previously. For instance, the mood induced by the sad music lingers during the break and makes the happy music less effective, but the effect of the happy music does not linger. A good way to spot differential carryover is by graphing the data by serial position (e.g., first or second) as well as condition. In Figure 8.4 we have depicted the situation in which sadness lingers, but happiness does not (participants have been averaged together). Simple order effects would create parallel lines on a position by treatment graph. The convergence of the lines in Figure 8.4 indicates differential carryover.

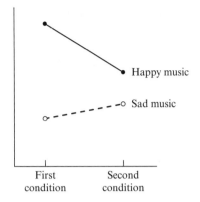

Figure 8.4 Graph of cell means as a function of type of music and serial position

In this graph a main effect of position is benign (indicating simple order effects), but a significant position by treatment interaction is worrisome. The real problem with differential carryover is that it can make it look like there is a difference between your two conditions when there isn't one, or it can suppress a difference that is really there, or even reverse its direction. If you have already run your study and discover this problem, you have the option of using only the first condition for each participant and performing an independent-groups ANOVA. All the power of repeated measures is lost, but you avoid the misleading effects of differential carryover.

DON'T FORGET

The Major Uses for the Mixed Design

1. Two or more groups (getting different treatments) are being measured over time (but if measurements are taken only twice, it can be preferable to deal with difference scores or ANCOVA).
2. There are two or more repeated treatments, and participants are categorized into two or more groups based on individual differences.
3. There are two experimental factors of interest, but it is only convenient to repeat treatments (or match participants) for one of the factors.
4. There is one factor that involves repeated measures given successively and counterbalanced over the participants. Adding order of treatment as a second (between-subjects) factor creates a mixed design.

THE TWO-WAY REPEATED-MEASURES ANOVA

Let us return to a popular form of the mixed design and see how it can be made even more powerful. Consider an experiment in which the participants in one group take an experimental drug expected to aid weight loss, whereas those in the other group take a placebo. The weights of participants in both groups are measured before the drug or placebo is given, and then at several points during treatment. We have already discussed the power of comparing linear trends. However, additional power can be attained by matching participants into pairs before randomly assigning them to the treatments. Obviously, participants would be matched on initial weight, but other factors, like gender and body type, could be used to attain even better matches. Such matching would create a design with one RB factor (drug condition) and one RM factor (time). This design is analyzed as a two-way RM ANOVA. Of course, a design with two RM factors would also be analyzed as a two-way RM ANOVA.

This design is fairly common in cognitive psychology, where it is easy, for instance, to combine words in a list that are categorized as low, medium, or high in frequency of usage, and also as happy, sad, or neutral (each participant gets a recall score for each of the nine types of words). Or, participants may perform three different tasks each presented at four levels of difficulty. Two-way RM designs can get tricky if the counterbalancing of successive conditions is required, so such designs usually involve only two or three levels per factor. Fortunately, understanding the calculation of a two-way RM ANOVA is easier than you might think, especially if you learned something about calculating a three-way ANOVA in the previous chapter.

A one-way RM ANOVA is calculated like a two-way ANOVA, in which the participants are different levels of a "subjects" factor. Similarly, the two-way RM ANOVA is calculated like a three-way ANOVA with subjects as the third factor. For instance, if there are three tasks, four difficulty levels, and 10 participants, then each participant is measured $3 \cdot 4 = 12$ times, and there are a total of 120 cells in the three-way matrix (one score per cell). It is not possible to calculate SS_w, but SS_{total}, which equals $SS_{between-cells}$, can be broken down into the following components, in this example: SS_{task}, $SS_{difficulty}$, $SS_{task \times difficulty}$, $SS_{subject \times task}$, $SS_{subject \times difficulty}$, and $SS_{subject \times task \times difficulty}$. After each SS is divided by its df to form the MSs, F_{task} equals $MS_{task}/MS_{subject \times task}$, $F_{difficulty}$ equals $MS_{difficulty}/MS_{subject \times difficulty}$, and $F_{task \times difficulty}$ equals $MS_{task \times difficulty}/MS_{subject \times task \times difficulty}$. In other words, each of the three effects in the two-way RM ANOVA uses a different error term; in each case the error term involves the interaction between the subject factor and the effect being tested. A three-way RM ANOVA is analyzed like a four-way ANOVA with subjects as the fourth factor, and so on.

Putting It Into Practice

1. Test the RM simple effects for the data in Table 8.2 by performing separate one-way RM ANOVAs for each instruction group (take the more conservative approach and do not use the RM error term from the mixed design ANOVA).
   (a) Which of the simple effects is significant at the .05 level?
   (b) Will either of your conclusions in 1a change if you make no assumptions about sphericity?

2. The data from the second exercise of Chapter 3 are reproduced in the following table.

Participant #	No Imagery	Imagery
1	8	14
2	11	15
3	7	5
4	10	16
5	9	9
6	15	16
7	7	8
8	16	20

   (a) Perform a one-way RM ANOVA on these data, and compare the F ratio you obtain with the matched t value you found previously.
   (b) Assume that this study was counterbalanced such that participants 1, 2, 4, and 8 received the "no imagery" condition first, and the remaining participants received the "imagery" condition first. Perform the mixed-design ANOVA, using order as the between-groups factor, and test all three F ratios for significance.
   (c) What does the interaction in 2b tell you about possible order effects? What effect does removing the interaction from the error term have on the main effect of the RM factor (compare the RM F ratio in 2b with the F ratio in 2a)?
   (d) Average the "no imagery" scores separately for participants who had "no imagery" first and for those who had that condition second. Do the same for the "imagery" scores, and then graph these averages (in the manner of Figure 8.4) so that on the horizontal axis you have "had the condition first" and "had the condition second," and the two lines are "no imagery" and "imagery." What does this graph tell you about the possibility of differential carryover effects? What can you do about the problem at this point?

3. After being sleep deprived, participants are given either a placebo or a caffeine pill and required to solve arithmetic problems under four levels of distraction. The number of errors committed for each condition for each participant is given in the following table.

(continued)

	Participant #	None	Mild	Moderate	Strong
Placebo participants	1	2	5	11	10
	2	0	8	4	9
	3	7	9	13	12
	4	3	12	10	11
Caffeine participants	5	3	7	8	6
	6	2	6	6	9
	7	5	8	7	7
	8	4	9	5	8

(a) Perform the mixed-design ANOVA, and test all three F ratios for significance.

(b) Graph the cell means, and explain the results in 3a in terms of the effects you can see on the graph.

(c) Calculate the F ratio for the interaction of group by linear trend (create a linear trend score for each participant, and then perform an ordinary one-way ANOVA on the trend scores of the two groups).

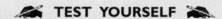

🪶 TEST YOURSELF 🪶

1. **Imagine a study in which there are two repeated conditions, and both the matched t and repeated-measures ANOVA are calculated. Which of the following will be true?**

   (a) The critical F will be the same as the critical t.

   (b) The p values will be the same for both tests.

   (c) The RM ANOVA will have a greater chance of statistical significance than the matched t.

   (d) The matched t will have a greater chance of statistical significance than the RM ANOVA.

2. **One disadvantage of a repeated-measures ANOVA (as compared to an independent-groups ANOVA on the same data) is**

   (a) the reduction of degrees of freedom in the error term.

   (b) the reduction in the numerator of the F ratio.

   (c) the reduction in the size of the error term.

   (d) the reduction in alpha.

3. **If an independent-groups ANOVA and a repeated-measures ANOVA are performed on the same data, which of the following will be the same for both analyses?**
   (a) The numerator of the F ratio
   (b) The denominator of the F ratio
   (c) The critical F
   (d) None of the above

4. **Which of the following is likely to cause a simple order effect?**
   (a) Carryover from one treatment to the next
   (b) Fatigue
   (c) The use of randomized blocks
   (d) All of the above

5. **Differential carryover effects can be eliminated by**
   (a) counterbalancing.
   (b) using a Latin-Square design.
   (c) matching participants in blocks.
   (d) using only two repeated conditions.

6. **If you have seven different conditions to present successively in a repeated-measures design, how many orders would be required for a digram-balanced Latin Square Design?**
   (a) 7
   (b) 14
   (c) 28
   (d) 56

7. **When the within-subjects factor in a mixed design has only two levels, the F ratio for the interaction of the two factors is equal to**
   (a) the main effect of the between-groups factor.
   (b) the main effect of the within-subjects factor.
   (c) a one-way ANOVA on the difference scores.
   (d) zero.

8. **An increase in person-to-person variability in a mixed design (all else remaining equal) will cause a reduction in the F ratio associated with**
   (a) the main effect of the between-groups factor.
   (b) the main effect of the within-subjects factor.
   (c) the interaction of the two factors.
   (d) both b and c.

(continued)

9. **Even when an experiment is fully counterbalanced, simple order effects can reduce the power of the ANOVA by**

   (a) increasing the size of the error term.

   (b) decreasing the separation of the means for the different conditions.

   (c) leading to a violation of sphericity.

   (d) all of the above.

10. **Consider a mixed design in which the order of treatments is the between-groups factor. If you have only simple order effects in your data (e.g., a practice effect) and they are large, this is likely to produce**

    (a) a significant main effect of your treatment.

    (b) a significant main effect of the order factor.

    (c) a significant order by treatment interaction.

    (d) all of the above.

Answers: 1. b, 2. a; 3. a; 4. b; 5. c; 6. b; 7. c; 8. a; 9. a; 10. c.

Nine

NONPARAMETRIC STATISTICS

M uch of this book is concerned with the argument that even when the results of your experiment look impressive those results may be due entirely to lucky accidents while sampling from the population, and that such results would not be obtained were the experiment performed on the entire population. You have seen that the way to counter that argument is to conduct an NHT and demonstrate that the null hypothesis can be rejected with a good deal of confidence (e.g., at the .05 level). The tests we have presented in this book so far have all been based on dependent variables that can be measured rather precisely, and that can be assumed to follow a (roughly) normal distribution in the population. However, there are plenty of possible experiments for which you would like to conduct on NHT, but there is no precisely measured variable.

TESTS FOR CATEGORICAL DATA

For instance, imagine that babies are tested to see if they have color preferences at the age of 6 months. Pairs of identical toys are colored so that one member of each pair is colored red and its twin is colored yellow. Each baby is then classified as preferring either red or yellow toys, according to the amount of time spent looking at or touching the various toys. Let's say that after 10 babies are tested it is shown that 8 babies prefer red and 2 babies prefer yellow. It looks like 6-month-old babies, in general, may prefer red toys, but it can be argued that this result is just an accident and that a replication is just as likely to show a preference for yellow. An NHT would be useful in this case, but the variable being measured has only two values: red and yellow (we can say it is *dichotomous*). The variable is categorical and cannot be said to have any distribution, let alone a normal distribution. Nonetheless, it is easy to see that 9 out of 10 babies preferring red is even less likely by chance than 8 out of 10 and 10 out of 10 is less likely still. It seems like we should be able to find a p value from the laws of chance and compare it to alpha—and indeed we can. A series of independent, dichotomous events represents the simplest situation calling for nonparametric statistics, so we will describe this case first and then proceed to more complicated cases.

The Binomial Distribution

Even when our DV is dichotomous (e.g., preferring red or yellow toys), there will still be a null hypothesis distribution—it just won't be very smooth unless we are dealing with a very large sample size (e.g., hundreds of babies). With a sample of 10 babies (i.e., $N = 10$), there are 11 possible outcomes to our experiment: Anywhere from 0 to 10 babies can prefer red. Each possible outcome has a different probability, and if we make a few simple assumptions we can easily find each of these 11 probabilities and draw the distribution. First, we need to state H_0; if the null hypothesis is that the babies will have no preference we can say that the probability (P) of preferring red is .5 for each baby. This means that the probability of preferring yellow (Q, or $1 - P$, because there are no other possibilities) is also .5 (we arbitrarily chose to focus on red; everything would come out the same if we focused instead on yellow). Let's say that X stands for the number of babies who prefer red. To find the probability for each possible value of X will require a few very basic rules of probability, which we describe next.

We have been dealing with probability throughout this book, but always in terms of a smooth, continuous distribution. For instance, if you select one man at random from a population, the probability that he will be taller than 71 inches is equal to the proportion of the male height distribution above that value. We can use areas of the ND to find this proportion because height can be measured so precisely that, with a large population, the distribution is quite smooth. However, when we are dealing with dichotomous events and ordinary sample sizes our distribution will not be smooth. We will need to base our probabilities instead on *discrete mathematics*. For the most part this involves sophisticated ways to count up events. This can get complicated because the same event can often occur in many different ways.

For example, in the color preferences experiment one possible event is that five babies prefer red and five prefer yellow. However, this event can occur because the first five babies tested prefer red, or the last five, or because the babies alternate, and so on. There are actually 252 different patterns in which five of the babies prefer red. In the classical approach to probability, the probability of some event A, symbolized as $p(A)$, is the number of outcomes that result in event A divided by the total number of possible outcomes. In our example the total number of outcomes is found by noting that for each baby there are two outcomes, and that these are multiplied together: two times two times two . . . a total of 10 times (i.e., 2^{10}). Therefore, the total number of outcomes is 1,024. The probability that 5 of the 10 babies will prefer red, therefore, is $252/1{,}024 = .246$. Note that the lowest p can ever get is zero (e.g., the probability that 11 out of the 10 babies will prefer red is zero because there is no way that this can happen), and the highest p can get is 1.0 (the probability that the number of babies preferring red will be between 0 and 10 is 1.0).

We didn't show you how to calculate that there are 252 patterns in which five babies prefer red. This involves the use of combinations and permutations. We will not take the space for that topic here, but virtually any introductory text on probability will cover that topic in great detail. We will simply show you the NHD for the color preference experiment (see Figure 9.1). This distribution is called the *binomial distribution* for $P = .5$ and $N = 10$. It applies to a wide range of circumstances, including the flipping of a fair coin 10 times, after which you count the number of heads (or tails).

Let's return to the question we posed when we introduced the toy color experiment: Would eight babies preferring red allow us to reject the null hypothe-

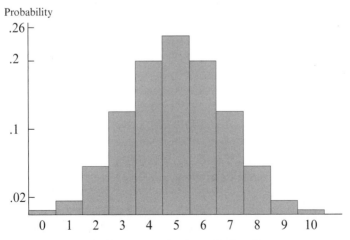

Figure 9.1 The binomial distribution for $N = 10$; $P = .5$

sis? The one-tailed p value for this experiment is the sum of the probabilities for 8, 9, and 10 babies preferring red from the distribution in Figure 9.1. If you don't want to do the combinatoric calculations needed to find these probabilities you can look in a book that has tables for the binomial distribution. In this case the calculations are so easy we'll show them. The easiest probability for this problem is all 10 babies preferring red; there is only one way this can happen, so p equals 1/1,024, or .0009766. For 9 babies there are 10 ways this can happen—any one of the babies can prefer yellow—so p equals 10/1,024 or .009766.

For eight babies preferring red we need to know how many *different* pairs of babies can prefer yellow. The number of possible pairs is given by Formula 5.8 (10 · 9/2 = 45), so p equals 45/1,024, or .0439. Adding these three probabilities yields about .055. As this p is not less than .05, the null hypothesis *cannot* be rejected. Note that the two-tailed p, which is more appropriate in this case, is about .11—not even on the borderline of significance. However, if 80 out of 100 babies preferred red, the results would have reached significance easily. We'll discuss the effect of sample size in the context of more complex tests later in this chapter.

The Rules of Probability

Adding the probabilities for 8, 9, and 10 babies to get our (one-tailed) p value illustrates an important rule of probability: the *addition rule*. When two or more events are all *mutually exclusive* the probability that any one of them will occur is equal to the sum of their probabilities. For two events, this is stated as P(A or B) = P(A) + P(B). For instance, the probability of drawing either an ace *or* a picture card from an ordinary deck of 52 playing cards (there are four aces and 12 picture cards) is 4/52 (i.e., .0769) plus 12/52 (.2308), which equals 16/52 or .3077. However, if two events are not mutually exclusive (e.g., drawing a playing card that is a club or a picture card), the addition rule must be modified. You would have to add the probabilities, and then subtract the overlap (the probability that both events will occur simultaneously). This is stated symbolically as

$$P(A \text{ or } B) = P(A) + P(B) - P(A \text{ and } B)$$

The probability of drawing a club is 13/52 and the probability of drawing a picture card is 12/52, but there are three picture cards that are also clubs. So the probability of drawing a club *or* a picture card is 13/52 plus 12/52 minus 3/52, which equals 22/52 or .423.

Another important rule of probability is the *multiplication rule*. If two events are independent (i.e., the occurrence of one of the events does not affect the probability for the other event), the probability that both will occur is the product of the two probabilities—that is, P(A and B) = P(A) · P(B). This rule can be easily extended to any number of mutually independent events. The probability that 10 babies in a row will prefer red is .5 · .5 · .5 . . . or .5^{10}, which equals .0009766. This is the same result we found by counting, earlier in this chapter (i.e., 1/1,024). The rules of probability are summarized in Rapid Reference 9.1.

The multiplication rule must be modified when events are not independent. The modified rule involves

Rapid Reference 9.1

Probability Rules

1. Probability ranges from 0 (cannot occur) to 1.0 (certain to occur).
2. Addition rule for mutually exclusive events: P(A or B) = P(A) + P(B).
3. Addition rule for overlapping events: P(A or B) = P(A) + P(B) − P(A and B).
4. Multiplication rule for independent events: P(A and B) = P(A) · P(B).

conditional probability, but we will not cover that topic in this book. An example of nonindependent events occurs in the context of sampling. When sampling from a population you must replace each selection before making another one (so that a given individual could be selected twice for the same sample) or your selections will not be truly independent. Fortunately, when your sample is much smaller than the population, sampling *without replacement* is essentially the same as sampling *with replacement* (the probability of randomly selecting the same individual twice for the same sample is so tiny), so no one actually samples with replacement.

The Normal Distribution Approximation

If you look again at Figure 9.1 you can see that the shape of this distribution is similar to the ND. As N gets larger the bars get thinner, and the binomial distribution gets smoother. As N approaches infinity the binomial distribution becomes the ND. Even with N as small as 20, the ND is a good appropriation for the binomial distribution, especially if $P = .5$. If the events were X, the baby grows up to be left-handed, and Y, the baby grows up to be right-handed, P would be less than .2, and the distribution would be rather skewed (e.g., the bar for 0 would be much higher than the bar for 10). A larger N is needed before the ND becomes a reasonable approximation. For small values of P, the product of N and P should be at least about 10 before the ND is used.

Using the ND to approximate the binomial distribution obviates the need to find and add various probabilities, but you need to know the mean and SD of the corresponding ND. These can be found easily. The mean of the ND is NP and the SD is $\sqrt{(NPQ)}$. Any value for X can be converted to a z score with the following formula:

$$z = \frac{X - NP}{\sqrt{NPQ}} \qquad (9.1)$$

(For small N—say, less than 40—a correction to the above formula is recommended, because the binomial distribution is not smooth and continuous. The *continuity correction* involves reducing the absolute value of the numerator of Formula 9.1 by .5.) Applying Formula 9.1 (with continuity correction) to our babies example, we get

$$z = \frac{|X - NP| - .5}{\sqrt{NPQ}} = \frac{|8 - 10(.5)| - .5}{\sqrt{10(.5)(.5)}} = \frac{|8 - 5| - .5}{\sqrt{2.5}} = \frac{2.5}{1.58} = 1.58$$

From Table A.1 we can see that the area beyond 1.58 is .0571, which is very close to the probability we found earlier by counting (.055). Even with N as small as 10 the ND can serve as a pretty good approximation.

The Sign Test

The binomial test, whether used in its exact form (adding up the appropriate probabilities of the binomial distribution) or in terms of the ND approximation, has many applications in the social sciences involving dichotomous events (e.g., does the gender balance among chief executive officers reflect a selection bias?). A particularly useful application of the binomial test is to evaluate the significance of an RM or matched-pairs experiment in which the DV cannot be measured precisely. Imagine that you have some treatment for enhancing creativity in children. Children are matched in pairs based on the creativity of drawings they have already produced in an art class. Then, one member of each pair is selected at random to get the new treatment, and the other member gets a control condition. Each child produces a drawing after the treatment or control condition is finished. It may not be possible to measure the creativity of each drawing in any precise way, but it is reasonable to suppose that a panel of artists could decide for each matched pair of children which drawing expressed the greater creativity (without knowing, of course, which child received the new treatment in each case).

For, say, 20 pairs of children the data from the experiment would boil down to the number of pairs (X) for which the treated child produced the more creative drawing. Say in this case that X equals 16. We can test the significance of this result with Formula 9.1 (and the continuity correction). Assuming that the null hypothesis is that the treatment and control children are equally likely to produce the more creative drawing, $P = .5$.

$$z = \frac{|16 - 20(.5)| - .5}{\sqrt{20(.5)(.5)}} = \frac{6 - .5}{\sqrt{5}} = \frac{5.5}{2.236} = 2.46$$

The one-tailed p for this z is .0069, and the two-tailed p is .0138. The result is easily significant at the .05 level with a two-tailed test.

In addition to dealing with situations in which precise measurement is not possible, nonparametric tests, including the binomial test, can be used when the DV has been measured precisely (i.e., on an interval or ratio scale) but its distribution is very far from the ND, and N is too small for you to rely on the CLT. Suppose you are looking at the effects of certain kinds of hints on problem solving. Each participant solves one problem with a hint and one without (assume that the experiment is properly counterbalanced and that the hint for one problem is not relevant to the other problem). For 16 participants the hint decreases solution time slightly, but for 4 participants the hint is confusing and greatly *increases* solution time. It is not likely that these 20 scores come from any distribution that looks like the ND, nor would the results be likely to attain significance were they submitted to an RM t test, anyway. However, you already know from the creativity experiment that 16 outcomes in one direction and 4 in the other will lead to a significant binomial test. In the kind of situation just described, the binomial test is usually called the *sign test,* because the magnitudes of the difference scores are being ignored, and only their signs (i.e., negative or positive) are being used for the significance test.

The One-Way Chi-Square Test

What if you wanted to test the babies with red, yellow, and blue toys? Or you want to test four magazine covers to see which, if any, would be preferred by a sample of potential consumers. A binomial distribution won't help you. With more than two categories you would need a *multinomial distribution,* and the determination of the probabilities becomes much more complicated. Fortunately, with any number of categories the various frequencies can be reduced to a single statistic that follows, approximately, a well-known distribution. That statistic is called the chi-square statistic (symbolized by the Greek letter chi—pronounced *kie* to rhyme with *eye* in English—being squared, like this: χ^2), because it follows the chi-square distribution. The chi-square statistic simply measures the (squared) discrepancies between the frequencies actually *obtained* in each category (symbolized by f_o, where the subscript "O" stands for "obtained"), and the frequencies *expected* by the null hypothesis (symbolized by f_e). The entire formula is as follows:

$$\chi^2 = \sum \frac{(f_o - f_e)^2}{f_e} \tag{9.2}$$

The summation sign indicates that the formula is calculated separately for each category, and then these amounts are added up. We will illustrate the use of this formula for an experiment in which each of 40 babies is categorized as preferring either red, yellow, blue, or green toys. The observed frequencies are given in the following table (see table 9.1).

The expected frequencies have also been filled in based on the null hypothesis that the 40 babies would be equally divided among the four colors (note that both the f_o's and the f_e's must sum to the same number, the total N). Applying Formula 9.2 to the data in Table 9.1, we get

$$\chi^2 = \frac{(16-10)^2}{10} + \frac{(6-10)^2}{10} + \frac{(11-10)^2}{10} + \frac{(7-10)^2}{10}$$

$$= \frac{36}{10} + \frac{16}{10} + \frac{1}{10} + \frac{9}{10} = \frac{62}{10} = 6.2$$

In order to decide whether to reject the null hypothesis (i.e., no color preference), we must compare our calculated χ^2 to the appropriate critical value. Like the t distribution, the χ^2 distribution varies according to one parameter, the number of degrees of freedom (symbolized as df by social scientists, and the Greek letter nu, ν, by mathematicians). Unlike the t distribution, df for χ^2 depends only on the number of categories (often symbolized as k), and not at all on the number of participants (N). Actually, df equals $k - 1$, so for this example, df $= 4 - 1 = 3$. The critical value of χ^2 for the .05 level and df $= 3$ can be found in Table A.7; $\chi^2_{.05}(3)$ $= 7.82$. Because $\chi^2_{calc} < \chi^2_{crit}$ (i.e., $6.2 < 7.82$), H_o cannot be rejected for this example.

Table 9.1 Observed and Expected Frequencies for a One-Way Chi-Square Test

	Red	Yellow	Blue	Green
f_o	16	6	11	7
f_e	10	10	10	10

The Tails of the Chi-Square Distribution

Figure 9.2 depicts the χ^2 distribution with 3 df. As df gets larger, the mean of the distribution shifts to the right and the amount of positive skewing reduces. As the number of df approaches infinity, the χ^2 distribution becomes identical to the ND. Note that, as in the case of ANOVA, the chi-square test usually uses only the positive tail of its distribution. A very small value for the chi-square statistic (in the left tail) indicates that the observed frequencies are unusually close to the expected frequencies given the possibilities for sampling error. However, this closeness between the f_e's and f_o's only serves to support the null hypothesis in the kind of chi-square applications we have been describing.

On the other hand, there are cases for which researchers use the left tail of the χ^2 distribution exclusively. For example, let's say a logic problem has four possible answers, and a psychologist might devise an elaborate, theoretical model that predicts what percentage of participants will choose each of the four answers. In this case, the f_e's, which would be determined by multiplying each predicted percentage by the N of the sample, represent not H_o, but rather H_A, the alternative hypothesis. A very small χ^2 value would indicate good agreement with the theoretical model and offer support for the H_A. Unfortunately, it is rarely possible for social scientists to create such quantitative models, though a greater effort in this direction could prove beneficial to the behavioral sciences. Although in most cases the f_e's represent the null hypothesis, they need not involve an equal division of N among the categories, as in this next example.

Finding the Expected Frequencies

Imagine that a major newspaper in the city of Springfield wants to check to see if its subscribers are the same politically as the population of the city. The political affiliations of 3,000 randomly selected subscribers are determined, and the results

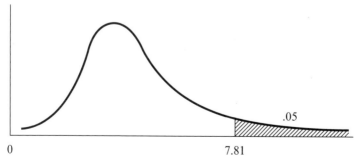

Figure 9.2 The chi-square distribution for df = 3

are 2,000 Democrats, 700 Republicans, and 300 Independents. The expected frequencies would not be, however, 1000 in each category. If the H_o is that the newspaper's readers are the same politically as the city population, the f_e's should reflect voter registration in that city. If 60% of the voters are Democrats, 20% Republicans, and 20% Independents, the f_e's would be 1,800, 600, and 600, respectively. Of course, with such large frequencies, the results will easily attain significance. This points out the need for an effect size measure to accompany your chi-square statistic. Indeed, if you multiply all of your frequencies by some constant C, the value of χ^2 will be multiplied by C as well. An effect size measure that does not change when multiplied by C will be discussed in the context of a more complex categorical design that will be described shortly.

Comparison to the Binomial Test

So far we have been discussing what is often called the one-way chi-square test, also known as the *goodness of fit* test. All of the k categories fall along a single dimension (e.g., colors, political parties). In general, the two-way chi-square test can answer more interesting questions, as you will see in the next section. In the meantime, it is useful to point out that in the two-category case the one-way chi-square test produces the same p value as the ND approximation to the binomial test. In fact, squaring the z from the binomial test gives you the value of your chi-square test in the two-category case (the χ^2 distribution with one df is just the normal distribution after being squared). In cases where you would apply the continuity correction to Formula 9.1 you can apply the same correction to Formula 9.2 (just reduce the magnitude of each $f_o - f_e$ difference by .5 before squaring).

The one-way chi-square test requires the same assumptions as the ND approximation to the binomial test: The expected frequencies should not be too small (they should average out to at least 5), and all of the observations should be mutually independent (if each baby sees two toys in each color, the baby should *not* be counted twice—that is, once for each type of toy). Categories should be chosen carefully so that every participant falls into a category but no participant falls into two categories at the same time.

The Two-Way Chi-Square Test

A psychologist suspects that boys whose parents are divorced (DBs) will start more fights with peers than boys from families with no divorce (NDBs). Ten DBs and 20 NDBs are monitored in playground settings for 1 month, at the end of which the data are as follows for DBs: 0, 0, 0, 0, 0, 0, 1, 3, 4, 8. For NDBs there are 18 zeroes and two ones. Although a t test may have been planned, the data are very far

Table 9.2 Observed Frequencies for a Two-Way Chi-Square Test

	NDB	DB
No fights	18	6
Started fights	2	4

from being consistent with the distributional assumptions of a *t* test. A reasonable alternative would be to categorize each boy as having started at least one fight, or having not started any fights. Next, a two-way *contingency table* can be formed by *cross-classifying* the boys by both divorce background and fight-starting, as in Table 9.2.

These data are now in a form that can be analyzed by a *two-way chi-square test,* but first we have to find the expected frequencies. A naive approach would be to divide the total number of boys ($N = 30$) by the number of cells in the table, so that all the f_e's would be 7.5. This does not conform to any reasonable null hypothesis. First, we don't expect equal numbers of DBs and NDBs because we deliberately sampled more of the latter (reflecting their greater proportion in the population). Second, we don't expect half of the boys to start fights; even in the Db group less than half of the boys start fights. The appropriate null hypothesis for this kind of design is that the two variables are *independent* of each other. For this example, that would mean that DB and NDB boys would have the same proportion of fight-starters. What proportion would that be? It will help to look at a table in which the sums for both rows and both columns have been filled in.

Finding the Expected Frequencies

If you look at the row sums in Table 9.3, you'll see that, overall, four times as many boys did not start fights (24) as did (6). If the two variables are independent we would expect the same 4 to 1 ratio to occur for both DBs and NDBs. At the same time, there are twice as many NDBs as DBs (you can see this in the column sums), so the f_e's should also follow a 2 to 1 ratio across each row. We have already included in Table 9.3 f_e's (in parentheses) that meet these requirements. Notice that

Table 9.3 Observed and Expected Frequencies for a Two-Way Chi-Square Test

	NDB	DB	Row Sum
No fights	18(16)	6(8)	24
Started fights	2(4)	4(2)	6
Column sum	20	10	30

the f_e's exhibit a lack of association between the two variables. Therefore, the two-way chi-square test is often referred to as a *test of association* as well as a *test of independence* of the two variables. The further the f_e's are from the f_o's, the more likely you are to reject the null hypothesis and suggest that there is indeed a relationship between the two variables. Finding f_e's that have a 4 to 1 ratio going down each column and a 2 to 1 ratio going across each row and add up to the same column and row totals as the f_o's may not seem easy, but fortunately there's a very simple formula that does the trick. For any cell in the table, f_e is found by multiplying the sum of that cell's row by the sum of that cell's column and dividing by N (i.e., $f_e = S_R \cdot S_C / N$). For instance, f_e for the lower right cell (DBs who start fights) is $6 \cdot 10/30 = 60/30 = 2$.

Calculating an Example

Once you have found the f_e's, the discrepancy between the f_e's and f_o's can be quantified by the same chi-square formula you used for the one-way test (Formula 9.2). In the two-way case the summation sign indicates that the calculation is performed for each cell of the table, and then these results are summed. This formula was originally devised by Karl Pearson (whose correlation coefficient was described in Chapter 4), so the test is often called Pearson's chi-square test. We will apply this test to the data in Table 9.3:

$$\chi^2 = \frac{(18-16)^2}{16} + \frac{(6-10)^2}{8} + \frac{(2-4)^2}{4} + \frac{(4-2)^2}{2}$$

$$= \frac{4}{16} + \frac{4}{8} + \frac{4}{4} + \frac{4}{2} = 3.75$$

In order to look up the appropriate critical value for our example we need to know the df for our contingency table. For a two-way table the df equals the number of rows minus one $(r-1)$ times the number of columns minus one $(c-1)$. For this example, df $= (r-1)(c-1) = (2-1)(2-1) = 1$. Therefore, the .05 critical value is 3.84. Because our calculated (or observed) chi-square value is less than this we cannot reject the null hypothesis. Perhaps divorce has no association with the starting of fights by boys, and the results in Table 9.3 look as promising as they do because of sampling error.

DON'T FORGET

In the two-way chi-square test, the expected frequency for a cell is found by multiplying the sum for the row that the cell is in by the sum for the column that the cell is in, and then dividing by the total N. The expected frequencies must add up to the same row and column sums (and total N) as the observed frequencies.

Fisher's Exact Test

If you divide all of the entries in Table 9.3 by two, the f_e's become so small that the accuracy of using the chi-square distribution is questionable. An alternative is to perform an "exact" test by adding up probabilities of the multinomial distribution. This test, originally designed by Fisher (for whom the F distribution was named), is called *Fisher's Exact test,* and it was quite tedious to perform before the advent of modern statistical software. Technically, this test is only appropriate when both the row and column sums are fixed in advance (in our last example the column but not the row sums were determined by the experimenter), but you are likely to see this test performed whenever the f_e's are quite small.

The Phi Coefficient

If you double all of the entries in Table 9.3, the value for χ^2 will also double (it will become 7.5) and become significant at the .05—even the .01—level. But the proportions will not have changed. There ought to be a measure that reflects the relative proportions and is not affected by the total sample size, and there is. For a 2×2 table the appropriate strength of association (i.e., correlational) measure is called the *phi coefficient* (symbolized by the Greek letter ϕ). The square of this coefficient follows the simple formula below:

$$\phi^2 = \frac{\chi^2}{N} \tag{9.3}$$

Because multiplying all entries in a 2×2 table by the same constant (C) results in both χ^2 and N being multiplied by C, ϕ^2 remains the same. Like r^2_{pb} (see Chapter 4), ϕ^2 gives you a sense of the proportion of variance accounted for and is unrelated to the total N. Like r_{pb}, ϕ is a Pearson correlation coefficient, which can be calculated if you assign arbitrary numbers to the categories of both variables (e.g., 0 for NDB, 1 for DB; 0 for no fights, 1 for start fights). For Table 9.3, ϕ^2 is

$$\phi^2 = \frac{\chi^2}{N} = \frac{3.75}{30} = .125$$

Therefore, ϕ equals $\sqrt{.125}$, which equals .354. This amount of correlation is considered moderately large, which is why the results in Table 9.3 were very nearly significant even with an N of only 30.

Larger Contingency Tables

The preceding example illustrated the use of a chi-square test when one's data are not well suited for a parametric test. However, the two-way chi-square test is also used quite often to examine the relation between two measures that are already

---

DON'T FORGET

··

The Assumptions for Categorical Tests

1. The categories are mutually exclusive and exhaustive—all observations should fall into a category, but not more than one category.
2. All cases should be independent of all others. A participant could be measured twice, as in the sign test, but each participant should be sampled independently of the others.
3. To use the normal or chi-square distributions as approximations, it is best if the expected frequency for each category is at least about 5.

---

categorical. Returning to our example of the political affiliations for newspaper readers in Springfield, suppose that the city has four major newspapers and the question is not whether the readers of each newspaper are representative of the city's electorate, but whether the political makeup of the four newspapers readerships are the same. In other words, are the relative proportions of Democrats, Republicans, and Independents the same among the subscribers for all four newspapers? The contingency table would have either three rows and four columns, or the reverse. The df for this table would be $(3-1)(4-1) = 2 \cdot 3 = 6$. It is important to note that a chi-square test on the data from the 3×4 table just described would only be valid if no one in the study was a subscriber to more than one newspaper; otherwise, one person would be counted more than once and the observations would not be completely independent. Although ϕ as described above cannot be calculated for a 3×4 table, a modified version, Cramer's ϕ can be found instead (see B. Cohen, 2000).

A Categorical Test for Agreement

We have illustrated two major ways that categorical data can arise. First, precise measurements from an interval/ratio scale can be assigned to a few categories (e.g., low, medium, and high) to avoid making any assumptions about the distribution of the DV. For this reason, the tests described in this chapter are often called *distribution-free* tests. Second, the data may already be categorized for you, as when people register with a particular political party, or affiliate with a particular religion. There is a third case, in which clear categories may exist, but the researcher must decide into which category each participant falls. Because the choice of category could depend to some extent on the subjective judgment of the researcher, there may be a need to check to see whether two different judges would agree on their choices of categories for the different participants. For instance, based on their responses to a projective psychological test, female execu-

tives can be categorized as to their major psychological need: affiliation, achievement, or power. However, before we trust the categorizations of one researcher
it is important to demonstrate that, given the guidelines of the study, two different judges will agree nearly all of the time on their choices. The amount of agreement can be assessed with the aid of a two-way contingency table, as shown in
Table 9.4.

Cohen's Kappa

The columns represent the judgments of the first rater, and the rows represent the
judgments of the second rater. For example, looking at the row and column sums
you can see that the first rater placed eight women in the Affiliation group; the
second rater placed nine in that group. Seven women were categorized as mainly
needing affiliation by both raters, 13 as needing achievement, and 10 as needing
power. In all, the two judges agreed on 30 of the 40 women, or 75%, which is a
reasonable amount of agreement. However, this percentage is inflated by the fact
that the two raters would be expected to have some agreement by chance, even if
both were categorizing the women at random. The chance amount of agreement
can be found by first finding the f_e's just for the cells on the diagonal that represent agreement of the two raters. These f_e's are found by multiplying row and sum
totals and dividing by N just as we did for the two-way chi-square test. The relevant f_e's were put in parentheses in Table 9.4. J. Cohen (1960), who later did pioneering work on power, created a measure called kappa (symbolized as κ, the
lower-case Greek letter k) to correct the sum of f_e's on the diagonal for the
amount of agreement expected by chance (as measured by the sum of f_e's on
the diagonal). Cohen's κ is found by the following formula:

$$\kappa = \frac{\sum f_o - \sum f_e}{N - \sum f_e} \tag{9.4}$$

The corrected amount of agreement is only about 66%, which is somewhat
low if you want to proceed with confidence based on the categorizations of just

Table 9.4 Observed and Expected Frequencies for Interrater Agreement

	Affiliation	Achievement	Power	Row Sum
Affiliation	7(1.8)	2	0	9
Achievement	1	13(4.05)	4	18
Power	0	3	10(4.55)	13
Column sums	8	18	14	40

one rater (you might use two raters and eliminate participants for whom the raters disagree). An even smaller κ would suggest that you should make your rating guidelines clearer, give your raters more training or practice, or abandon your variable as not being reliably measurable. With a higher κ you might confidently proceed with a two-way classification in which the "needs" categories are crossed with a categorization of how successful these women are in their organization.

TESTS FOR ORDINAL DATA

There are many attributes of people that cannot be measured precisely, but differ in terms of amount (i.e., quantitatively) rather than category (i.e., qualitatively). For instance, it is clear that some people have greater leadership potential or more charisma, even though these attributes cannot be measured precisely. If we assign people to levels as having a great deal of charisma, a moderate amount of charisma, and very little charisma, we are using what is called an *ordinal scale* (as described in Chapter 1). If a coach ranks her athletes in terms of their value to the team, she is also using an ordinal scale. Although ordinal scales do not provide the precise measurements required for parametric statistics (like the *t* test), they contain more information than categorical scales; in fact, significance tests based on ordinal scales often have nearly as much power (i.e., probability of yielding significant results when there is some effect to be found) as their parametric counterparts (see Rapid Reference 9.2 at the end of this chapter for a list of ordinal tests discussed herein and the parametric tests they can replace). We will begin our description of ordinal tests with the ordinal counterpart to the two-group *t* test.

The Mann-Whitney Test

Let's return to the example concerning the impact of divorce on the aggressiveness of young boys. This time, instead of counting fights we will suppose that after observing the boys daily in the playground for a month the psychologist ranks the boys for aggressiveness, so that the boy ranked 1 is the most aggressive, and the boy ranked 30 is the least. Note that the DB and NDB boys are being ranked together, ideally by an observer who does not know which boys have divorced parents. The best possible result for the researcher is that the 10 DB boys occupy the top 10 ranks for aggressiveness followed by the 20 NDB boys. This is extremely unlikely to happen by accident when the null hypothesis is true (H_o: there is no difference in aggressiveness between DB and NDB boys). One way to quantify the difference in ranks between the two groups is to compare the sum of ranks for the smaller group (in this case, the DBs) to what we would expect to get on the average for that group when the null hypothesis is true. In order to understand what to expect for a sum of ranks for a subgroup, let's first take a look at the sum of ranks for all the boys combined. If there are a total of N boys, the sum of the N ranks will be

$$S_N = \frac{N(N+1)}{2} \tag{9.5}$$

For a total of 30 boys, $S_N = (30 \cdot 31)/2 = 930/2 = 465$. Now let's look at the sum of ranks for the DBs in the best case (best with respect to finding the predicted effect); the DBs will be ranked 1 to 10, so S_{DB} will be $(10 \cdot 11)/2 = 110/2 = 55$. In the worst case the DBs will be ranked 21 to 30, and S_{DB} will be 255 (we got this by subtracting the sum of 1 to 20 from the sum of 1 to 30). According to H_o what we would expect for S_S (the sum of ranks for the smaller group) is midway between the best and worst cases. For this example the expected $\overline{S}_S$ is $(55 + 255)/2 = 310/2 = 155$. The general formula for the average sum of ranks for the smaller group is $\overline{S}_S = .5n_S (N + 1)$, where n_S is the size of the smaller group, and N is the size of both groups combined. For our example $S_S = .5 \cdot 10(31) = .5 \cdot 310 = 155$, just as we had found by averaging the best and worst cases. The difference between the actual S_S and the average S_S can be divided by the standard deviation of S_S to create a z score, as in the following formula:

$$z = \frac{S_S - .5(n_S)(N + 1)}{\sqrt{\dfrac{n_S n_L (N + 1)}{12}}} \tag{9.6}$$

where n_L is the size of the larger group (if the two subgroups are the same size, n, then $n_S = n_L = n$, and the sum of ranks for either group can be used as S_S).

Dealing with Ties

Sometimes it will be impossible to distinguish between two or more boys. If you are careful with your ranking such ties can be accounted for without changing the sum of the ranks. Suppose that the 10 DBs occupy the first 10 ranks (i.e., no NDB is more aggressive than any of the DBs), but the middle four are indistinguishable. The first step is to assign ranks to all 10 anyway, even though these ranks must be assigned arbitrarily to the middle four: 1, 2, 3, *4, 5, 6, 7,* 8, 9, 10 (the middle four have been italicized). The next step is to replace all of the italicized (i.e., tied) ranks by their average, which in this case is 5.5[i.e., $(4 + 5 + 6 + 7)/4 = 22/4$]. The ranks will be 1, 2, 3, 5.5, 5.5, 5.5, 5.5, 8, 9, 10; the sum of these ranks will be the same as the sum of the ranks numbered 1 to 10 without ties.

Suppose that DB and NDB boys alternate in the first 20 ranks, so that DB boys occupy all the odd ranks from 1 to 20, leaving the even ranks from 1 to 20 and all of the ranks from 21 to 30 to the NDBs. In that case, S_s will be 100, and the z score for testing this sum will be

$$z = \frac{100 - .5(10)(31)}{\sqrt{\dfrac{(10)(20)(31)}{12}}} = \frac{100 - 155}{\sqrt{\dfrac{6200}{12}}} = \frac{-55}{22.73} = -2.42$$

This z score is easily significant at the .05 level (the sign of the z score is not helpful—you have to look at your data to see if the ranking is going in the direction you predicted).

Assumptions of the Mann-Whitney Test

The use of the normal distribution for Formula 9.6 is reasonable when the total N is at least about 20. For smaller samples Mann and Whitney worked out exact probabilities (based on combinations and permutations of the possible rankings) for a statistic they called U (Mann & Whitney, 1947), which is based on S_s. This version of the test is called the Mann-Whitney U test. Wilcoxon (1949) created tables of critical values for S_s, so his name is associated with this test as well (a table for *Wilcoxon's rank-sum test* can be found in B. Cohen, 2000). When the normal approximation is used, as in Formula 9.6, the test is often referred to simply as the *Mann-Whitney* (M-W) test. Any version of this test assumes that the cases being ranked are independent (e.g., if five schizophrenic patients and five art students each produce *two* paintings for an experiment, the 20 paintings could be ranked together, but they would *not* all be mutually independent).

It is also assumed that the variable that forms the basis of the ranking (e.g., aggressiveness, creativity, charisma) is continuous; ties may occur due to a lack of precision in measurement, but not because two cases are exactly the same for that variable. A high percentage of ties will decrease the accuracy of the test. This is why it can be problematic to use a 5-point ordinal scale (e.g., very aggressive, somewhat aggressive, average, somewhat passive, very passive) to measure all of your participants; it is likely that there will be too many ties (see Siegel & Castellan, 1988, about how to correct for ties). Probably the most common use of the M-W test does not involve directly ranking participants, but rather taking data that were meant for a two-group t test and ranking them (this is very easy to do with interval/ratio data and not likely to involve many ties). Converting your data to ranks is recommended as an alternative to a data transformation when your data are extremely skewed, or otherwise nonnormal, and your groups are quite small.

Finally, the null hypothesis for the M-W test is not that the two groups have the same population means, but that the population distributions represented by the two groups are *identical*. Therefore, a significant M-W test could occur because the two population distributions differ in shape or spread, rather than mean. Because a finding that your two groups differ in any way is usually interesting, this lack of specificity is generally not considered a drawback of the M-W test. The other ordinal tests described below also test the null hypothesis that all population distributions involved are identical.

> ## CAUTION
>
> When ranking cases, some of which are tied, begin by giving preliminary ranks by numbering all cases consecutively, ignoring ties. Then average the ranks for a set of cases that are tied, and give the average rank to each of the tied cases in that set.

The Kruskal-Wallis Test

A test very similar to the M-W test can be used when you are ranking cases from three or more groups, or converting the data from a one-way ANOVA to ranks. The test begins with ranking all of the participants together and dealing with ties as in the M-W test. Kruskal and Wallis (1952) devised a statistic called H that is based on the sums of ranks for each group. Hence, the test is called the *Kruskal-Wallis H test,* or just the Kruskal-Wallis (K-W) test for short. The formula for H is as follows:

$$H = \frac{12}{N(N+1)} \sum_{i=1}^{k} \left(\frac{S_i^2}{n_i} \right) - 3(N+1), \tag{9.7}$$

where N is the total number of participants, n_i is the number of participants in the ith group, S_i is the sum of ranks for the ith group, and k is the number of different groups. When all of the subgroups contain at least five cases, H follows a χ^2 distribution quite well, with $k - 1$ degrees of freedom. For tables needed to perform an exact test when your samples are too small or for a formula that corrects for excessive ties, see Siegel and Castellan (1988).

As you might guess, the K-W test involves the same assumptions as the M-W test. In fact, if you apply H to a two-group case it will be equal to the square of the z score from the M-W test (we invite you to try this on our DB/NDB example). As in the case of the one-way ANOVA, it often makes sense to follow a significant K-W test with M-W (or K-W) tests for each pair of groups, with some adjustment to the alpha for each comparison if there are more than three groups. Finally, it is good to know that when data meant for a t test or one-way ANOVA are converted to ranks, the M-W and K-W tests usually have nearly as much power as their parametric counterparts, without the possible risk of an inflated Type I error rate if the distributional assumptions of the parametric tests are severely violated.

Wilcoxon's Test for Matched Pairs

One of the best ways to improve power is by employing repeated measures or matching, and such designs can certainly be analyzed with nonparametric methods. Earlier in this chapter we showed you how the sign test could be used for a matched design. However, in some cases an ordinal statistic can have considerably more power than the sign test and still avoid the distributional assumptions of the matched *t* test. Let's return to the example in which children were matched in pairs, after which one random member of each pair was given a creativity treatment, and then the paintings for each pair of children were compared. The sign test is appropriate if all you can determine is which of the two paintings is more creative. Suppose, however, that in addition to determining the direction (i.e., sign) of each creativity discrepancy you could compare the sizes of the discrepancies well enough to put them in order (perhaps with occasional ties). The next step would be to rank order all of the discrepancies (regardless of direction), handling ties as you would in the M-W test. For instance, the largest discrepancy would be ranked 1; let's say that its sign is positive because it favors the creative member of the pair (which direction is considered positive is an arbitrary decision and won't affect the outcome of the test). Imagine that the next two discrepancies are tied, and that one is positive and the other negative; both are given the rank of 2.5.

After all of the ranks have been assigned, the ranks are summed *separately* for the negative and positive differences (this is just like in the M-W test—you rank all the cases together but keep track of which group each case belongs to so ranks can be summed separately for each group). Whichever sum is smaller (negative or positive) is the *T* statistic for the *matched-pairs signed-ranks test,* often called *Wilcoxon's T test,* after the statistician who first created tables for this test. When you are dealing with at least 15 to 20 pairs of participants, *T* has a fairly normal distribution and can therefore be converted to a z score with the following formula:

$$z = \frac{T - .25N(N+1)}{\sqrt{\dfrac{N(N+1)(2N+1)}{24}}} \tag{9.8}$$

where N is the number of pairs (i.e., the number of discrepancies that are being ranked).

Dealing with Ties

If you are dealing with fewer than 15 pairs, many introductory statistics texts have tables for Wilcoxon's T that you can use to perform an exact test. If you have more than a few ties and therefore need a correction factor, see Spiegel and Castellan (1988). There is one kind of tie that is particularly problematic with this kind of test. If for a specific pair it is impossible to say which painting is more creative, that pair must be given a zero. If there is just one zero, that pair should be eliminated from the analysis. If there are several zeroes they can all be eliminated—as is usually recommended for the sign test—but for the Wilcoxon T test a more conservative solution is recommended. If there is an odd number of zeroes, delete one of them. Half of an even number of zeroes should be arbitrarily assigned to be positive and the other half negative, and all should be included in the ranking (of course, all of the zeroes will be tied with each other).

Comparisons to Other Tests

Ranking discrepancies that can't be quantified precisely is difficult, which probably accounts for why Wilcoxon's T is rarely used in that way. The more common use for this test is as an alternative to the matched t test. Suppose each participant solves two similar puzzles under different conditions, and solution times differ wildly (sometimes the participant gets it right away, sometimes not). If there are only 10 participants, the matched t test may not be appropriate. However, there is no need to throw away quantitative information and merely determine which condition had the shorter time. The differences between the conditions can be rank-ordered easily (ties are unlikely) and the sum of ranks found for each direction (i.e., condition 1 has the longer time, or condition 2 has the longer time). Wilcoxon's T test can then be applied (an exact table is suggested for this example because $N = 10$). The Wilcoxon test will usually have as much as 90% of the power of the matched t test; the sign test will have considerably less power.

The Friedman Test

What if each participant solves three problems, each under a different condition? If the data are not appropriate

CAUTION

An assumption of ordinal tests is that the variable being measured ordinally is actually continuous, so that ties should be rare. Although there are correction factors for ordinal tests when ties do occur, a large percentage of ties will diminish the accuracy of the p values associated with those tests.

for a one-way RM test, they can be converted to ranks and submitted to a simple nonparametric test. The test we will describe is called the *Friedman test,* having been invented by Milton Friedman, who later won the Nobel Prize for economics. The key element is that scores are not ranked among participants, but rather separately for each participant across conditions. For instance, suppose that participants solve a puzzle with a reward for quick solution, or with no reward and distracting noise, or both a reward and distraction. For each participant the three conditions are ranked in order of solution time. Then these ranks are summed across participants for each condition. If participants are consistent with each other (which would lead to a small interaction in an RM ANOVA), the sum of ranks should be considerably lower for some conditions (e.g., "distraction" gets mostly ones and a few twos—assuming the longest time gets ranked "1") and higher for others (e.g., "reward" gets mostly threes and a few twos). The more the sums differ for the different conditions, the larger will be Friedman's test statistic, which we call F_r. The formula for F_r is as follows:

$$F_r = \frac{12}{Nc(c+1)} \sum_{i=1}^{c} S_i^2 - 3N(c+1), \qquad (9.9)$$

where N is the number of different participants or blocks (not the total number of observations), c is the number of conditions (3 in our example), and S_i is the sum of ranks for the ith condition (add up the squared sums, multiply by the factor in front of the summation sign, and then subtract the factor beginning with $3N$). If N is at least about 8, F_r will follow the chi-square distribution fairly well, with degrees of freedom equal to $c - 1$. For smaller samples, you can use a table to perform an exact test (see Spiegel & Castellan, 1988).

The Friedman test is often thought of as an expansion of Wilcoxon's matched-pairs test, but if you were to try to perform a Friedman test with just two conditions, you would see that in that case, the Friedman test is equivalent to the sign test (without the continuity correction, the square of the z score for the sign test will equal F_r). Ranking two conditions as "1" and "2" for each participant is no more (or less) precise than assigning a plus or minus to each participant according to which condition the participant is better on. Therefore, a significant Friedman test with more than two conditions can be followed by Friedman or sign tests for each pair, adjusting alpha if there are more than three conditions.

The Spearman Correlation Coefficient

We described the use of Cohen's κ to quantify the amount of agreement between two judges who are assigning cases to categories. But what about the psychologist who was ranking boys for aggressiveness? How can we quantify his or her agreement with a second psychologist ranking the same set of boys? Actually, this is easy. We need only calculate the ordinary Pearson correlation coefficient for the two sets of ranks. When the two variables consist of ordinal data, the correlation coefficient that results from applying Pearson's formula is often called the *Spearman correlation* (r_S) or the *rank correlation coefficient*. As with the point-biserial r (r_{pb}) and the phi coefficient (ϕ), the special symbol, r_S, reminds us that although this is a Pearson correlation coefficient, it is calculated for data involving at least one variable that was not measured on an interval or ratio scale. Although there is a shortcut formula for calculating r_S, based on the differences of ranks, the use of modern calculators and statistical tables make this shortcut less important, so we will not bother to present it here.

When to Use Ranks for Correlation

The Spearman correlation is appropriate whenever both variables consist of ranks (e.g., boys are ranked for aggressiveness and for leadership potential), or even when just one of the variables is ordinal (e.g., you want to correlate aggressiveness rank with grade average). In the latter case, you would convert the interval/ratio data (e.g., grade averages) to ranks before finding the correlation. Even when both variables are measured on interval/ratio scales, it can be preferable to rank order both variables and find r_S, rather than calculating r directly. For instance, a few extreme outliers can have a devastating effect on r, but their impact can be reduced by converting the data to ranks. When you do this, the highest score on one variable can be very far from the next highest, but in terms of ranking it is just one rank higher.

Also, recall that Pearson's r measures only the degree of *linear* relationship. If the relationship between two variables follows a curve, even a curve that keeps rising, Pearson's r can be deceptively low. A curvilinear correlation coefficient can be calculated if that is what you are interested in, or the data can be transformed to create a fairly linear relationship. However, ranking the scores may lead to the answer you want. The correlation of the ranks will give the relationship credit for being *monotonic* (whenever X goes up, Y goes up, and vice versa), even if it's far from linear. In fact, if the relationship is perfectly monotonic, r_S will equal 1.0. Therefore, if it is the degree of monotonicity rather than the linearity of the relationship that you wish to measure, r_S will serve you better than Pearson's r.

Determining Statistical Significance for Spearman's r

Although r_S can be found by applying the ordinary Pearson correlation formula to ranked data, the distribution of r_S is not the same as the distribution of r that is calculated for interval/ratio data, unless the sample size is extremely large (the-

Rapid Reference 9.2

Parametric and Corresponding Ordinal Tests

Parametric Test	Corresponding Ordinal Test
Independent-groups t test	Mann-Whitney test
RM or matched t test	Wilcoxon T (signed-ranks) test
Independent-groups ANOVA	Kruskal-Wallis (H) test
RM or randomized-blocks ANOVA	Friedman test
Pearson correlation	Spearman (rank) correlation

oretically, infinite). You cannot use the *t* value from Formula 4.4 (or 4.4'). Special tables or approximating formulas must be used to determine the significance of Spearman's *r* for small sample sizes (see Siegel & Castellan, 1988). In general, it is easier to obtain a high correlation with ranks than it is with interval/ratio data, so the critical values for r_s are higher than the corresponding critical values for *r*. Perfect Spearman correlation requires only that ordinal positions match across two variables, but perfect Pearson correlation requires, in addition, that the variables have a perfect *linear* relationship (see Rapid References 9.2).

Putting It Into Practice

1. The data below come from the second exercise in Chapter 3, in which you were asked to calculate an RM *t* test.

Participant #	No Imagery	Imagery
1	8	14
2	11	15
3	7	5
4	10	16
5	9	9
6	15	16
7	7	8
8	16	20

(a) Perform the sign test using the exact probabilities of the binomial distribution (follow the example in which 8 of 10 babies prefer red). Is the probability less than .05 for a one-tailed test? For a two-tailed test? Compare your results to the RM t test you calculated in Chapter 3. Which test seems to have more power given that these data are not inconsistent with the assumptions of the RM t test?

(b) Perform the sign test using the normal approximation and the correction for continuity (even though N is too small for a good approximation in this case). Is the test significant at the .05 level, one-tailed? Two-tailed?

(c) Perform the Wilcoxon test using the normal approximation (even though N is too small for a good approximation in this case). Is the test significant at the .05 level, one-tailed? Two-tailed?

(d) Calculate the Spearman correlation for the data above. Does the magnitude of the correlation suggest good matching between the two sets of scores?

2 One hundred low self-esteem students participated in an experiment, in which the independent variable was whether the person running the experiment appeared to be rude, needy, friendly, or just normal (i.e., neutral). Each student was asked to return for a follow-up experiment "to help the research," without additional compensation. The number of students who agreed or didn't agree to return in each condition are shown in the table below.

	Rude	Needy	Friendly	Neutral
Agree to return	18	16	10	16
Do not agree	7	9	15	9

(a) Perform separate one-way chi-square tests for the students who agreed to return and for those who did not. Did the type of experimenter make a significant difference in each case?

(b) Perform a two-way chi-square test to determine whether type of experimenter affects the proportion of students who agree to return. Are the results significant at the .05 level? What would the chi-square statistic equal if every entry in the above table were doubled? Would the results be significant in that case?

(c) Perform a 2 × 2 chi-square test deleting the "needy" and "neutral" conditions. Are the results significant? Calculate the phi coefficient. Does the association between the two variables appear to be small, medium, or large?

3. Boys are classified as having experienced parental divorce (DB) or not (NDB). The number of fights initiated by each boy during school recess is recorded for a period of 3 months. The data are as follows: DB: 3, 5, 0, 9, 1, 7, 4; NDB: 0, 2, 1, 0, 2, 0, 3, 1, 0.

(a) Perform the Mann-Whitney test for these data, using the normal approximation. Are the results significant with a .05, two-tailed test?

(b) Perform the Kruskal-Wallis test on these data. Explain the relation between H and the z you found in 3a.

4. Perform Friedman tests on the two RM simple effects referred to in the first exercise of the previous chapter. Did you reach the same statistical conclusion in each case as in the previous exercise?

🖋 TEST YOURSELF 🖋

1. **A series of dichotomous events will follow the binomial distribution only if**

    (a) the events are normally distributed.

    (b) the two outcomes are equally likely.

    (c) the number of events is large.

    (d) the events are independent of each other.

2. **Compared to the matched t test, a sign test on the same data**

    (a) usually has less power.

    (b) usually leads to more Type I errors.

    (c) requires more stringent assumptions.

    (d) is easier to calculate, but always leads to the same statistical decision.

3. **A friend of yours is at a carnival and betting on a wheel that stops in 1 of 10 places, numbered 1 to 10. Imagine that your friend will lose if the number comes up either odd or higher than 8 on the next spin. What is your friend's probability of winning?**

    (a) .2

    (b) .4

    (c) .5

    (d) .6

4. **The critical value of the chi-square statistic for a one-way test increases as**

    (a) the number of categories increases.

    (b) N increases.

    (c) alpha increases.

    (d) all of the above.

5. **Suppose you have read about a one-way chi-square test with four categories, in which the chi-square statistic turned out to be .03. Without further information, which of the following could you conclude?**

    (a) A calculation error has been made.

    (b) N must have been small.

    (c) The null hypothesis could be rejected at the .05 level.

    (d) The observed frequencies are similar to the expected frequencies.

6. **In a two-way chi-square test of independence involving 96 participants classified into six religious categories and four political preferences, how many degrees of freedom will be associated with the test?**

   (a) 4

   (b) 15

   (c) 18

   (d) 24

7. **To perform the Mann-Whitney test,**

   (a) the scores are ranked separately for each group.

   (b) the scores are combined into one large group before ranking.

   (c) the two groups must be the same size.

   (d) the ranks for one group are added to the ranks for the other group.

8. **To perform the Wilcoxon signed-rank test you must first**

   (a) rank-order the difference scores separately for positive and negative differences.

   (b) rank-order the difference scores while ignoring their signs.

   (c) rank-order the scores before finding the differences.

   (d) delete any nonzero difference scores that are tied.

9. **The size of the Kruskal-Wallis test statistic, H, increases as the sums of ranks for each group**

   (a) increase.

   (b) decrease.

   (c) become more alike.

   (d) become more different.

10. **Suppose that 10 participants are each measured under four conditions. Before you apply the formula for the Friedman test,**

    (a) all 40 scores are ranked together.

    (b) the 10 scores in each condition are ranked separately.

    (c) the four scores for each participant are ranked separately.

    (d) the ranks are summed separately for each participant.

Answers: 1. d; 2. a; 3. b; 4. a; 5. d; 6. b; 7. b; 8. b; 9. d; 10. c.

Appendix A

Statistical Tables

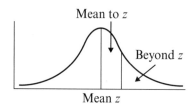

Mean to z

Beyond z

Mean z

Table A.1 Areas under the Standard Normal Distribution

z	Mean to z	Beyond z	z	Mean to z	Beyond z
.00	.0000	.5000	.22	.0871	.4129
.01	.0040	.4960	.23	.0910	.4090
.02	.0080	.4920	.24	.0948	.4052
.03	.0120	.4880	.25	.0987	.4013
.04	.0160	.4840	.26	.1026	.3974
.05	.0199	.4801	.27	.1064	.3936
.06	.0239	.4761	.28	.1103	.3897
.07	.0279	.4721	.29	.1141	.3859
.08	.0319	.4681	.30	.1179	.3821
.09	.0359	.4641	.31	.1217	.3783
.10	.0398	.4602	.32	.1255	.3745
.11	.0438	.4562	.33	.1293	.3707
.12	.0478	.4522	.34	.1331	.3669
.13	.0517	.4483	.35	.1368	.3632
.14	.0557	.4443	.36	.1406	.3594
.15	.0596	.4404	.37	.1443	.3557
.16	.0636	.4364	.38	.1480	.3520
.17	.0675	.4325	.39	.1517	.3483
.18	.0714	.4286	.40	.1554	.3446
.19	.0753	.4247	.41	.1591	.3409
.20	.0793	.4207	.42	.1628	.3372
.21	.0832	.4168	.43	.1664	.3336

Table A.1 Continued

z	Mean to z	Beyond z	z	Mean to z	Beyond z
.44	.1700	.3300	.79	.2852	.2148
.45	.1736	.3264	.80	.2881	.2119
.46	.1772	.3228	.81	.2910	.2090
.47	.1808	.3192	.82	.2939	.2061
.48	.1844	.3156	.83	.2967	.2033
.49	.1879	.3121	.84	.2995	.2005
.50	.1915	.3085	.85	.3023	.1977
.51	.1950	.3050	.86	.3051	.1949
.52	.1985	.3015	.87	.3078	.1922
.53	.2019	.2981	.88	.3106	.1894
.54	.2054	.2946	.89	.3133	.1867
.55	.2088	.2912	.90	.3159	.1841
.56	.2123	.2877	.91	.3186	.1814
.57	.2157	.2843	.92	.3212	.1788
.58	.2190	.2810	.93	.3238	.1762
.59	.2224	.2776	.94	.3264	.1736
.60	.2257	.2743	.95	.3289	.1711
.61	.2291	.2709	.96	.3315	.1685
.62	.2324	.2676	.97	.3340	.1660
.63	.2357	.2643	.98	.3365	.1635
.64	.2389	.2611	.99	.3389	.1611
.65	.2422	.2578	1.00	.3413	.1587
.66	.2454	.2546	1.01	.3438	.1562
.67	.2486	.2514	1.02	.3461	.1539
.68	.2517	.2483	1.03	.3485	.1515
.69	.2549	.2451	1.04	.3508	.1492
.70	.2580	.2420	1.05	.3531	.1469
.71	.2611	.2389	1.06	.3554	.1446
.72	.2642	.2358	1.07	.3577	.1423
.73	.2673	.2327	1.08	.3599	.1401
.74	.2704	.2296	1.09	.3621	.1379
.75	.2734	.2266	1.10	.3643	.1357
.76	.2764	.2236	1.11	.3665	.1335
.77	.2794	.2206	1.12	.3686	.1314
.78	.2823	.2177	1.13	.3708	.1292

(continued)

Table A.1 Continued

z	Mean to z	Beyond z	z	Mean to z	Beyond z
1.14	.3729	.1271	1.50	.4332	.0668
1.15	.3749	.1251	1.51	.4345	.0655
1.16	.3770	.1230	1.52	.4357	.0643
1.17	.3790	.1210	1.53	.4370	.0630
1.18	.3810	.1190	1.54	.4382	.0618
1.19	.3830	.1170	1.55	.4394	.0606
1.20	.3849	.1151	1.56	.4406	.0594
1.21	.3869	.1131	1.57	.4418	.0582
1.22	.3888	.1112	1.58	.4429	.0571
1.23	.3907	.1093	1.59	.4441	.0559
1.24	.3925	.1075	1.60	.4452	.0548
1.25	.3944	.1056	1.61	.4463	.0537
1.26	.3962	.1038	1.62	.4474	.0526
1.27	.3980	.1020	1.63	.4484	.0516
1.28	.3997	.1003	1.64	.4495	.0505
1.29	.4015	.0985	1.65	.4505	.0495
1.30	.4032	.0968	1.66	.4515	.0485
1.31	.4049	.0951	1.67	.4525	.0475
1.32	.4066	.0934	1.68	.4535	.0465
1.33	.4082	.0918	1.69	.4545	.0455
1.34	.4099	.0901	1.70	.4554	.0446
1.35	.4115	.0885	1.71	.4564	.0436
1.36	.4131	.0869	1.72	.4573	.0427
1.37	.4147	.0853	1.73	.4582	.0418
1.38	.4162	.0838	1.74	.4591	.0409
1.39	.4177	.0823	1.75	.4599	.0401
1.40	.4192	.0808	1.76	.4608	.0392
1.41	.4207	.0793	1.77	.4616	.0384
1.42	.4222	.0778	1.78	.4625	.0375
1.43	.4236	.0764	1.79	.4633	.0367
1.44	.4251	.0749	1.80	.4641	.0359
1.45	.4265	.0735	1.81	.4649	.0351
1.46	.4279	.0721	1.82	.4656	.0344
1.47	.4292	.0708	1.83	.4664	.0336
1.48	.4306	.0694	1.84	.4671	.0329
1.49	.4319	.0681	1.85	.4678	.0322

Table A.1   Continued

z	Mean to z	Beyond z	z	Mean to z	Beyond z
1.86	.4686	.0314	2.22	.4868	.0132
1.87	.4693	.0307	2.23	.4871	.0129
1.88	.4699	.0301	2.24	.4875	.0125
1.89	.4706	.0294	2.25	.4878	.0122
1.90	.4713	.0287	2.26	.4881	.0119
1.91	.4719	.0281	2.27	.4884	.0116
1.92	.4726	.0274	2.28	.4887	.0113
1.93	.4732	.0268	2.29	.4890	.0110
1.94	.4738	.0262	2.30	.4893	.0107
1.95	.4744	.0256	2.31	.4896	.0104
1.96	.4750	.0250	2.32	.4898	.0102
1.97	.4756	.0244	2.33	.4901	.0099
1.98	.4761	.0239	2.34	.4904	.0096
1.99	.4767	.0233	2.35	.4906	.0094
2.00	.4772	.0228	2.36	.4909	.0091
2.01	.4778	.0222	2.37	.4911	.0089
2.02	.4783	.0217	2.38	.4913	.0087
2.03	.4788	.0212	2.39	.4916	.0084
2.04	.4793	.0207	2.40	.4918	.0082
2.05	.4798	.0202	2.41	.4920	.0080
2.06	.4803	.0197	2.42	.4922	.0078
2.07	.4808	.0192	2.43	.4925	.0075
2.08	.4812	.0188	2.44	.4927	.0073
2.09	.4817	.0183	2.45	.4929	.0071
2.10	.4821	.0179	2.46	.4931	.0069
2.11	.4826	.0174	2.47	.4932	.0068
2.12	.4830	.0170	2.48	.4934	.0066
2.13	.4834	.0166	2.49	.4936	.0064
2.14	.4838	.0162	2.50	.4938	.0062
2.15	.4842	.0158	2.51	.4940	.0060
2.16	.4846	.0154	2.52	.4941	.0059
2.17	.4850	.0150	2.53	.4943	.0057
2.18	.4854	.0146	2.54	.4945	.0055
2.19	.4857	.0143	2.55	.4946	.0054
2.20	.4861	.0139	2.56	.4948	.0052
2.21	.4864	.0136	2.57	.4949	.0051

(continued)

Table A.1 **Continued**

z	Mean to z	Beyond z	z	Mean to z	Beyond z
2.58	.4951	.0049	2.83	.4977	.0023
2.59	.4952	.0048	2.84	.4977	.0023
2.60	.4953	.0047	2.85	.4978	.0022
2.61	.4955	.0045	2.86	.4979	.0021
2.62	.4956	.0044	2.87	.4979	.0021
2.63	.4957	.0043	2.88	.4980	.0020
2.64	.4959	.0041	2.89	.4981	.0019
2.65	.4960	.0040	2.90	.4981	.0019
2.66	.4961	.0039	2.91	.4982	.0018
2.67	.4962	.0038	2.92	.4982	.0018
2.68	.4963	.0037	2.93	.4983	.0017
2.69	.4964	.0036	2.94	.4984	.0016
2.70	.4965	.0035	2.95	.4984	.0016
2.71	.4966	.0034	2.96	.4985	.0015
2.72	.4967	.0033	2.97	.4985	.0015
2.73	.4968	.0032	2.98	.4986	.0014
2.74	.4969	.0031	2.99	.4986	.0014
2.75	.4970	.0030	3.00	.4987	.0013
2.76	.4971	.0029	3.20	.4993	.0007
2.77	.4972	.0028	3.40	.4997	.0003
2.78	.4973	.0027			
2.79	.4974	.0026	3.60	.4998	.0002
2.80	.4974	.0026			
2.81	.4975	.0025	3.80	.4999	.0001
2.82	.4976	.0024	4.00	.49997	.00003

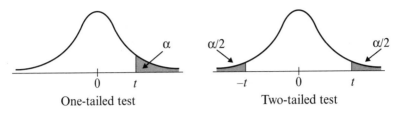

One-tailed test   Two-tailed test

Table A.2 Critical Values of the t Distribution

	Level of Significance for One-Tailed Test					
	.10	.05	.025	.01	.005	.0005
	Level of Significance for Two-Tailed Test					
df	.20	.10	.05	.02	.01	.001
1	3.078	6.314	12.706	31.821	63.657	636.620
2	1.886	2.920	4.303	6.965	9.925	31.599
3	1.638	2.353	3.182	4.541	5.841	12.924
4	1.533	2.132	2.776	3.747	4.604	8.610
5	1.476	2.015	2.571	3.365	4.032	6.869
6	1.440	1.943	2.447	3.143	3.707	5.959
7	1.415	1.895	2.365	2.998	3.499	5.408
8	1.397	1.860	2.306	2.896	3.355	5.041
9	1.383	1.833	2.262	2.821	3.250	4.781
10	1.372	1.812	2.228	2.764	3.169	4.587
11	1.363	1.796	2.201	2.718	3.106	4.437
12	1.356	1.782	2.179	2.681	3.055	4.318
13	1.350	1.771	2.160	2.650	3.012	4.221
14	1.345	1.761	2.145	2.624	2.977	4.140
15	1.341	1.753	2.131	2.602	2.947	4.073
16	1.337	1.746	2.120	2.583	2.921	4.015
17	1.333	1.740	2.110	2.567	2.898	3.965
18	1.330	1.734	2.101	2.552	2.878	3.922
19	1.328	1.729	2.093	2.539	2.861	3.883
20	1.325	1.725	2.086	2.528	2.845	3.850
21	1.323	1.721	2.080	2.518	2.831	3.819
22	1.321	1.717	2.074	2.508	2.819	3.792
23	1.319	1.714	2.069	2.500	2.807	3.768
24	1.318	1.711	2.064	2.492	2.797	3.745
25	1.316	1.708	2.060	2.485	2.787	3.725
26	1.315	1.706	2.056	2.479	2.779	3.707
27	1.314	1.703	2.052	2.473	2.771	3.690

(continued)

Table A.2 Continued

df	Level of Significance for One-Tailed Test					
	.10	.05	.025	.01	.005	.0005
	Level of Significance for Two-Tailed Test					
	.20	.10	.05	.02	.01	.001
28	1.313	1.701	2.048	2.467	2.753	3.674
29	1.311	1.699	2.045	2.462	2.756	3.659
30	1.310	1.697	2.042	2.457	2.750	3.646
40	1.303	1.684	2.021	2.423	2.704	3.551
60	1.296	1.671	2.000	2.390	2.660	3.460
120	1.289	1.658	1.980	2.358	2.617	3.373
∞	1.282	1.645	1.960	2.326	2.576	3.291

Table A.3 Critical Values of the F Distribution for $\alpha = .05$

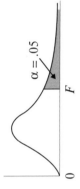

$\alpha = .05$

df Numerator

df Denominator	1	2	3	4	5	6	7	8	9	10	12	15	20	25	30	40	60	120	∞
3	10.13	9.55	9.28	9.12	9.01	8.94	8.89	8.85	8.81	8.79	8.74	8.70	8.66	8.63	8.62	8.59	8.57	8.55	8.53
4	7.71	6.94	6.59	6.39	6.26	6.16	6.09	6.04	6.00	5.96	5.91	5.86	5.80	5.77	5.75	5.72	5.69	5.66	5.63
5	6.61	5.79	5.41	5.19	5.05	4.95	4.88	4.82	4.77	4.74	4.68	4.62	4.56	4.52	4.50	4.46	4.43	4.40	4.36
6	5.99	5.14	4.76	4.53	4.39	4.28	4.21	4.15	4.10	4.06	4.00	3.94	3.87	3.83	3.81	3.77	3.74	3.70	3.67
7	5.59	4.74	4.35	4.12	3.97	3.87	3.79	3.73	3.68	3.64	3.57	3.51	3.44	3.40	3.38	3.34	3.30	3.27	3.23
8	5.32	4.46	4.07	3.84	3.69	3.58	3.50	3.44	3.39	3.35	3.28	3.22	3.15	3.11	3.08	3.04	3.01	2.97	2.93
9	5.12	4.26	3.86	3.63	3.48	3.37	3.29	3.23	3.18	3.14	3.07	3.01	2.94	2.89	2.86	2.83	2.79	2.75	2.71
10	4.96	4.10	3.71	3.48	3.33	3.22	3.14	3.07	3.02	2.98	2.91	2.85	2.77	2.73	2.70	2.66	2.62	2.58	2.54
11	4.84	3.98	3.59	3.36	3.20	3.09	3.01	2.95	2.90	2.85	2.79	2.72	2.65	2.60	2.57	2.53	2.49	2.45	2.40
12	4.75	3.89	3.49	3.26	3.11	3.00	2.91	2.85	2.80	2.75	2.69	2.62	2.54	2.50	2.47	2.43	2.38	2.34	2.30
13	4.67	3.81	3.41	3.18	3.03	2.92	2.83	2.77	2.71	2.67	2.60	2.53	2.46	2.41	2.38	2.34	2.30	2.25	2.21
14	4.60	3.74	3.34	3.11	2.96	2.85	2.76	2.70	2.65	2.60	2.53	2.46	2.39	2.34	2.31	2.27	2.22	2.18	2.13
15	4.54	3.68	3.29	3.06	2.90	2.79	2.71	2.64	2.59	2.54	2.48	2.40	2.33	2.28	2.25	2.20	2.16	2.11	2.07
16	4.49	3.63	3.24	3.01	2.85	2.74	2.66	2.59	2.54	2.49	2.42	2.35	2.28	2.23	2.19	2.15	2.11	2.06	2.01

(continued)

Table A.3 Continued

										df Numerator									
df Denominator	1	2	3	4	5	6	7	8	9	10	12	15	20	25	30	40	60	120	∞
17	4.45	3.59	3.20	2.96	2.81	2.70	2.61	2.55	2.49	2.45	2.38	2.31	2.23	2.18	2.15	2.10	2.06	2.01	1.96
18	4.41	3.55	3.16	2.93	2.77	2.66	2.58	2.51	2.46	2.41	2.34	2.27	2.19	2.14	2.11	2.06	2.02	1.97	1.92
19	4.38	3.52	3.13	2.90	2.74	2.63	2.54	2.48	2.42	2.38	2.31	2.23	2.16	2.11	2.07	2.03	1.98	1.93	1.88
20	4.35	3.49	3.10	2.87	2.71	2.60	2.51	2.45	2.39	2.35	2.28	2.20	2.12	2.07	2.04	1.99	1.95	1.90	1.84
21	4.32	3.47	3.07	2.84	2.68	2.57	2.49	2.42	2.37	2.32	2.25	2.18	2.10	2.04	2.01	1.96	1.92	1.87	1.31
22	4.30	3.44	3.05	2.82	2.66	2.55	2.46	2.40	2.34	2.30	2.23	2.15	2.07	2.02	1.98	1.94	1.89	1.84	1.78
23	4.28	3.42	3.03	2.80	2.64	2.53	2.44	2.37	2.32	2.27	2.20	2.13	2.05	2.00	1.96	1.91	1.86	1.81	1.76
24	4.26	3.40	3.01	2.78	2.62	2.51	2.42	2.36	2.30	2.25	2.18	2.11	2.03	1.97	1.94	1.89	1.84	1.79	1.73
25	4.24	3.39	2.99	2.76	2.60	2.49	2.40	2.34	2.28	2.24	2.16	2.09	2.01	1.95	1.92	1.87	1.82	1.77	1.71
26	4.23	3.37	2.98	2.74	2.59	2.47	2.39	2.32	2.27	2.22	2.15	2.07	1.99	1.94	1.90	1.85	1.80	1.75	1.69
27	4.21	3.35	2.96	2.73	2.57	2.46	2.37	2.31	2.25	2.20	2.13	2.06	1.97	1.92	1.88	1.84	1.79	1.73	1.67
28	4.20	3.34	2.95	2.71	2.56	2.45	2.36	2.29	2.24	2.19	2.12	2.04	1.96	1.91	1.87	1.82	1.77	1.71	1.65
29	4.18	3.33	2.93	2.70	2.55	2.43	2.35	2.28	2.22	2.18	2.10	2.03	1.94	1.90	1.85	1.81	1.75	1.70	1.64
30	4.17	3.32	2.92	2.69	2.53	2.42	2.33	2.27	2.21	2.16	2.09	2.01	1.93	1.88	1.84	1.79	1.74	1.68	1.62
40	4.08	3.23	2.84	2.61	2.45	2.34	2.25	2.18	2.12	2.08	2.00	1.92	1.84	1.78	1.74	1.69	1.64	1.58	1.51
60	4.00	3.15	2.76	2.53	2.37	2.25	2.17	2.10	2.04	1.99	1.92	1.84	1.75	1.69	1.65	1.59	1.53	1.47	1.39
120	3.92	3.07	2.68	2.45	2.29	2.17	2.09	2.02	1.96	1.91	1.83	1.75	1.66	1.60	1.55	1.50	1.43	1.35	1.25
∞	3.84	3.00	2.60	2.37	2.21	2.10	2.01	1.94	1.88	1.83	1.75	1.67	1.57	1.51	1.46	1.39	1.32	1.22	1.00

Table A.4 Critical Values of the Studentized Range Statistic (q) for α = .05

df for Error Term	Number of Groups (or number of steps between ordered means)																		
	2	3	4	5	6	7	8	9	10	11	12	13	14	15	16	17	18	19	20
1	17.97	26.98	32.82	37.08	40.41	43.12	45.40	47.36	49.07	50.59	51.96	53.20	54.33	55.36	56.32	57.22	58.04	58.83	59.56
2	6.08	8.33	9.80	10.88	11.74	12.44	13.03	13.54	13.99	14.39	14.75	15.08	15.38	15.65	15.91	16.14	16.37	16.57	16.77
3	4.50	5.91	6.82	7.50	8.04	8.48	8.85	9.18	9.46	9.72	9.95	10.15	10.35	10.52	10.69	10.84	10.98	11.11	11.24
4	3.93	5.04	5.76	6.29	6.71	7.05	7.35	7.60	7.83	8.03	8.21	8.37	8.52	8.66	8.79	8.91	9.03	9.13	9.23
5	3.64	4.60	5.22	5.67	6.03	6.33	6.58	6.80	6.99	7.17	7.32	7.47	7.60	7.72	7.83	7.93	8.03	8.12	8.21
6	3.46	4.34	4.90	5.30	5.63	5.90	6.12	6.32	6.49	6.65	6.79	6.92	7.03	7.14	7.24	7.34	7.43	7.51	7.59
7	3.34	4.16	4.68	5.06	5.36	5.61	5.82	6.00	6.16	6.30	6.43	6.55	6.66	6.76	6.85	6.94	7.02	7.10	7.17
8	3.26	4.04	4.53	4.89	5.17	5.40	5.60	5.77	5.92	6.05	6.18	6.29	6.39	6.48	6.57	6.65	6.73	6.80	6.87
9	3.20	3.95	4.41	4.76	5.02	5.24	5.43	5.59	5.74	5.87	5.98	6.09	6.19	6.28	6.36	6.44	6.51	6.58	6.64
10	3.15	3.88	4.33	4.65	4.91	5.12	5.30	5.46	5.60	5.72	5.83	5.93	6.03	6.11	6.19	6.27	6.34	6.40	6.47
11	3.11	3.82	4.26	4.57	4.82	5.03	5.20	5.35	5.49	5.61	5.71	5.81	5.90	5.98	6.06	6.13	6.20	6.27	6.33

(continued)

Table A.4 Continued

df for Error Term	Number of Groups (or number of steps between ordered means)																		
	2	3	4	5	6	7	8	9	10	11	12	13	14	15	16	17	18	19	20
12	3.08	3.77	4.20	4.51	4.75	4.95	5.12	5.27	5.39	5.51	5.61	5.71	5.80	5.88	5.95	6.02	6.09	6.15	6.21
13	3.06	3.73	4.15	4.45	4.69	4.88	5.05	5.19	5.32	5.43	5.53	5.63	5.71	5.79	5.86	5.93	5.99	6.05	6.11
14	3.03	3.70	4.11	4.41	4.64	4.83	4.99	5.13	5.25	5.36	5.46	5.55	5.64	5.71	5.79	5.85	5.91	5.97	6.03
15	3.01	3.67	4.08	4.37	4.59	4.78	4.94	5.08	5.20	5.31	5.40	5.49	5.57	5.65	5.72	5.78	5.85	5.90	5.96
16	3.00	3.65	4.05	4.33	4.56	4.74	4.90	5.03	5.15	5.26	5.35	5.44	5.52	5.59	5.66	5.73	5.79	5.84	5.90
17	2.98	3.63	4.02	4.30	4.52	4.70	4.86	4.99	5.11	5.21	5.31	5.39	5.47	5.54	5.61	5.67	5.73	5.79	5.84
18	2.97	3.61	4.00	4.28	4.49	4.67	4.82	4.96	5.07	5.17	5.27	5.35	5.43	5.50	5.57	5.63	5.69	5.74	5.79
19	2.96	3.59	3.98	4.25	4.47	4.65	4.79	4.92	5.04	5.14	5.23	5.31	5.39	5.46	5.53	5.59	5.65	5.70	5.75
20	2.95	3.58	3.96	4.23	4.45	4.62	4.77	4.90	5.01	5.11	5.20	5.28	5.36	5.43	5.49	5.55	5.61	5.66	5.71
24	2.92	3.53	3.90	4.17	4.37	4.54	4.68	4.81	4.92	5.01	5.10	5.18	5.25	5.32	5.38	5.44	5.49	5.55	5.59
30	2.89	3.49	3.85	4.10	4.30	4.46	4.60	4.72	4.82	4.92	5.00	5.08	5.15	5.21	5.27	5.33	5.38	5.43	5.47
40	2.86	3.44	3.79	4.04	4.23	4.39	4.52	4.63	4.73	4.82	4.90	4.98	5.04	5.11	5.16	5.22	5.27	5.31	5.36
60	2.83	3.40	3.74	3.98	4.16	4.31	4.44	4.55	4.65	4.73	4.81	4.88	4.94	5.00	5.06	5.11	5.15	5.20	5.24
120	2.80	3.36	3.68	3.92	4.10	4.24	4.36	4.47	4.56	4.64	4.71	4.78	4.84	4.90	4.95	5.00	5.04	5.09	5.13
∞	2.77	3.31	3.63	3.86	4.03	4.17	4.29	4.39	4.47	4.55	4.62	4.68	4.74	4.80	4.85	4.89	4.93	4.97	5.01

Source: Adapted from Pearson & Hartley, Biometrika Tables for Statisticians 1966, Vol. I, third edition, Table 29, by permission of the Biometrika Trustees.

Table A.5 Power as a Function of δ and Significance Criterion (α)

δ	One-Tailed Test (α)			
	.05	.025	.01	.005
	Two-Tailed Test (α)			
	.10	.05	.02	.01
0.5	.14	.08	.03	.02
0.6	.16	.09	.04	.02
0.7	.18	.11	.05	.03
0.8	.21	.13	.06	.04
0.9	.23	.15	.08	.05
1.0	.26	.17	.09	.06
1.1	.29	.20	.11	.07
1.2	.33	.22	.13	.08
1.3	.37	.26	.15	.10
1.4	.40	.29	.18	.12
1.5	.44	.32	.20	.14
1.6	.48	.36	.23	.16
1.7	.52	.40	.27	.19
1.8	.56	.44	.30	.22
1.9	.60	.48	.33	.25
2.0	.64	.52	.37	.28
2.1	.68	.56	.41	.32
2.2	.71	.60	.45	.35
2.3	.74	.63	.49	.39
2.4	.77	.67	.53	.43
2.5	.80	.71	.57	.47
2.6	.83	.74	.61	.51
2.7	.85	.77	.65	.55
2.8	.88	.80	.68	.59
2.9	.90	.83	.72	.63
3.0	.91	.85	.75	.66
3.1	.93	.87	.78	.70
3.2	.94	.89	.81	.73
3.3	.95	.91	.84	.77
3.4	.96	.93	.86	.80

(continued)

Table A.5 Continued

	One-Tailed Test (α)			
	.05	.025	.01	.005
	Two-Tailed Test (α)			
δ	.10	.05	.02	.01
3.5	.97	.94	.88	.82
3.6	.97	.95	.90	.85
3.7	.98	.96	.92	.87
3.8	.98	.97	.93	.89
3.9	.99	.97	.94	.91
4.0	.99	.97	.94	.92
4.1	.99	.98	.96	.94
4.2	.99	.99	.97	.95
4.3	a	.99	.98	.96
4.4		.99	.98	.97
4.5		.99	.99	.97
4.6		a	.99	.98
4.7			.99	.98
4.8			.99	.99
4.9			a	.99
5.0				.99

[a]The power at and below this point is greater than .995.

Table A.6 Power of ANOVA (α = .05)

df_w	(ϕ)								
	1.0	1.2	1.4	1.6	1.8	2.0	2.2	2.6	3.0
$k = 2$									
4	.20	.26	.33	.41	.49	.57	.65	.78	.88
8	.24	.32	.41	.51	.61	.70	.78	.89	.96
12	.26	.35	.44	.55	.65	.74	.81	.92	.97
16	.26	.36	.46	.57	.67	.76	.83	.93	.98
20	.27	.37	.47	.58	.68	.77	.84	.94	.98
30	.28	.38	.48	.59	.69	.78	.85	.94	.98
60	.29	.39	.50	.61	.71	.79	.86	.95	.99
∞	.29	.40	.51	.62	.72	.81	.88	.96	.99
$k = 3$									
4	.18	.23	.30	.38	.46	.54	.62	.76	.86
8	.23	.32	.42	.52	.63	.72	.80	.92	.97
12	.26	.36	.47	.58	.69	.78	.86	.95	.99
16	.27	.38	.49	.61	.72	.81	.88	.96	.99
20	.28	.39	.51	.63	.74	.83	.89	.97	.99
30	.29	.41	.53	.65	.76	.85	.91	.98	*
60	.31	.43	.55	.68	.78	.87	.92	.98	*
∞	.32	.44	.57	.70	.80	.88	.94	.99	*
$k = 4$									
4	.17	.23	.29	.37	.45	.53	.61	.75	.86
8	.24	.33	.43	.54	.65	.75	.83	.94	.98
12	.27	.38	.50	.62	.73	.82	.89	.97	.99
16	.29	.40	.53	.66	.77	.86	.92	.98	*
20	.30	.42	.55	.68	.79	.87	.93	.99	*
30	.32	.45	.58	.71	.82	.90	.95	.99	*
60	.34	.47	.61	.74	.84	.92	.96	.99	*
∞	.36	.50	.64	.77	.87	.93	.97	*	*

(continued)

Table A.6 Continued

df$_w$	(ϕ)								
	1.0	1.2	1.4	1.6	1.8	2.0	2.2	2.6	3.0
$k = 5$									
4	.17	.22	.29	.36	.45	.53	.61	.75	.86
8	.24	.34	.45	.56	.67	.77	.85	.96	.99
12	.28	.39	.52	.65	.76	.85	.92	.98	*
16	.30	.43	.56	.69	.81	.89	.94	.99	*
20	.32	.45	.59	.72	.83	.91	.96	.99	*
30	.34	.48	.63	.76	.86	.93	.97	*	*
60	.37	.52	.67	.80	.89	.95	.98	*	*
∞	.40	.55	.71	.83	.92	.96	.99	*	*

*Power ≥ .995. Reprinted with permission from *The Journal of the American Statistical Association*. Copyright © 1967 by the American Statistical Association. All rights reserved.

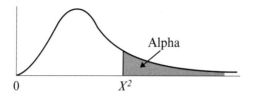

Table A.7 Critical Values of the χ^2 Distribution

df	Alpha (area in the upper tail)				
	.10	.05	.025	.01	.005
1	2.71	3.84	5.02	6.63	7.88
2	4.61	5.99	7.38	9.21	10.60
3	6.25	7.81	9.35	11.35	12.84
4	7.78	9.49	11.14	13.28	14.86
5	9.24	11.07	12.83	15.09	16.75
6	10.64	12.59	14.45	16.81	18.55
7	12.02	14.07	16.01	18.48	20.28
8	13.36	15.51	17.54	20.09	21.96
9	14.68	16.92	19.02	21.67	23.59
10	15.99	18.31	20.48	23.21	25.19
11	17.28	19.68	21.92	24.72	26.75
12	18.55	21.03	23.34	26.22	28.30
13	19.81	22.36	24.74	27.69	29.82
14	21.06	23.69	26.12	29.14	31.32
15	22.31	25.00	27.49	30.58	32.80
16	23.54	26.30	28.85	32.00	34.27
17	24.77	27.59	30.19	33.41	35.72
18	25.99	28.87	31.53	34.81	37.15
19	27.20	30.14	32.85	36.19	38.58
20	28.41	31.41	34.17	37.56	40.00
21	29.62	32.67	35.48	38.93	41.40
22	30.81	33.92	36.78	40.29	42.80
23	32.01	35.17	38.08	41.64	44.18
24	33.20	36.42	39.37	42.98	45.56
25	34.38	37.65	40.65	44.31	46.93
26	35.56	38.89	41.92	45.64	48.29
27	36.74	40.11	43.19	46.96	49.64

(continued)

Table A.7 Continued

df	Alpha (area in the upper tail)				
	.10	.05	.025	.01	.005
28	37.92	41.34	44.46	48.28	50.99
29	39.09	42.56	45.72	49.59	52.34
30	40.26	43.77	46.98	50.89	53.67
40	51.80	55.76	59.34	63.69	66.78
50	63.16	67.50	71.42	76.16	79.50
60	74.40	79.08	83.30	88.39	91.96
70	85.53	90.53	95.03	100.43	104.23
80	96.58	101.88	106.63	112.34	116.33
90	107.56	113.14	118.14	124.12	128.31
100	118.50	124.34	129.56	135.81	140.18

Appendix B: Answers to Putting It Into Practice Exercises

Chapter I

1. (a) mode = 97.8; median = 96.9; mean = 96.08; negatively skewed

   (b) range = 99.7 − 89.5 + .1 = 10.2 + .1 = 10.3

   $$\text{mean deviation (MD)} = \frac{\sum |X_i - \mu|}{N} = \frac{56}{25} = 2.24$$

   $$\sigma = \sqrt{\frac{\sum (X_1 - \mu)^2}{N}} = \sqrt{\frac{182.8}{25}} = 2.70$$

2. (a) Histogram:

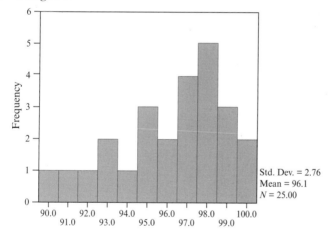

Temps

Std. Dev. = 2.76
Mean = 96.1
N = 25.00

Stemplot:

89	5					
90	8					
91	7					
92						
93	0	2				
94	3	5	8			

95	3	7				
96	4	6	9			
97	1	4	6	8	8	9
98	2	5	7			
99	0	6	7			

Boxplot:

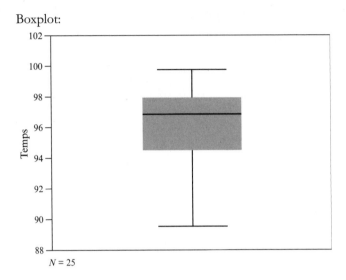

$N = 25$

(b) PR for 95.0 = 32; PR for 98.6 = 84

(c) 30th percentile = 94.7; 65th = 97.8

3. (a) $z = \dfrac{95.0 - 96.08}{2.7} = -.40$ $z = \dfrac{98.6 - 96.08}{2.7} = +.933$

(b) $+1.5 = \dfrac{X - 96.08}{2.7}$; $X = +1.5\,(2.7) + 96.08 = 4.05 + 96.08 = 100.13$

$-.8 = \dfrac{X - 96.08}{2.7}$; $X = -.8\,(2.7) + 96.08 = -2.16 + 96.08 = 93.92$

4. (a) area above $z = -.4$ is .1544 + .5 = .6544, so 65.44%

area above $z = .93$ is .1762, so 17.62%

(b) area beyond $z = .4$ is .1554, so 15.54%

(c) The actual PR of 32 is larger than what you get from assuming a normal distribution (about 15.5) because the distribution is negatively skewed. The normal distribution is not a very good approximation in this case.

Chapter 2

1. (a) $\overline{X} = 96.08$, $\sigma = 2.70$

$$z = \frac{96.08 - 98.6}{\dfrac{2.7}{\sqrt{25}}} = \frac{-2.52}{.54} = -4.67$$

This z is larger in magnitude than the critical value (1.96), so the result is significant at the .05 level (two-tailed).

(b) $z = \dfrac{-2.52}{\dfrac{2.7}{\sqrt{100}}} = -9.33$

For $\alpha = .01$, $z_{\text{crit}} = 2.33$ (one-tailed), or 2.58 (two-tailed). In either case these results are significant at the .01 level. (Optional: Because the sample size was 4 times larger for part b than part a, the z-score was multiplied by 2 [i.e., the square root of 4].)

(c) $\sigma_{\overline{x}} = \dfrac{2.7}{\sqrt{25}}$; $\mu = \overline{X} \pm z_{\text{crit}}\sigma_{\overline{x}} = 96.08 \pm 1.96 \,(.54)$; so $\mu = 96.08 \pm 1.06$

Therefore, the 95% CI goes from 95.02 to 97.14 (note that the sum of these two limits is 192.16, which is exactly twice as large as the sample mean, as will always be the case). Because the population mean tested in part a (98.6) is not in this 95% CI, we know that the sample mean differs significantly from this population mean at the .05 level.

(d) $\sigma_{\overline{x}} = \dfrac{2.7}{\sqrt{100}}$; $\mu = \overline{X} \pm z_{\text{crit}}\sigma_{\overline{x}} = 96.08 \pm 2.58 \,(.27)$; so $\mu = 96.08 \pm .7$

Therefore, the 99% CI goes from 95.38 to 96.78.

2. (a) $\overline{X} = 6.5625$

(b) $\sigma = 4.873$; $\sigma_{\overline{x}} = \dfrac{4.873}{\sqrt{16}} = 1.22$

$\mu = \overline{X} \pm z_{\text{crit}}\sigma_{\overline{x}} = 6.56 \pm 1.96 \,(1.22)$; so $\mu = 6.56 \pm 2.39$

Therefore, the 95% CI goes from 4.17 to 8.95.

(c) Yes, you can reject the null hypothesis at the .05 level (two-tailed) because 9 is not contained in the 95% CI in part b.

Chapter 3

1. (a) *Younger: Modeling vs. Tutorial*

   $n_1 = 52; n_2 = 45; s_1 = 6.69; s_2 = 7.19; s_1^2 = 44.76; s_2^2 = 51.70$

   Pooled-variances *t* test:

   $$s_p^2 = \frac{(n_1 - 1)s_1^2 + (n_2 - 1)s_2^2}{n_1 + n_2 - 2} = \frac{(52-1)44.76 + (45-1)51.70}{52 + 45 - 2}$$

   $$= \frac{4557.56}{95} = 47.97$$

   $$t = \frac{\overline{X}_1 - \overline{X}_2}{\sqrt{s_p^2\left(\dfrac{1}{n_1} + \dfrac{1}{n_2}\right)}} = \frac{36.74 - 32.14}{\sqrt{47.97\left(\dfrac{1}{52} + \dfrac{1}{45}\right)}} = \frac{4.6}{\sqrt{1.988}}$$

   $$= \frac{4.6}{1.41} = 3.26$$

   df = 95, α = .05, two-tailed t_{crit} = 1.99 < 3.26; therefore, the difference is significant.

   Separate-variances *t* test:

   $$t = \frac{\overline{X}_1 - \overline{X}_2}{\sqrt{\dfrac{s_1^2}{n_1} + \dfrac{s_2^2}{n_2}}} = \frac{4.6}{\sqrt{\dfrac{44.76}{52} + \dfrac{51.70}{45}}} = \frac{4.6}{\sqrt{2.01}} = \frac{4.6}{1.418} = 3.24$$

   Older: Modeling vs. Tutorial

   $n_1 = 20; n_2 = 30; s_1 = 8.51; s_2 = 7.29; s_1^2 = 72.42; s_2^2 = 53.14$

   Pooled-variances *t* test:

   $$t = \frac{(29.63 - 26.04)}{\sqrt{60.77\left(\dfrac{1}{20} + \dfrac{1}{30}\right)}} = \frac{3.59}{\sqrt{5.0642}} = \frac{3.59}{2.25} = 1.60$$

   df = 48, α = .05, two-tailed t_{crit} = 2.01 > 1.60; therefore, the difference is not significant.

Separate-variances t test:

$$t = \frac{29.63 - 26.04}{\sqrt{\dfrac{72.42}{20} + \dfrac{53.14}{30}}} = \frac{3.59}{\sqrt{5.392}} = \frac{3.59}{2.32} = 1.55$$

Modeling: Younger vs. Older

$n_1 = 52; n_2 = 20; s_1 = 6.69; s_2 = 8.51; s_1^2 = 44.76; s_2^2 = 72.42$

Pooled-variances t test:

$$t = \frac{(36.74 - 29.63)}{\sqrt{52.27\left(\dfrac{1}{52} + \dfrac{1}{20}\right)}} = \frac{7.11}{\sqrt{3.6187}} = \frac{7.11}{1.9023} = 3.74$$

df = 70, α = .05, two-tailed t_{crit} = 2.0 < 3.74; therefore, the difference is significant.

Separate-variances t test:

$$t = \frac{36.74 - 29.63}{\sqrt{\dfrac{44.76}{52} + \dfrac{72.42}{20}}} = \frac{7.11}{\sqrt{4.4818}} = \frac{7.11}{1.9023} = 3.32$$

Tutorial: Younger vs. Older

$n_1 = 45; n_2 = 30; s_1 = 7.19; s_2 = 7.29; s_1^2 = 51.70; s_2^2 = 53.14$

Pooled-variances t test:

$$t = \frac{(32.14 - 26.04)}{\sqrt{52.27\left(\dfrac{1}{45} + \dfrac{1}{30}\right)}} = \frac{6.10}{\sqrt{2.9038}} = \frac{6.10}{1.704} = 3.58$$

df = 73, α = .05, two-tailed t_{crit} = 2.0 < 3.58; therefore, the difference is significant.

Separate-variances t test:

$$t = \frac{32.14 - 26.04}{\sqrt{\dfrac{51.70}{45} + \dfrac{53.14}{30}}} = \frac{6.10}{\sqrt{2.92}} = \frac{6.10}{1.71} = 3.57$$

Because the variances are very similar for the four groups, the pooled-variances t test seems more appropriate. Based on the results above, method makes a significant difference for younger but not older participants. However, this does not imply that the method effect is significantly greater for the younger group than the older group. A two-way ANOVA is needed to test that difference, as shown in Chapter 7.

(b) $g = \dfrac{(\overline{X}_1 - \overline{X}_2)}{s_p}$

Younger: Modeling vs. Tutorial: $g = \dfrac{4.6}{\sqrt{47.97}} = \dfrac{4.6}{6.926} = 0.66$; between moderate and large

Older: Modeling vs. Tutorial: $g = \dfrac{3.59}{\sqrt{60.77}} = \dfrac{3.59}{7.796} = 0.46$; moderate

Modeling: Younger vs. Older: $g = \dfrac{7.11}{\sqrt{52.27}} = \dfrac{7.11}{7.229} = 0.98$; quite large

Tutorial: Younger vs. Older: $g = \dfrac{6.10}{\sqrt{52.27}} = \dfrac{6.10}{7.229} = 0.84$; large

(c) $\mu_1 - \mu_2 = \overline{X}_1 - \overline{X}_2 \pm t_{crit} s_{\overline{X}_1 - \overline{X}_1} = 4.6 \pm 1.99\,(1.41)$; so $\mu = 4.6 \pm 2.8$

Therefore, the 95% CI goes from 1.8 to 7.4.

2. (a)

Participant	No Imagery	Imagery	D $\Sigma(\text{q·p})$
1	8	14	6
2	11	15	4
3	7	5	-2
4	10	16	6
5	9	9	0
6	15	16	1
7	7	8	1
8	16	20	4

$\Sigma D = 20$; $n = 8$, $s_D = 2.93$, $\overline{D} = \dfrac{20}{8} = 2.5$

$\Sigma d^2 = \dfrac{116}{7}$

$$t = \frac{\overline{D}}{\frac{S_D}{\sqrt{N}}} = \frac{2.5}{\frac{2.93}{\sqrt{8}}} = \frac{2.5}{1.036} = 2.41$$

$t_{.05}(7) = 2.365$; $t_{.01}(7) = 3.499$; $2.365 < 2.41 < 3.499$; therefore, the results are significant at the .05 level (two-tailed), but not the .01 level.

(b) $\mu_{\text{lower}} = \overline{D} - t_{.01}s_{\overline{D}} = 2.5 - 3.499(1.036) = 2.5 - 3.62 = -1.12$

$\mu_{\text{upper}} = \overline{D} + t_{.01}s_{\overline{D}} = 2.5 + 3.499(1.036) = 2.5 + 3.62 = +6.12$

Because zero is contained in the 99% CI (-1.12 to $+6.12$), we know that the null hypothesis cannot be rejected at the .01 level, two-tailed— consistent with the result in part a.

(c) No, you cannot say that imagery instructions *caused* an increase in recall, because the results could easily be due to a practice effect (participants perform better the second time they do the task, because of the experience they gained from the first time).

Chapter 4

1. (a)

No Image	Image	XY
8	14	112
11	15	165
7	5	35
10	16	160
9	9	81
15	16	240
7	8	56
16	20	320

$\Sigma X = 83$; $\Sigma Y = 103$; $\Sigma XY = 1169$; $\overline{X} = 10.375$; $\overline{Y} = 12.875$; $s_x = 3.462$; $s_y = 5.027$; $s_x^2 = 11.98$; $s_y^2 = 25.27$

$$r = \frac{\frac{1}{N-1}\left(\sum XY - N\overline{X}\overline{Y}\right)}{s_x s_y} = \frac{\frac{1}{8-1}[1169 - (8 \cdot 10.375 \cdot 12.875)]}{17.4}$$

$$= \frac{14.34}{17.4} = .824$$

$$t = \frac{r\sqrt{N-2}}{\sqrt{1-r^2}} = \frac{.824\sqrt{8-2}}{\sqrt{1-.824^2}} = \frac{2.018}{\sqrt{.321}} = 3.56$$

$t_{.05}(6) = 2.447 < 3.56$; therefore, the results are significant at the .05 level.

$t_{.01}(6) = 3.707$; the results are not significant at the .01 level.

(b) $\overline{X} = 10.375$; $\overline{Y} = 12.875$; $s_x = 3.462$; $s_y = 5.027$; $s_x^2 = 11.98$; $s_y^2 = 25.27$

$$t = \frac{(\overline{X}_1 - \overline{X}_2)}{\sqrt{\dfrac{s_1^2 + s_2^2}{N} - \dfrac{2rs_1 s_2}{N}}}$$

$$t = \frac{(10.375 - 12.875)}{\left(\dfrac{11.98 + 25.27}{8} - \dfrac{2 \cdot .824 \cdot 3.462 \cdot 5.027}{8}\right)^2}$$

$$t = \frac{-2.5}{\sqrt{4.65625 - 3.584125}} = \frac{-2.5}{\sqrt{1.072}} = 2.41$$

This formula yields exactly the same answer as the direct-difference method presented in the previous chapter (unless you rounded off too much during intermediate steps).

(c) Yes, the correlation can be significant, but the RM t test can fail to reach significance because the numerator (the difference of the two means) is too small. On the other hand, the correlation can be fairly low and not significant, but the RM t test can reach significance because its numerator is quite large.

2. (a)

$$r = \frac{\dfrac{1}{10-1}[197 - (10 \cdot 5.2 \cdot 3.2)]}{2.936 \cdot 2.3} = \frac{\dfrac{1}{9}(30.6)}{6.7528} = \frac{3.4}{6.7528} = .503$$

(b) $t = \dfrac{r\sqrt{N-2}}{\sqrt{1-r^2}} = \dfrac{.503\sqrt{10-2}}{\sqrt{1-.503^2}} = \dfrac{.503\sqrt{8}}{\sqrt{1-.253}} = \dfrac{1.423}{.8643} = 1.646$

$t_{.05}(8) = 2.306 > 1.646$; therefore, the results are not significant at the .05 level.

(c)

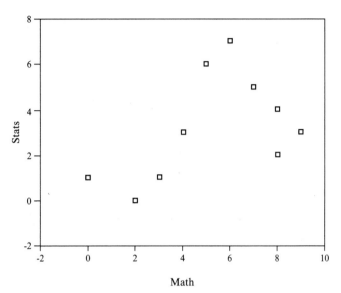

No. Pearson's *r* is not a very good way to summarize the relation between the two variables, because the relationship has a curvilinear component.

(d) $b_{yx} = \dfrac{s_y}{s_x} r = \dfrac{2.3}{2.936} .503 = .7834 \cdot .503 = .394$

$a_{yx} = \overline{Y} - b_{yx}\overline{Y} = 3.2 - .394\,(5.2) = 3.2 - 2.05 = 1.15$

$Y' = .394X + 1.15$

$Y' = .394(6) + 1.15 = 2.36 + 1.15 = 3.51$

3.   Younger: Modeling vs. Tutorial:

$$r_{pb} = \sqrt{\dfrac{t^2}{t^2 + df}} = \sqrt{\dfrac{3.26^2}{3.26^2 + 95}} = \sqrt{\dfrac{10.63}{105.63}} = \sqrt{.1006} = .317; g = .67$$

Older: Modeling vs. Tutorial: $r_{pb} = \sqrt{\dfrac{1.6^2}{1.6^2 + 48}} = .225; g = .46$

Modeling: Younger vs. Older: $r_{pb} = \sqrt{\dfrac{3.74^2}{3.74^2 + 70}} = .408; g = .98$

Tutorial: Younger vs. Older: $r_{pb} = \sqrt{\dfrac{3.58^2}{3.58^2 + 73}} = .386; g = .84$

Notice that as g gets larger, r_{pb} gets larger (however, although there is no limit to how large g can get, r_{pb} cannot be more than 1.0). The square of r_{pb} is approximately equal to the square of g divided by g-squared plus 4 (the approximation improves with larger sample sizes).

Chapter 5

1. $N_T = 44; n = 11; k = 4$

(a) $F = \dfrac{ns_{\bar{x}}^2}{\dfrac{\sum s^2}{k}} = \dfrac{11 \cdot 8.67}{\dfrac{157}{4}} = \dfrac{95.37}{39.25} = 2.43 \qquad df_{bet} = k - 1; df_w = N_T - k$

(b) $F_{.05}(3, 40) = 2.84 > 2.43$, so cannot reject null hypothesis.

(c) $LSD = t_{.05} \sqrt{\dfrac{2MS_w}{n}} = 2.021 \sqrt{\dfrac{2 \cdot 39.25}{11}}$

$\qquad = 2.021 \sqrt{7.136} = 2.021 \cdot 2.67 = 5.4$

Only placebo and Prozac differ by more than 5.4 points.

(d) $HSD = q_{.05} \sqrt{\dfrac{MS_w}{n}} = 3.79 \sqrt{\dfrac{39.25}{11}} = 3.79 \sqrt{3.568} = 3.79 \cdot 1.89 = 7.16$

None of the pairs differ by more than 7.16 points.

(e) HSD and LSD can produce different results because HSD is more conservative (i.e., it raises the critical value and does a better job of keeping the experiment-wise alpha down to .05). With three groups, HSD is unnecessarily conservative, but with four or more groups, LSD is considered too liberal, so HSD is preferred. Of course, in this example, it wouldn't be legitimate to use LSD anyway because the ANOVA was not significant.

(f) With four groups, there are six different pairs to test (i.e., $4 \cdot 3/2 = 12/2$), so $c = 6$.

$$\alpha_{pc} = \frac{\alpha_{EW}}{c} = \frac{.05}{6} = .0083$$

(g) $\eta^2 = \dfrac{df_{bet}F}{df_{bet}F + df_w} = \dfrac{3 \cdot 2.43}{3 \cdot 2.43 + 40} = \dfrac{7.29}{47.29} = .154$

so 15.4% of the variance in depression is accounted for by the drug conditions.

2. $\quad L = .5\ (9) + .5\ (8) - .5\ (4) - .5\ (3) = 4.5 + 4 - 2 - 1.5 = 5$

$$SS_{contrast} = \frac{nL^2}{\sum c^2} = \frac{11 \cdot 5^2}{.5^2 + .5^2 + .5^2 + .5^2} = \frac{275}{1} = 275 = MS_{contrast}$$

$$F = \frac{MS_{contrast}}{MS_w} = \frac{275}{39.25} = 7.0.$$

If planned, $F_{crit} = F_{.05}\ (1, 40) = 4.08$. Because $7.0 > 4.08$, the contrast is significant at the .05 level. The planned contrast was significant, even though the omnibus ANOVA was not. This contrast takes advantage of the fact that the means being averaged together are relatively close together. The contrast F is much higher than the ANOVA F, because much of the SS_{bet} from the ANOVA is included in the contrast, which has only one df in its numerator.

If not planned, $F_s = df_{bet} \cdot F_{.05}\ (3, 40) = 3 \cdot 2.84 = 8.52$. Because $7.0 < 8.52$, this contrast is not significant by Scheffé's test (which will always be the case when the omnibus ANOVA is not significant, as in this example). The advantage of planning a contrast in advance is that your calculated F can be considerably higher than the ANOVA F, while the critical value for the contrast is not very much higher than the critical F for the ANOVA (4.08 vs. 2.84, in this example). If a contrast was not planned, you are supposed to use Scheffé's test, which greatly increases your critical value (8.52 vs. 4.08, in this example).

3. (a) $F = \dfrac{ns_{\bar{x}}^2}{\dfrac{\sum s^2}{k}} = \dfrac{24 \cdot 183.84}{\dfrac{11668}{.5}} = \dfrac{5515.2}{2333.6} = 2.36$

$df_{between} = k - 1 = 4$

$df_{within} = N_T - k = 120 - 5 = 115$

$F_{.05}$ (4, 115) = 2.45 > 2.36, so cannot reject null hypothesis.

(b) $L = -\dfrac{1}{2}(50) - \dfrac{1}{2}(70) + \dfrac{1}{3}(82) + \dfrac{1}{3}(86) + \dfrac{1}{3}(85)$

$= -25 - 35 + 27.33 + 28.67 + 28.33 = -60 + 84.33 = 24.33$

$$SS_{contrast} = \frac{24 \cdot 24.33^2}{.5^2 + .5^2 + .33^2 + .33^2 + .33^2} = \frac{14,210.67}{.833}$$

$$= 17,052.8 = MS_{contrast}$$

$$F = \frac{MS_{contrast}}{MS_w} = \frac{17,052.8}{2333.6} = 7.31.$$

$F_{.05}(1, 115) = 3.92$. Because 7.31 > 3.92, the contrast is significant at the .05 level.

(c) $L = -2 (50) + -1 (70) + 0 (82) + 1 (86) + 2 (85)$

$= -100 - 70 + 86 + 170 = 86$

$$SS_{linear} = \frac{24(86^2)}{-2^2 + -1^2 + 0^2 + 1^2 + 2^2} = \frac{177,504}{10} = 17,750.4 = MS_{linear}$$

$$F_{linear} = \frac{MS_{linear}}{MS_w} = \frac{17,750.4}{2333.6} = 7.61.$$

$F_{.05}(1, 115) = 3.92$. Because 7.61 > 3.92, the linear trend is significant at the .05 level.

$SS_{bet} = df_{bet} \cdot MS_{bet} = 4 \cdot 5515.2 = 22,060.8.$

$SS_{residual} = SS_{bet} - SS_{linear} = 22,060.8 - 17,750.4 = 4,310.4$

$df_{residual} = df_{bet} - df_{linear} = 4 - 1 = 3$, so $MS_{residual} = \dfrac{4310.4}{3} = 1436.8$

$$F_{residual} = \frac{MS_{residual}}{MS_w} = \frac{1436.8}{2333.6} = .62$$

There is no evidence of significant higher-order trends.

Chapter 6

1. (a) From Table A.5, $\delta = 2.8$; $d = \dfrac{1}{.7} = 1.43$.

$$n = 2\left(\dfrac{\delta}{d}\right)^2 = 2\left(\dfrac{2.8}{1.43}\right)^2 = 2 \cdot 1.96^2 = 2 \cdot 3.84 = 7.7$$

Therefore, eight subjects would be needed in each group to have suffi-cient power.

Based on the n found above, we would look under $df_w = 12$ (as our first guess) in the $k = 2$ section of Table A.6, and estimate $\phi = 2.18$ to corre-spond with .8 power; $f = d/2 = 1.43/2 = .715$.

$$n = \left(\dfrac{\phi}{f}\right)^2 = \left(\dfrac{2.18}{.715}\right)^2 = 3.05^2 = 9.3$$

This estimate implies that df_w would be closer to 16, and therefore that ϕ would be closer to 2.11. This revised ϕ leads to a sample size of 8.7, which is consistent with $df_w = 16$. Thus, the sample size estimate from Table A.6 is about 9. This estimate is higher than the one from Table A.5, because Table A.6 takes into consideration that the critical value for $df_w = 16$ is 2.12, rather than 1.96.

(b) $n_b = \dfrac{2n_1 n_2}{n_1 + n_2} = \dfrac{2 \cdot 4 \cdot 8}{4 + 8} = \dfrac{64}{12} = 5.33$

$\delta = \sqrt{\dfrac{5.33}{2}}\,1.43 = 1.633 \cdot 1.43 = 2.34$

From Table A.5, power is about .65 for a .05, two-tailed test.

$\Phi = f\sqrt{n} = .714\sqrt{5.33} = 1.65$

Looking in the $k = 2$ section of Table A.6 between $df_w = 8$ and $df_w = 12$, a ϕ of 1.65 corresponds to about .56 power, a somewhat lower esti-mate than the one given by the normal approximation in Table A.5.

(c) From Table A.5, $\delta = 3.85$.

$3.85 = d\sqrt{\dfrac{5.33}{2}} = d \cdot 1.633$

Therefore, $\mathbf{d} = 3.85/1.633 = 2.36$. You can see that $\mathbf{d}$ would have to be extremely large to have that much power with a .01 alpha and small sample sizes.

(d) mean difference/.7 = 2.36, so the difference must be $.7 \cdot 2.36 = 1.65$ degrees.

2. (a) From Table A.5, $\delta = 2.6$; you are given that $\mathbf{d} = .5$ (i.e., means differ by half of an SD).

$$n = 2\left(\frac{\delta}{d}\right)^2 = 2\left(\frac{2.6}{.5}\right)^2 = 2 \cdot 5.2^2 = 2 \cdot 27.04 = 54.08$$

Therefore, about 54 participants would be needed in each group to have a reasonable amount of power with a medium effect size.

(b) $2.6 = \sqrt{\dfrac{1}{1-.4}} \sqrt{\dfrac{n}{2}} \cdot .5 = .5\sqrt{1.67}\sqrt{\dfrac{n}{2}} = .645\sqrt{\dfrac{n}{2}}$;

so $\sqrt{\dfrac{n}{2}} = \dfrac{2.6}{.645} = 4.03$

Therefore, $n = 2 \cdot 4.03^2 = 2 \cdot 16.224 = 32.45$. The matching of subjects allowed the size of each sample to be reduced from 54 to about 33 without reducing power.

(c) From Table A.5, $\delta = 2.48$.

$$2.48 = \sqrt{\dfrac{1}{1-\rho}} \sqrt{\dfrac{18}{2}} \cdot .5 = .5 \cdot 3 \sqrt{\dfrac{1}{1-\rho}} = 1.5\sqrt{\dfrac{1}{1-\rho}}$$

so $\sqrt{\dfrac{1}{1-\rho}} = \dfrac{2.48}{1.5} = 1.653$

Therefore, $\rho = 1 - (1/1.653^2) = 1 - .366 = .634$. To have adequate power with relatively small samples and a medium effect size, a rather high degree of matching is needed.

3. (a) $3.1 = .35\sqrt{N-1}$; so $\sqrt{N-1} = \dfrac{3.1}{.35} = 8.86$

Therefore, $N = 8.86^2 + 1 = 78.45 + 1 = 79.45$; about 80 cases would be needed to achieve the stated level of power, with $\rho = .35$.

(b) From Table A.5, $\delta = 2.8$.

$$2.8 = \rho\sqrt{26-1} = 5\rho; \text{ so } \rho = \frac{2.8}{5} = .56$$

The effect size has to be large to have .8 power with a fairly small sample.

4. (a) Given $k = 4$; $n = 9$; $f = .5$. $df_w = (4 \cdot 9) - 4 = 36 - 4 = 32$, $\Phi = f\sqrt{n} = .5\sqrt{9} = 1.5$.

Looking in the $k = 4$ section of Table A.6 with df_w about 30, a ϕ of 1.5 corresponds to about .65 power (about midway between the entries for 1.4 and 1.6, which are .58 and .71, respectively).

(b) With an f of .2 and $k = 4$, it is a good guess to use the bottom (i.e., infinite) row of the $k = 4$ section of Table A.6. A ϕ of 1.4 corresponds to .64 power, so we will use 1.42 for .65 power.

$$1.42 = .2\sqrt{n}; \text{ so, } \sqrt{n} = \frac{1.42}{.2} = 7.1$$

Therefore, $n = 7.1^2 = 50.4$. About 51 subjects are needed in each of the four groups, which corresponds to a df_w of 200, which is consistent with assuming an infinite df_w to look up our value for ϕ.

(c) Given $k = 4$ and $n = 9$, so $df_w = 32$. Looking in the $k = 4$ section of Table A.6 along the $df_w = 30$ row, we see that a ϕ of 1.8 corresponds to the desired power of .82.

$$1.8 = f\sqrt{9} = 3f; \text{ so } f = \frac{1.8}{3} = .6$$

To obtain power as high as .82 with only 9 participants per group, f has to be quite large (i.e., 6).

Chapter 7

1. (a)

	Placebo	St. John's Wort	Elavil	Prozac	Row Means
Men	9	8	4	3	6
Women	8	2	5	1	4
Column means	8.5	5	4.5	2	Grand mean: 5

$n = 11; N_T = 88; c = 4; r = 2; df_w = rc(n-1) = 4 \cdot 2 \, (11-1) = 80$

$SS_{\text{between-cell}} = N_T \sigma^2 \ (\textit{cell means}) = 88 \cdot 8 = 704$

$SS_{\text{drug}} = N_T \sigma^2 \ (8.5, 5, 4.5, 2) = 88 \cdot 5.375 = 473$

$SS_{\text{gender}} = N_T \sigma^2 \ (6, 4) = 88 \cdot 2 = 176$

$SS_{\text{inter}} = SS_{\text{between-cell}} - SS_{\text{row}} - SS_{\text{column}} = 704 - 176 - 473 = 55$

$MS_{\text{gender}} = \dfrac{SS_{\text{gender}}}{df_{\text{gender}}} = \dfrac{176}{1} = 176; \ MS_{\text{drug}} = \dfrac{SS_{\text{drug}}}{df_{\text{drug}}} = \dfrac{473}{3} = 157.67$

$df_{\text{inter}} = (r-1)(c-1) = (2-1)(4-1) = 3; \ MS_{\text{inter}} = \dfrac{SS_{\text{inter}}}{df_{\text{inter}}}$

$= \dfrac{55}{3} = 18.33$

$F_{\text{gender}} = \dfrac{MS_{\text{gender}}}{MS_w} = \dfrac{176}{32} = 5.5; \ F_{\text{drug}} = \dfrac{MS_{\text{drug}}}{MS_w} = \dfrac{157.67}{32} = 4.93;$

$F_{\text{inter}} = \dfrac{MS_{\text{inter}}}{MS_w} = \dfrac{18.33}{32} = .57$

$F_{.05}(1, 80) = 3.96 < 5.5$, so the main effect of gender is significant at the .05 level. $F_{.05} \ (3, 80) = 2.72 < 4.93$, so the main effect of drug is also significant at the .05 level. However, F_{inter} is less than 1.0, so it cannot be significant.

(b) Men:

$$F = \dfrac{ns_{\bar{x}}^2}{MS_w} = \dfrac{11 \cdot 8.67}{32} = \dfrac{95.37}{32} = 2.98$$

$F_{.05}(3, 40) = 2.84 < 2.98$, so the simple main effect of drug is significant for the men.

Women:

$$F = \frac{11 \cdot 10}{32} = \frac{110}{32} = 3.44$$

$3.44 > 2.84$, so the simple main effect of drug is also significant for the women.

(c) $L = (8 - 2) - (4 - 5) = 6 - (-1) = 6 + 1 = 7$

$$SS_{contrast} = \frac{11 \cdot 7^2}{1^2 + 1^2 + 1^2 + 1^2} = \frac{539}{4} = 134.75 = MS_{contrast}$$

$$F = \frac{MS_{contrast}}{MS_w} = \frac{134.75}{32} = 4.21; F_{.05}(1, 80) = 3.96.$$

Because $4.21 > 3.96$, this interaction contrast would be significant if planned.

$F_S = df_{inter} \cdot F_{.05}(3, 80) = 3 \cdot 2.72 = 8.16 > 4.21$, so this contrast would not be significant by Scheffé's test (consistent with the fact that the interaction in the entire ANOVA was not significant).

2. (a) $N_T = 147$

Marginal means: Younger = 34.44; Older = 27.835; Modeling = 33.185; Tutorial = 29.09

$SS_{between-cell} = N_T \sigma^2$ (*cell means*) $= 147 \cdot 15.1625 = 2228.9$

$SS_{age} = N_T \sigma^2 (34.44, 27.835) = 147 \cdot 10.906 = 1603.2$

$SS_{method} = N_T \sigma^2 (33.185, 29.09) = 147 \cdot 4.192 = 616.3$

$SS_{inter} = SS_{between-cell} - SS_{row} - SS_{column} = 2228.9 - 1603.2 - 616.3 = 9.4$

Because the df for all of the above effects is 1,

$MS_{age} = 1603.2; MS_{method}\ 616.3; MS_{inter} = 9.4$

$$MS_w = \frac{(52-1)6.69^2 + (45-1)7.19^2 + (20-1)8.51^2 + (30-1)7.29^2}{52 + 45 + 20 + 30 - 4}$$

$$= \frac{7474.35}{143} = 52.27$$

$$F_{age} = \frac{1603.2}{52.27} = 30.67; F_{method} = \frac{616.3}{52.27} = 11.79; F_{inter} = \frac{9.4}{52.27} = .18$$

$F_{.05}(1, 143) = 3.90$. The two main effects are easily significant at the .05 level, but the interaction is obviously not close to significance.

(b)
$$\frac{\dfrac{1}{52} + \dfrac{1}{45} + \dfrac{1}{20} + \dfrac{1}{30}}{4} = \frac{.1248}{4} = .0312;$$

therefore, the harmonic mean of the cell sizes $= 1/.0312 = 32.055$. There are four cells, so N_H (the adjusted total N) $= 4 \cdot 32.055 = 128.22$. Recalculating the SSs with 128.22 in place of 147 yields the following results:

$SS_{age} = 1398.4$; $SS_{method} = 537.5$; $SS_{inter} = 8.2$, which leads to the following adjusted F ratios:

$$F_{age} = \frac{1398.4}{52.27} = 26.75; \quad F_{method} = \frac{537.5}{52.27} = 10.28; \quad F_{inter} = \frac{8.2}{52.27} = .16$$

All of the F ratios are somewhat smaller, as is generally the case with an unbalanced factorial ANOVA (the analysis of unweighted means effectively subtracts the overlapping of the different effects).

3. (a) This is a $4 \times 2 \times 2$ ANOVA, so there are a total of 16 cells. Assuming a balanced design, $n = 128/16 = 8$, and $df_w = 128 - 16 = 112$. The numerator MSs are created by dividing each given SS by its corresponding df, as shown below:

$$MS_{relax} = \frac{64.4}{1} = 64.4; \quad MS_{dark} = \frac{31.6}{1} = 31.6; \quad MS_{emotion} = \frac{223.1}{3}$$

$$= 74.367$$

$$MS_{emo \times relax} = \frac{167.3}{3} = 55.77; \quad MS_{emo \times dark} = \frac{51.5}{3} = 17.17; \quad MS_{rel \times dark}$$

$$= \frac{127.3}{1} = 127.3$$

$$MS_{emo \times rel \times dark} = \frac{77.2}{3} = 25.73$$

SS_w is found by subtracting $SS_{between-cells}$ from SS_{total}, which was given (2,344). $SS_{between-cells}$ is found by summing the seven numerator SSs that were given. $SS_{between-cells} = 64.4 + 31.6 + 223.1 + 167.3 + 51.5 + 127.3$

+ 77.2 = 742.4. Therefore, SS_w = 2344 – 742.4 = 1,601.6, and MS_w = 1,601.6/112 = 14.3. The F ratios are

$$F_{relax} = \frac{64.4}{14.3} = 4.5; \quad F_{dark} = \frac{31.6}{14.3} = 2.21; \quad F_{emotion} = \frac{74.367}{14.3} = 5.2;$$

$$F_{emo \times relax} = \frac{55.77}{14.3} = 3.9$$

$$F_{emo \times dark} = \frac{17.17}{14.3} = 1.2; \quad F_{rel \times dark} = \frac{127.3}{14.3} = 8.9;$$

$$F_{emo \times rel \times dark} = \frac{25.73}{14.3} = 1.8$$

$F_{.05}(1, 112)$ = 3.92, so the main effect of relax and its interaction with dark are significant, but the main effect of dark is not. $F_{.05}(3, 112)$ = 2.68, so the main effect of emotion and its interaction with relax is significant, but the interaction of emotion and dark is not significant, nor is the three-way interaction.

(b) Hypothetical Means for Blood Pressure
     At room type = normal

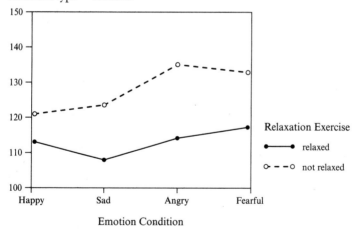

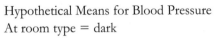

Hypothetical Means for Blood Pressure
At room type = dark

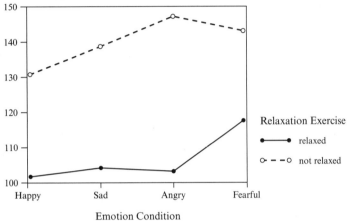

(c) The significant relax by dark interaction could be followed up by comparing the relax condition for the normal and dark rooms, and the no relax
condition for the two rooms. In addition (or alternatively), the two rooms
can be compared separately for the relax and no relax conditions. The significant main effect of emotion can be followed by comparing pairs of
emotion means, but the significant emotion by relax interaction suggests
that it may be preferable to test the simple main effect of emotion separately for the relax and no relax conditions. Depending on which of these
simple main effects reaches significance, the emotion means can be compared separately for the relax and/or the no relax condition.

4. Cell Means for Eye Movements
    At instructions = subvocal

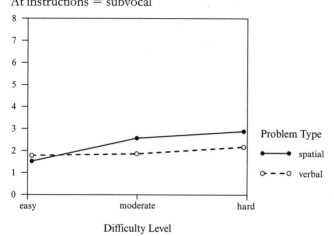

Difficulty Level

Cell Means for Eye Movements
At instructions = imagery

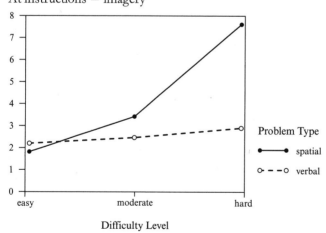

Difficulty Level

Yes, there appears to be a three-way interaction, because the problem
type by difficult interaction is much larger for the group given imagery
instructions than it is for the group given subvocalization instructions.

Chapter 8

1. (a) *Expect Sound* ($N_T = 18$, $n = 6$, $c = 3$)

$$SS_{total} = N_T \sigma^2 \text{ (all scores)} = 18 \cdot 1.444 = 26$$

$$SS_{subject} = N_T \sigma^2 \text{ (subject means)} = 18 \cdot .926 = 16.67$$

$$SS_{RM} = N_T \sigma^2 (1.167, 1.833, 2.0) = 18 \cdot .13 = 2.33$$

$$SS_{sub \times RM} = SS_{total} - SS_{sub} - SS_{RM} = 26 - 16.67 - 2.33 = 7$$

$$MS_{RM} = \frac{SS_{RM}}{df_{RM}} = \frac{2.33}{2} = 1.167$$

$$df_{sub \times RM} = (c-1)(n-1) = 2 \cdot 5 = 10$$

$$MS_{sub \times RM} = \frac{7}{10} = .7$$

$$F = \frac{MS_{RM}}{MS_{sub \times RM}} = \frac{1.167}{7} = 1.667$$

$$F_{.05}(2, 10) = 4.10$$

1.667 < 4.1, so this effect is not significant.

Source	SS	df	MS	F	p
Subject	16.67	5			
Treatment	2.33	2	1.167	1.667	>.05
Interaction	7	10	.7		
Total	26	17			

Ignore Sound ($N_T = 18$, $n = 6$, $c = 3$)

Source	SS	df	MS	F	p
Subject	13.33	5			
Treatment	32.33	2	16.165	13.10	<.01
Interaction	12.34	10	1.234		
Total	58	17			

Reject null hypothesis; this effect is significant.

(b) No. Ignore Sound is not significant, not assuming sphericity can only make it further from reaching significance. For Expect Sound, the conservatively adjusted critical value (based on $\varepsilon = .5$) is $F_{.05}(1, 5) = 6.61$. Because $13.1 > 6.61$, this effect is significant without making any assumption about sphericity in the population.

2. (a)

Source	SS	df	MS	F	p
Subject	230.75	7			
Treatment	25	1	25	5.83	.046
Interaction	30	7	4.286		
Total	285.75	15			

The matched t was 2.41 for these data; $2.41^2 = 5.81$. The slight discrepancy with the F found above is due to rounding off.

(b)

	Participant #	No Imagery	Imagery	Subject Means	Order Means
No image first	1	8	14	11	13.75
	2	11	15	13	
	4	10	16	13	
	8	16	20	18	
		$\overline{X} = 11.25$	$\overline{X} = 16.25$		
Imagery first	3	7	5	6	9.5
	5	9	9	9	
	6	15	16	15.5	
	7	7	8	7.5	
		$\overline{X} = 9.5$	$\overline{X} = 9.5$		
Column means		10.375	12.875	11.625	

From part a, we know that $SS_{total} = 285.75$, $SS_{RM} = 25$, and $SS_{sub} = 230.75$.

$$SS_{order} = N_T \sigma^2(13.75, 9.5) = 16 \cdot 4.5156 = 72.25$$

$$SS_w = SS_{sub} - SS_{order} = 230.75 - 72.25 = 158.5$$

$$SS_{between-cells} = N_T \sigma^2(11.25, 9.5, 16.25, 9.5) = 16 \cdot 7.641 = 122.25$$

$$SS_{inter} = SS_{between-cells} - SS_{RM} - SS_{groups} = 122.25 - 25 - 72.25 = 25$$

$$SS_{within-cells} = SS_{total} - SS_{between-cells} = 285.75 - 122.25 = 163.5$$

$$SS_{sub \times RM} = SS_{within-cells} - SS_w = 163.5 - 158.5 = 5$$

$$MS_{RM} = \frac{25}{1} = 25 \quad MS_{order} = \frac{72.25}{1} = 72.25 \quad MS_{inter} = \frac{25}{1} = 25$$

$$df_w = N_s - k = 8 - 2 = 6; \ MS_w = \frac{158.5}{6} = 26.417$$

$$df_{sub \times RM} = (N_s - k)(c - 1) = 6 \cdot 1 = 6; \ MS_{sub \times RM} = \frac{5}{6} = .833$$

$$F_{order} = \frac{MS_{order}}{MS_w} = \frac{72.25}{26.417} = 2.735 \quad F_{RM} = \frac{MS_{RM}}{MS_{sub \times RM}} = \frac{25}{.833} = 30.0$$

$$F_{inter} = \frac{MS_{inter}}{MS_{sub \times RM}} = \frac{25}{.833} = 30.0 \quad F_{.05}(1, 6) = 5.99$$

The main effect of the RM factor (imagery vs. no imagery) is significant, and so is the order by treatment interaction. The main effect of order, however, is not significant. For the next problem, we will show how the results of a mixed design look in a summary table.

(c) The significant order by treatment interaction tells you that order effects influenced your data. Fortunately, the lack of a main effect of order suggests that you have only simple order effects, rather than differential carry-over effects. Removing the interaction from the error term resulted in an increase in the F ratio for the main effect of treatment—from a barely significant 5.83 to 30.

(d) Cell Means by Type of Instructions and Order

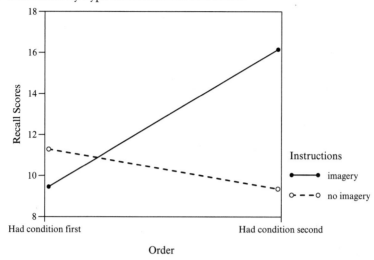

The interaction in the graph suggests differential carry-over effects (being in the second position has a very different effect on the Imagery condition as compared to the No Imagery condition). In this case, the interaction falls short of significance, but that is not surprising given the very small sample sizes. You could use the data only from each participant's first condition, but in this case you would lose your imagery effect. It would be best to redesign the experiment based on matching pairs of subjects to avoid carry-over effects (once given imagery instructions, it would be difficult to not use those instructions, even when asked not to).

3. (a)

	Participant #	None	Mild	Moderate	Strong	$\overline{X}_{subj}$	$\overline{X}_{group}$
Placebo	1	2	5	11	10	7.00	
	2	0	8	4	9	5.25	
	3	7	9	13	12	10.25	7.875
	4	3	12	10	11	9.00	
$\overline{X}_{cell}$		3	8.5	9.5	10.5		

	Participant #	None	Mild	Moderate	Strong	$\overline{X}_{subj}$	$\overline{X}_{group}$
Caffeine	5	3	7	8	6	6.00	
	6	2	6	6	9	5.75	
	7	5	8	7	7	6.75	6.25
	8	4	9	5	8	6.50	
$\overline{X}_{cell}$		3.5	7.5	6.5	7.5		
$\overline{X}_{RM}$		3.25	8.0	8.0	9.0	$\overline{X}_{G} = 7.0625$	

Source	SS	df	MS	F	p
Between-cells	198.875				
Subject	81.875				
RM	160.375	3	53.458	15.971	<.05
Group	21.125	1	21.125	2.086	>.05 (n.s.)
Interaction	17.375	3	5.792	1.73	>.05 (n.s.)
Within-group	60.75	6	10.125		
Sub × RM	60.25	18	3.347		
Total	319.875	31			

$F_{.05}(1, 6) = 5.99$ $F_{.05}(3, 18) = 3.16$

(b) Cell Means for Number of Errors

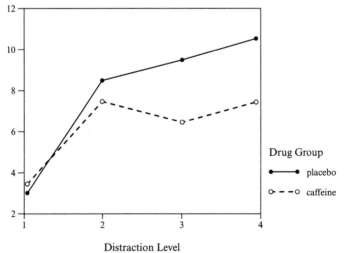

You can see some interaction in the graph, but it is not dramatic, so it is not surprising that the interaction is not near significance. You can see some main effect of drug group, but with small sample sizes and a between-group comparison (i.e., no repeated measures on this factor), it is again not surprising that this effect falls short of significance. However, the main effect of distraction level is rather strong, especially between none and mild. Given the extra power of repeated measures, this effect is easily significant.

(c)

	Participant #	None	Mild	Moderate	Strong	Linear
Placebo	1	2	5	11	10	30
	2	0	8	4	9	23
	3	7	9	13	12	19
	4	3	12	10	11	22
Caffeine	5	3	7	8	6	10
	6	2	6	6	9	21
	7	5	8	7	7	5
	8	4	9	5	8	8

Source	SS	df	MS	F	p
Linear trend	312.5	1	312.5	8.89	.025
Within-group	211.0	6	35.167		
Total	523.5	7			

Chapter 9

1. (a)

No Imagery	Imagery	Imagery–No Imagery (Sign)
8	14	+
11	15	+
7	5	−
10	16	+
9	9	(0)
15	16	+
7	8	+
16	20	+

The zero difference is deleted, so there are only seven events that could be either plus or minus. The total number of possibilities, therefore, is $2^7 = 128$. For these data there is only one minus sign. There are seven ways that that can happen, so the probability of getting one minus sign is $7/128 = .0547$. However, we must add the more extreme result of getting no minus signs, which can happen only one way, so its probability is $1/128 = .0078$. The total one-tailed $p = .0547 + .0078 = .0625$. This p is not less than .05, so the results are not significant with a one-tailed test, and certainly not with a two-tailed test ($p = 2 \cdot .0625 = .125$). The RM t was equal to 2.41, which has a p just a little less than .05. The sign test throws away all the quantitative information concerning the differences, and generally has less power, which is why it failed to reach significance, even though the RM t test was significant.

(b) $z = \dfrac{|X - NP| - .5}{\sqrt{NPQ}} = \dfrac{|1 - 7 \cdot .5| - .5}{\sqrt{7 \cdot .5 \cdot .5}} = \dfrac{|1 - 3.5| - .5}{\sqrt{1.75}} = \dfrac{2}{1.323} = 1.51$

$z_{.05}$, 1-tailed $= 1.645 > 1.51$, so cannot reject null hypothesis; a result that is not significant with a one-tailed test will not be significant with a two-tailed test.

(c)

Imagery–No Imagery	Positive Ranks	Negative Ranks
6	1.5	
4	3.5	
−2		5
6	1.5	
0		
1	6.5	
1	6.5	
4	3.5	
Sum of ranks	23	5

The smaller sum is 5, so $T = 5$.

$z = \dfrac{T - .25N(N + 1)}{\sqrt{\dfrac{N(N + 1)(2N + 1)}{24}}} = \dfrac{5 - .25 \cdot 7(7 + 1)}{\sqrt{\dfrac{7(7 + 1)(14 + 1)}{24}}} = \dfrac{5 - 14}{\sqrt{35}}$

$= \dfrac{-9}{5.916} = -1.52$

Notes that the z from Wilcoxon's test happens to be very similar to the z from the sign test on the same data, although often it will be considerably larger. The Wilcoxon test also fails to reach significance at the .05 level for either a one-tailed or two-tailed test.

(d) For Spearman's correlation, each set of scores is ranked separately:

Ranks for No Imagery	Ranks for Imagery
6	5
3	4
7.5	8
4	2.5
5	6
2	2.5
7.5	7
1	1

Pearson's r calculated for these two sets of ranks is .928, so $r_s = .928$. The Pearson's r for the original scores (i.e., not ranked) is .82, somewhat lower.

2. (a) *Agree to Return:*

$$\chi^2 = \sum \frac{(f_0 - f_e)^2}{f_e} = \frac{(18-15)^2}{15} + \frac{(16-15)^2}{15} + \frac{(10-15)^2}{15} + \frac{(16-15)^2}{15}$$

$$= \frac{36}{15} = 2.4$$

$\chi^2_{.05}(3) = 7.81$; $\chi^2_{obs} < \chi^2_{crit}$; therefore, do not reject null hypothesis.

Do Not Agree:

$$\chi^2 = \sum \frac{(f_0 - f_e)^2}{f_e} = \frac{(7-10)^2}{10} + \frac{(9-10)^2}{10} + \frac{(15-10)^2}{10} + \frac{(9-10)^2}{10}$$

$$= \frac{36}{10} = 3.6$$

$\chi^2_{.05}(3) = 7.81$; $\chi^2_{obs} < \chi^2_{crit}$; therefore, do not reject null hypothesis.

No, the type of experimenter did not make a significant difference in either case.

(b) $\dfrac{(18-15)^2}{15} + \dfrac{(16-15)^2}{15} + \dfrac{(10-15)^2}{15} + \dfrac{(16-15)^2}{15} + \dfrac{(7-10)^2}{10}$

$+ \dfrac{(9-10)^2}{10} + \dfrac{(15-10)^2}{10} + \dfrac{(9-10)^2}{10} = 6.0$

$\chi^2_{.05}(3) = 7.81$; $\chi^2_{obs} < \chi^2_{crit}$; therefore, do not reject null hypothesis.

If all of the entries were doubled, χ^2 would become $2 \cdot 6.0 = 12$ $> \chi^2_{.05}(3) = 7.81$, so in this case you could reject the null hypothesis.

(c) $\chi^2 = \sum \dfrac{(f_o - f_e)^2}{f_e} = \dfrac{(18-14)^2}{14} + \dfrac{(7-11)^2}{11} + \dfrac{(10-14)^2}{14} + \dfrac{(15-11)^2}{11}$

$= \dfrac{32}{14} + \dfrac{32}{11} = 5.2$

$\chi^2_{.05}(1) = 3.84 < 5.2$, so the results are significant at the .05 level.

$\Phi^2 = \chi^2/N = 5.2/50 = .104$, so $\Phi = \sqrt{.104} = .32$. As a correlation coefficient, .32 is a medium-sized effect.

3. (a) For the Mann-Whitney test, all of the scores (16 for this problem) are ranked with respect to each other as one big group, and then the ranks are separated according to which subgroup the score comes from, as shown below.

DB	Rank	NDB	Rank
3	5.5	0	14
5	3	2	7.5
0	14	1	10
9	1	0	14
1	10	2	7.5
7	2	0	14
4	4	3	5.5
		1	10
		0	14
Sum		39.5	96.5

$n_s = 7$; $n_L = 9$; $S_s = 39.5$; $S_L = 96.5$; $N = 16$

$$z = \frac{S_s - .5(n_s)(N + 1)}{\sqrt{\dfrac{n_s n_L (N + 1)}{12}}} = \frac{39.5 - .5(7)(16 + 1)}{\sqrt{\dfrac{7 \cdot 9(16 + 1)}{12}}} = \frac{-20}{\sqrt{89.25}} = -2.12$$

$2.12 > 1.96$ ($z_{.05}$, 2-tailed); therefore, reject the null hypothesis.

(b) Kruskal-Wallis test:

$$H = \frac{12}{N(N + 1)} \sum_{i=1}^{K} \left(\frac{S_i^2}{n_i} \right) - 3(N + 1) \qquad \sum_{i-1}^{K} = \frac{39.5^2}{7} + \frac{96.5^2}{9} = 1257.58$$

so $H = \dfrac{12}{16(16 + 1)} \cdot 1257.58 - 3(16 + 1) = 55.46 - 51 = 4.46$

If you square the z from 3a, you get $-2.12^2 = 4.49$, which differs from H only because of rounding error.

4.   For the Friedman test, scores are ranked among the several conditions separately for each subject, as shown for Table 8.2:

Expect	Classic	Popular	Noise
1	2	2.5	2.5
2	1.5	1.5	3
3	2	1	3
4	1	2.5	2.5
5	1.5	3	1.5
6	2.5	2.5	1
Sum	9.5	13	13.5

Ignore	Classic	Popular	Noise
1	1.5	1.5	3
2	1	2	3
3	1	2	3
4	1	2	3
5	1.5	1.5	3
6	2	1	3
Sum	8	10	18

Expect ($N = 6, c = 3$):

$$F_r = \frac{12}{Nc(c + 1)} \sum_{i=1}^{c} S_i^2 - 3N(c + 1)$$

$$= \frac{12}{6 \cdot 3(3 + 1)} [(9.5^2) + (13^2) + (13.5^2)] - 3 \cdot 6(3 + 1)$$

$$= \frac{12}{72}(441.5) - 72 = 73.583 - 72 = 1.583$$

Because $1.583 < \chi_{.05}^2(2) = 5.99$, the results are not significant for this group.

Ignore ($N = 6, c = 3$):

$$F_r = \frac{12}{72}[(8^2) + (10^2) + (18^2)] - 72 = \frac{1}{6}(488) - 72 = 81.33 - 72 = 9.33$$

Because $9.33 > \chi_{.05}^2(2) = 5.99$, the results are significant for this group.

These statistical conclusions agree with those in the first exercise of Chapter 8: significant for Ignore, but not significant for Expect.

References

Algina, J., & Keselman, H. J. (1997). Detecting repeated measures effects with univariate and multivariate statistics. *Psychological Methods, 2,* 208–218.

American Psychiatric Association. (1994). Diagnostic and statistical manual of mental disorders (4th ed.). Washington, DC: Author.

American Psychological Association. (2001). *Publication manual of the American Psychological Association* (5th ed.). Washington, DC: Author.

Behrens, J. T. (1997). Principles and procedures of exploratory data analysis. *Psychological Methods, 2,* 131–160.

Boik, R. J. (1979). Interactions, partial interactions, and interaction contrasts in the analysis of variance. *Psychological Bulletin, 86,* 1084–1089.

Cicchetti, D. V. (1972). Extension of multiple range tests to interaction tables in the analysis of variance: A rapid approximate solution. *Psychological Bulletin, 77,* 405–408.

Cohen, B. H. (2000). *Explaining psychological statistics* (2nd ed.). New York: Wiley.

Cohen, B. H. (2002). Calculating a factorial ANOVA from means and standard deviations. *Understanding Statistics, 1,* 191–203.

Cohen, J. (1960). A coefficient of agreement for nominal scales. *Educational and Psychological Measurement, 20,* 37–46.

Cohen, J. (1988). *Statistical power analysis for the behavioral sciences* (2nd ed.). Hillsdale, NJ: Lawrence Erlbaum.

Cohen, J. (1994). The earth is round ($p < .05$). *American Psychologist, 49,* 997–1003.

Cowles, M. (2001). *Statistics in psychology: An historical perspective* (2nd ed.). Mahwah, NJ: Lawrence Erlbaum.

Cumming, G., & Finch, S. (2001). A primer on the understanding, use, and calculation of confidence intervals that are based on central and noncentral distributions. *Educational and Psychological Measurement, 61,* 532–574.

Davidson, M. L. (1972). Univariate versus multivariate tests in repeated measures experiments. *Psychological Bulletin, 77,* 446–452.

Dunn, O. J. (1961). Multiple comparisons among means. *Journal of the American Statistical Association, 56,* 52–64.

Dunnett, C. W. (1964). New tables for multiple comparisons with a control. *Biometrics, 20,* 482–491.

Gist, M., Rosen, B., & Schwoerer, C. (1988). The influence of training method and trainee age on the acquisition of computer skills. *Personnel Psychology, 41,* 255–265.

Greenhouse, S. W., & Geisser, S. (1959). On methods in the analysis of profile data. *Psychometrika, 24,* 95–112.

Hayter, A. J. (1986). The maximum familywise error rate of Fisher's least significant difference test. *Journal of the American Statistical Association, 81,* 1000–1004.

Hedges, L. V. (1982). Estimation of effect size from a series of independent experiments. *Psychological Bulletin, 92,* 490–499.

Hochberg, Y. (1988). A sharper Bonferroni procedure for multiple tests of significance. *Biometrika, 75,* 800–803.

Howell, D. C. (2002). *Statistical methods for psychology* (5th ed.). Boston: Duxbury Press.

Huck, S. W., & McLean, R. A. (1975). Using a repeated measures ANOVA to analyze the data from a pretest-posttest design: A potentially confusing task. *Psychological Bulletin, 82,* 511–518.

Huynh, H., & Feldt, L. S. (1976). Estimation of the Box correction for degrees of freedom from sample data in randomized block and split-plot designs. *Journal of Educational Statistics, 1,* 69–82.

Huynh, H., & Mandeville, G. K. (1979). Validity conditions in repeated measures designs. *Psychological Bulletin, 86,* 964–973.

Keppel, G. (1991). *Design and analysis: A researcher's handbook* (3rd ed.). Englewood Cliffs, NJ: Prentice-Hall.

Kruskal, W. H., & Wallis, W. A. (1952). Use of ranks in one-criterion variance analysis. *Journal of the American Statistical Association, 47,* 583–621.

Likert, R. (1932). A technique for the measurement of attitudes. *Archives of Psychology, 140* (June), 5–53.

Mann, H. B., & Whitney, D. R. (1947). On a test of whether one of two random variables is stochastically larger than the other. *Annals of Mathematical Statistics, 18,* 50–60.

Maxwell, S. E., & Delaney, H. D. (2000). *Designing experiments and analyzing data: A model comparison perspective.* Mahwah, NJ: Lawrence Erlbaum Associates.

Myers, J. L., & Well, A. D. (2003). *Research design and statistical analysis* (2nd ed.). Mahwah, NJ: Lawrence Erlbaum Associates.

Pearson, E., & Hartley, H. (1966). *Biometrika tables for statisticians,* vol. 1 (3rd ed.). University Press.

Reichardt, C. S., & Gollob, H. F. (1999). Justifying the use and increasing the power of a *t* test for a randomized experiment with a convenience sample. *Psychological Methods, 4,* 117–128.

Rosenthal, R. (1979). The "file drawer problem" and tolerance for null results. *Psychological Bulletin, 86,* 638–641.

Rosenthal, R. (1993). Cumulating evidence. In G. Keren & C. Lewis (Eds.), *A handbook for data analysis in the behavioral sciences: Methodological issues* (pp. 519–559). Hillsdale, NJ: Lawrence Erlbaum.

Rozeboom, W. W. (1960). The fallacy of the null hypothesis significance test. *Psychological Bulletin, 57,* 416–428.

Schmidt, F. L. (1996). Statistical significance testing and cumulative knowledge in psychology. *Psychological Methods, 1,* 115–129.

Shaffer, J. P. (1986). Modified sequentially rejective multiple test procedures. *Journal of the American Statistical Association, 81,* 826–831.

Siegel, S., & Castellan, N. J., Jr. (1988). *Nonparametric statistics for the behavioral sciences* (2nd ed.). New York: McGraw-Hill.

Steiger, J. H., & Fouladi, R. T. (1997). Noncentrality interval estimation and the evaluation of statistical models. In L. L. Harlow, S. A. Mulaik, & J. H. Steiger (Eds.), *What if there were no significance tests?* (pp. 221–257). Hillsdale, NJ: Lawrence Erlbaum.

Tiku, M. L. (1967). Tables of the power of the *F* test. *Journal of the American Statistical Association, 62,* 525–539.

Tukey, J. W. (1969). Analyzing data: Sanctification or detective work? *American Psychologist, 24,* 83–91.

Tukey, J. W. (1977). *Exploratory data analysis.* Reading, MA: Addison-Wesley.

Wilcox, R. R. (1998). How many discoveries have been lost by ignoring modern statistical methods? *American Psychologist, 53,* 300–314.

Wilcoxon, F. (1949). *Some rapid approximate statistical procedures.* Stamford, CT: American Cyanamid Company, Stamford Research Laboratories.

Annotated Bibliography

Behrens, J. T. (1997). Principles and procedures of exploratory data analysis. *Psychological Methods, 2,* 131–160.

This article is a recent and very accessible summary of the most popular methods of exploratory data analysis. It also presents J. W. Tukey's philosophy that a researcher should approach data as a detective should examine a crime scene—that is, without preconceived ideas. Especially in the exploratory phases of research, one's emphasis should not be on trying to show how one's data fit some initial hypothesis; rather, one should allow the data to tell their own story by using a variety of techniques to reveal whatever patterns are already hidden in the data.

Cohen, B. H. (2000). *Explaining psychological statistics* (2nd ed.). New York: Wiley.

In some ways the book you are now reading is a briefer, more conceptual version of the text cited here, and it takes the same basic approach to teaching statistics. This text is recommended for further reading and more exercises on any of the topics covered in the present book, and to learn about some topics (e.g., multiple regression, analysis of covariance) that had to be left out of this book. It was written as a text for students in advanced undergraduate or master's-level statistics courses.

Cohen, J. (1988). *Statistical power analysis for the behavioral sciences* (2nd ed.). Hillsdale, NJ: Lawrence Erlbaum.

This book remains the definitive work on power for social scientists. It contains numerous tables for estimating power and effect size in many common experimental situations. Although progress has been made in making power analysis available by computer, this book is likely to be useful for some time to come.

Cowles, M. (2001). *Statistics in psychology: An historical perspective* (2nd ed.). Mahwah, NJ: Lawrence Erlbaum.

This very readable and sometimes entertaining book tracks the history of some of the most common statistical procedures and describes the personalities and historical contexts of the statisticians who created these procedures. The author does not shy away from describing some of the acrimonious personal conflicts that developed between rival statisticians.

L. L. Harlow, S. A. Mulaik, & J. H. Steiger (Eds.). (1997). *What if there were no significance tests?* Hillsdale, NJ: Lawrence Erlbaum.

This recent, edited volume contains chapters that argue for or against the use of null hypothesis testing or in favor of some alternative or supplementary procedure. It includes chapters by some of the best-known writers on statistical issues in the social sciences, such as Robert Abelson, Jacob Cohen, Richard Harris, and Paul Meehl.

The next three books are all advanced statistic texts (suitable for doctoral courses), which include a more rigorous treatment of topics in this Essentials book (e.g., expected mean squares for various ANOVA designs), greater detail on these topics (e.g., various follow-up tests, alternative procedures to use when assumptions are not met), and material on topics like logistic regression, nested designs, random effect factors, and others that are not covered in this book.

Howell, D. C. (2002). *Statistical methods for psychology* (5th ed.). Boston: Duxbury Press.

This book is particularly useful for its chapters on logistic regression (useful for predicting a binary outcome from several predictors) and log-linear analysis (useful for analyzing data from three-way and higher-order contingency tables).

Keppel, G., & Zedeck, S. (1989). *Data analysis for research designs: Analysis of variance and multiple regression/correlation approaches.* New York: W. H. Freeman.

This book takes the novel approach of illustrating how each ANOVA design can be analyzed by means of multiple regression, as well as the traditional way. By comparing the two approaches to the same designs, the authors demonstrate the intimate connections between ANOVA and regression, and deepen the reader's understanding of both types of procedures.

Myers, J. L., & Well, A. D. (2003). *Research design and statistical analysis* (2nd ed.). Mahwah, NJ: Lawrence Erlbaum.

This thorough and sophisticated text is not only an excellent advanced textbook but also a reference book to keep close at hand. It is particularly useful for its treatment of complex ANOVA designs, including those with nested or random effect factors, or counterbalancing.

Rosenthal, R. (1993). Cumulating evidence. In G. Keren & C. Lewis (Eds.), *A handbook for data analysis in the behavioral sciences: Methodological issues* (pp. 519–559). Hillsdale, NJ: Lawrence Erlbaum.

This chapter is a very useful introduction and practical guide to the topic of meta-analysis—the comparing or combining of separate but similar experiments. Reading this chapter will also increase your understanding of the information that can be derived from estimates of effect size and the procedure of null hypothesis testing.

Siegel, S., & Castellan, N. J., Jr. (1988). *Nonparametric statistics for the behavioral sciences* (2nd ed.). New York: McGraw Hill.

This book covers all of the common nonparametric statistical procedures in detail, explaining, for instance, what to do when some cases are tied. It also supplies significance tables for small samples.

Tukey, J. W. (1977). *Exploratory data analysis.* Reading, MA: Addison-Wesley.

This classic work is more relevant than ever. It contains a broad collection of methods for displaying data and identifying trends and patterns therein. Many of these methods have become fairly popular in recent years (e.g., boxplots), although they are probably still underutilized. The various methods introduced are copiously illustrated.

Wilcox, R. R. (1998). How many discoveries have been lost by ignoring modern statistical methods? *American Psychologist, 53,* 300–314.

This article is both easy to obtain, being in a very popular journal, and easy to read. It presents a strong argument for trimming one's data when outliers are a problem and using modified statistical procedures (robust statistics) on the trimmed data.

Index

Acknowledgments

Barry Cohen would like to acknowledge his wife Leona for typing the entire body of the manuscript, and for morally supporting him throughout the writing of this book. Brooke Lea would like to acknowledge Kathleen Dull and Heidi Schmidt for their brilliant and tireless contributions to this work, the Center for Cognitive Sciences at the University of Minnesota who hosted him while he worked on this book, and Jerome L. Myers for his inspiration. Both authors gratefully acknowledge the assistance of Tracey Belmont and her editorial program assistant, Isabel Pratt, and the production assistance of Deborah DeBlasi (Wiley) and Susan Dodson (GCI).

About the Authors

Barry Cohen, PhD, earned a BS in physics from Stony Brook University, and later a doctoral degree in experimental psychology from New York University, where he presently directs the master's program in psychology and teaches statistics on both the master's and doctoral levels. He has been teaching statistics for nearly 20 years and has previously published a graduate-level text on the subject (*Explaining Psychological Statistics,* now in its second edition, is published by John Wiley & Sons). He has completed a postdoctoral fellowship in the area of psychophysiology and has also published empirical research in this area. He is presently planning experiments exploring the mind-body relation and collecting data for a new book on the different ways to become a psychotherapist in the United States.

R. Brooke Lea, PhD, earned a BA in English from Haverford College before completing master's and doctoral degrees in cognitive psychology from New York University. While at NYU he learned statistics from several master teachers, including the first author of this book. After completing his dissertation on logical reasoning and comprehension, Brooke took a postdoctoral fellowship at the University of Massachusetts-Amherst, where he developed his research interests in reading and discourse processing. Brooke first taught statistics at Bowdoin College, and then at Macalester College, where he is currently associate professor of psychology. His research publications concern the comprehension processes that occur during reading, and psychological models of deduction.